MW00790412

RITUALS, MANTRAS AND SCIENCE

India's Scientific Heritage

General Editor: Dr L M Singhvi

11

Editorial Panel

Abhijit Das
Andrew Nicholas
Ashutosh Urs Strobel
B D Kulkarni
David Frawley
David Pingee
James T Glover
Jeremy Pickles
Kenneth R Williams
K V Sarma
M A Dhaky
Mark Gaskell
Navaratna S Rajaram
P K Srivathsa
R K Tiwari
Rajiv Malhotra
Sambhaji Narayan Bhavsar
Subhash Kak
Toke Lindegaard Knudsen
V V Bedekar
Vithal Nadkarni
W Bradstreet Stewart

RITUALS, MANTRAS AND SCIENCE

An Integral Perspective

JAYANT BURDE

Foreword by

FRITS STAAL

Professor Emeritus

University of California, Berkeley

MOTILAL BANARSIDASS PUBLISHERS
PRIVATE LIMITED • DELHI

First Edition: Delhi, 2004

© JAYANT BURDE
All Rights Reserved

ISBN: 81-208-2053-3

MOTILAL BANARSIDASS
41 U.A. Bungalow Road, Jawahar Nagar, Delhi 110 007
8 Mahalaxmi Chamber, 22 Bhulabhai Desai Road, Mumbai 400 026
120 Royapettah High Road, Mylapore, Chennai 600 004
236, 9th Main III Block, Jayanagar, Bangalore 560 011
Sanas Plaza, 1302 Baji Rao Road, Pune 411 002
8 Camac Street, Kolkata 700 017
Ashok Rajpath, Patna 800 004
Chowk, Varanasi 221 001

Printed in India
BY JAINENDRA PRAKASH JAIN AT SHRI JAINENDRA PRESS,
A-45 NARAINA, PHASE-I, NEW DELHI 110 028
AND PUBLISHED BY NARENDRA PRAKASH JAIN FOR
MOTILAL BANARSIDASS PUBLISHERS PRIVATE LIMITED,
BUNGALOW ROAD, DELHI 110 007

In Memory of

Uncle Shive and Aunt Kamala

FOREWORD

In this new book on Rituals, Mantras and Science, Jayant Burde generously acknowledges his debt to my 1989 book Rules without Meaning: Ritual Man and the Human Sciences (in the 1996 Indian edition: Ritual and Mantras. Rules without Meaning). I am pleased, of course, by such recognition but that is not the reason that I am writing this Preface. The reason is that Burde has gone significantly beyond what I had tried to do and has reached conclusions that are not only entirely new and unforeseen by me, but that are of special relevance today. But to begin with the beginning — the author has broadened the scope of the subject considerably. While my empirical foundation was largely confined to Vedic ritual, Burde has taken account of later developments such as Tantric ritual and Puja ceremo nies a well as compulsive (pathological) rituals, animal rites and other forms of instinctive behaviour. He has widened the comparison with other human activities that are similarly structured by including domains such as poetry. He has lifted the discussion to a new level by embedding it in an original theory of science. It is in this connection that he introduces clear distinctions and criteria for distinguishing science from pseudo-science and non-science.

In so doing he performs a service to the scholarly community but goes at the same time beyond the scholar's ivory tower and opens up a contemporary perspective. His analysis is relevant to the present situation in India where ritual traditions remain strong but claims about their supernatural effects have also risen to unprecedented heights. With a new educational program called "Vedic Mathematics", which is neither Vedic nor mathematics being pushed from above and for political reasons, Burde's work takes on a new dimension of relevance. Ritual, Mantras and Science should be studies and pondered not only by those who are interested in contemporary India, but by every thinking Indian.

—Frits Staal, Ph.D. (Madras)
Professor Emeritus
University of California at Berkeley

PREFACE

This book discusses the place of science in rituals and mantras. Though serious in tone, it is addressed to a general audience and all the tools necessary to understand the various concepts are introduced at appropriate places especially in Part II.

I hope that part from the common reader, the students of religion, science, philosophy and sociology will find the book interesting because it uses the less known approach of structural (syntactic) analysis. Frits Staal uses it in his seminal work *Ritual and Mantras: Rules without Meaning* in which he shows that there was, in ancient India,a science of ritual and mantras.

Staal's treatise was the most important stimulus which motivated me to write this book. This volume, however, differs from his book in some respects. First it is not confined to Vedic rituals but analyzes the structure of the contemporary rituals sourced from the Vedas, Puranas and tantra. Second, there are a few areas of disagreement which has made me take a route which differs from Staal's but which has enabled me to integrate religious rituals with rituals in general, pathological (compulsive) rituals and animal rituals. This has also led me to present a general theory of rituals which unifies all types of ritual activities. Third, the book discusses non-science, science and pseudo-science and shows how the scientific knowledge of different types including those related to supernatural powers and *siddhis,* which the ancient Indian text are believed to contain, can be categorized appropriately.

It is difficult to name all those who contributed to creation of this work, and to whom I am indebted. Prof Staal's influence is reflected throughout the book. The works of those authors listed in the Bibliography have been of great help. I must to particularly refer to the author whose writings in Indian languages provided me with wealth of information relating to current rituals.

I am grateful to Mr. Rajendra P. Jain of MLBD without whose help and encouragement the project would have remained a pipedream. In Dr. Bhavsar, who went through the manuscript and made valuable suggestions, I found a sincere guide.

I am thankful to my family and friends who encouraged me to write the book and rendered help in many ways. I must particular mention my niece Deepalakshmi who provided valuable help in solving computer-related problems.

My gratitude also goes to Mr. Yashwant Dusane who prepared the DTP manuscript and designed the figures.

—JAYANT BURDE

CONTENTS

PART I
RELIGIOUS RITUALS

CHAPTERS

PART II
ANALYTICAL TOOLS

THE PRONUNCIATION OF SANSKRIT/ INDIC LETTERS AND WORDS

1. Sanskrit vowels are pure such as are found in French, Italian and Spanish. (a, i, u, ṛ, ḷ) are short while (ā, ī, ū, ṝ, ḹ, e, o, ai, au) are long.
2. A dental consonant is one in which the tip of the tongue presses against the upper teeth.
3. A retroflex sound is pronounced with the tongue-tip curled back.
4. An aspirate is a consonant followed by the sound of 'h' e.g. gh in doghouse.
5. It is necessary to know the sounds only to recognize their differences in structural analysis. It is not necessary to pronounce the words exactly as Indians do, unless one is learning Sanskrit or an Indic language.
6. Some Indic languages have also borrowed certain sounds (used in mantras) from Dravidian languages. These are omitted to avoid complications.

a	f*u*n
ā	*a*rm
ai	*ai*sle (approximate)
au	c*ow* (approximate)
b	*b*ear
bh	aspirated b as in a*bh*or
c	*ch*est
ch	aspirated as in chur*chh*ill
ḍ	*d*en, but retroflex
d	*d*en but dental similar to th in *th*en
ḍh	aspirated ḍ resembling dh in a*dh*ere
dh	aspirated d
e	pl*ay*
g	*g*ive

gh	aspirated g, as in do*gh*ouse
ḥ	(slight aspiration of the preceding vowel)
h	*h*im
i	*i*n
ī	*see*
j	*j*et
jh	aspirated j as in lo*dgeh*ouse (approx)
k	*k*ill
kh	aspirated k similar to kh in wor*kh*ouse
ḷ	a short vowel resembling lry in reve*lry*
ḹ	similar to l, but longer. Usually not found in the text
l	*l*ip
ṃ	(nasalization of the preceding vowel)
m	*m*eet
ṅ	si*ng*
ṇ	a*nd*
ñ	ni*n*a (girl child) as in Spanish
n	*n*ever
o	n*o*
p	*p*en
ph	aspirated p similar to ph in u*ph*ill
ṛ	short retroflex vowel slightly resembling short 'i' in the third syllable in *ability*
ṝ	similar to r, but longer
r	*r*un, but more audible than in English resembling that in Italian
ś	*sh*e
ṣ	as in *sh*e but retroflex
s	*s*it
ṭ	*t*ip, but retroflex
t	wa*t*er, but dental
ṭh	aspirated ṭ similar to th in an*th*ill
th	aspirated t similar to th in *Th*ailand
u	p*u*t
ū	r*u*de
v	*v*ery
y	*y*es

ABBREVIATIONS

AV	:	Atharva Veda
BG	:	Bhagvad Gītā
ESP	:	Extrasensory Perception
GRS	:	General Ritual Structures
OCD	:	Obsessive-compulsive Disorder
PK	:	Psychokinesis
RV	:	Rig (Ṛg) Veda
SV	:	Sāma Veda
VS	:	Vājasaneyī Saṃhitā
YV	:	Yajur Veda

INTRODUCTION

Indians are proud of their ancestors who have made valuable contributions to the various fields of learning ; arts, literature, grammar, mathematics, astronomy, medicine and many others. Their most outstanding contribution is undoubtedly the decimal system of numbers and the concept of zero. Of course, a similar vigesimal numerical system (with twenty as the base) was used in the Maya in Central America much before, but the world at large did not benefit from it.

However, when the ancestral pride is excessive and rooted in superstition, it becomes ancestor worship. Many of us are guilty of regarding our forebears as gods. There are many Indians, some of them highly educated, who believe that rainfall will occur if you recite (in Sanskrit) a mantra such as the following a certain number of times, and perform some ancillary rituals.[1]

> O Varuṇa, we praise you. Release us from the fetters. We deserve to be protected by you. Always protect us.
>
> (RV 5 – 6 – 10)

(Varuṇa is the personification of all-investing sky)

If you try this method, you are likely to fail unless you recite the mantra when there are dark clouds in the sky, and even a child can tell you that it will soon start pouring. But if the rain-mantra fails, it does not dishearten the ancestor-worshippers : the failure can be easily rationalized. It can be contended that nobody in modern times knows exactly how the mantra should be chanted as prescribed in the ancient texts. The 'science' was lost in the Dark Ages.

They also believe that the ancient Indians were far advanced in science and technology. They built aeroplanes and missiles, and used radio and television. It is even suggested that they had mastered genetic engineering. According to the epic Mahābhārata, King Dhṛtarāṣṭra had 100 sons (Kauravas) from his wife Gāndhārī. Since this is not possible through the normal reproductive method, it has been suggested that some of the Kauravas were clones.

While many of us see a science, where none exists, in the ancient texts, most of us are not aware of the sciences which really prevailed in ancient India. How many of us know that the science of linguistics was born in India long ago, and the West accepted it as science only recenlty?

It must be mentioned that a true scientist is not a pathological skeptic; he has an open mind. If a number of experiments show that there exists a probability that the rain-mantra is effective or that some of the supernatural powers (siddhis) mentioned in Patañjali's Yoga Sūtra can be acquired, he will start developing a coherent theory for these phenomena, instead of ridiculing the claims.

But while there may not be much science *in* rituals and mantras, there can be a science *of* them, as we shall see later.

There are basically two methods of studying ritual. The first method is the most widely used, and is sometimes called the semantic approach. It is concerned with the meaning of ritual.

Suppose you observe a devotee who offers oblations to a god and utters a mantra, "O God, bestow upon me health and wealth". The ritual is quite intelligible and you understand its goal. However, not all rituals are so easy to understand. Suppose you find a priest utter the following incantation.

om yaṃ yiṃ yuṃ yauṃ yaḥ
oṃ a vāyavya ya vāyavyo ma vāyavya va vāyavya
yo vāyavya ca vāyavya ya vāyavyo

followed by a few gestures, which do not convey any meaning to you. The ritual makes no sense even to a person who knows Sanskrit, and needs to be interpreted. Several scholars from different fields may be involved in this task: the elders in the community who claim to have witnessed similar ceremonies before, scholars of religion, mythologists who interpret various symbols, sociologists who are particularly acquainted with the society in which the ritual prevails, social anthropologists, psychoanalysts, linguists, historians, and a host of other specialists who may have something to say about ritual. More often than not, no unanimous interpretation emerges. Depending up on the status of the interpreters a few interpretations may be considered important, and will find a place in the commentaries on rituals and mantras. As time passes, the ritual will be handed down to the next generation. The experts from the new generation will not only examine the ritual, but will also consult the earlier interpretative texts. They will write their own commentaries, adding their own views.

This process of interpreting and re-interpreting the ritual will continue generation after generation. After many centuries we will find that a given ritual has hundreds of interpretations, some of them diametrically opposite to others.

The other method of studying ritual is to analyze its structure or syntax. This method is of recent origin, and is still in infancy.

Suppose you find a devotee recite the following mantra:

hrīṃ strīṃ huṃ huṃ strīṃ hrīṃ hrīṃ strīṃ huṃ huṃ strīṃ hrīṃ

You do not understand its meaning, but after hearing it repeated several times you may observe some of its features.

1. 'Hrīṃ' occurs four times in the line.
2. 'Strīṃ' occurs four times in the line.
3. 'Huṃ' occurs four times in the line.
4. The mantra is repeated, say, 1000 times.
5. The mantra reads the same from the right to the left as it reads from the left to the right.
6. If you consult a person who knows Sanskrit, he is likely to say that these words are meaningless though he might recognize 'Strīṃ' as a variant of 'strī' which means woman.

In 1, 2, and 3 you have observed a structure called 'refrain' whose meaning you must have learnt in school while studying poetry.

In 4 you find that the whole mantra is repeated or 'iterated' several times.

In 5 you have come across a structure called palindrome or mirror image.

(6) will tell you that a mantra need not have a dictionary meaning.

You may observe other rituals and you will able to detect several structures some of which occur frequently. In the syntactic analysis you analyse structures of different rituals and try to find out if there are regular patterns and similarities. What you are trying to find out is whether structures, independent of meaning can tell you something about the general and special characteristics of rituals.

Frits Staal uses the syntactic method in this seminal work *Ritual and Mantras : Rules Without Meaning*. Staal had earlier studied the performance of Vedic Agnicayana ritual performed by Nambudri Brahmins in the South India. This is one of the śrauta rituals which are also called public or traditional rituals that are primarily dedicated to Agni (fire) and Soma. This ritual is almost extinct, though a few Nambudri Brahmins seem to have kept it alive. Staal's findings were recorded in two volumes entitled *AGNI – The Vedic Ritual Of The Fire Alter*. He found that the data which he gathered were extra-ordinary and "no one knew how to account for them" [2] He then tried a syntactic approach to analyze the bizarre data.

His main conclusions in *Ritual and Mantras* are 1. The Vedic ritual is pure activity without meaning or goal, performed for its own sake, 2. Language developed from mantras and 3. There was in Ancient India a science of ritual.

It was Staal's work which inspired me to write this book, but its scope is much broader than that of *Ritual and Mantras*.

First, in relation to rituals and mantras, the book discusses such topics as science, non-science and pseudo-science. Its approach may be called liberal agnosticism. It is agnostic because it recognizes the distinction between the knowable and the transcendental. It is liberal because it recognizes the human need for faith, so long as it is harmless, in the areas where science has no role to play. These include not only matters relating to God and after - life, but also samādhi, superconscious state and other experiences which are purely personal, and lie beyond the domain of social knowledge. Second, the structural analysis is not confined to Vedic rituals. I have discussed at length the syntax of mantras and rites which are prevalent today and which have Vedic, Purāṇic and tantric sources. All these rituals are found to have structural similarities. These common features form the basis of the science of (religious) ritual.

Like any other science, the ritual science has a scope for generalization. The word ritual is used in a generic sense to indicate any stylized and repetitive behavior ; social, religious, psychological and so on. The book analyzes the rituals in general and finds that there is a common ground between them.

Fourth, Staal has highlighted structural similarities between Vedic ritual and music. Unfortunately he has not fully exploited these findings. In fact rituals in general share a common structural core with music, verse, dance and gymnastics which have been called recreational rituals by some writers. Staal is however, more fascinated by the processes common to language and śrauta rituals, and thus moves in a different direction.

Finally, any science of ritual should be able to account for two phenomena: one, animals too perform rituals; second, there are compulsive rituals which are pathological and found among those suffering from the obsessive compulsive disorder (OCD). These two facts can be satisfactorily accommodated if we assume that ritual behavior is instinctual.

Part I makes a brief survey of ancient Indian culture. In addition to rituals and mantras (Chapter 2), it also discusses tantra and yoga (Chapter 3). Tantric rituals are unique in that the yantras (geometrical figures) used in them display spatial structures somewhat similar to those found in the temporal (time-related) structures of ritual acts and mantras. Yoga offers rich material – superconscious states, supernatural powers and liberation – which can be scrutinized to determine the status of yoga as science.

Part II deals with such topics as knowledge, sciences, meaning and interpretation, structures and rituals in general. Though these topics appear disparate, they provide the necessary tools for structural analysis. I have tried to sequence the material contained in them in such a way that they should appear as the links of the same chain.

Part III presents structural analysis of rituals and mantras, but also includes language, verse and music with which rituals patterns are compared. It is found that language (prose) is not ritual despite its closeness to śrauta rituals in certain aspects. Mantras are found to be a subclass of human utterances as well as rituals.

Worship rituals are studied in detail (Chapter 12) Of all the types of religious rituals, these are most amenable to what may be called abstract formulation. This is attested by the fact that the 'pūjas' (worship ceremonies) designed in recent years conform to the pūjā formula mentioned in Chapter 12.

The main conclusions of the book may be summarized as follows:

1. All rituals, religious (Vedic or otherwise), social, political and so forth have common structural patterns. Moreover, they include recreational rituals like verse, music, dance and gymnastics.
2. A science of ritual can be built in which rituals display a hierarchical structure.
3. A further unification with animal rituals and compulsive rituals is possible if we assume that ritual behavior is instinctual.
4. Some rituals like śrauta ritual and compulsive rituals appear meaningless or admit of innumerable interpretations. These can be treated as pure structures that are semantically irrelevant.
5. Language, despite its similarities with śrauta rituals is not ritual.
6. Mantras antedate language, and are a structural subclass of both, human utterances as well as rituals.

Part I

RELIGIOUS RITUALS

1

VEDIC AND ANCIENT INDIA

1.1 Aryans in India

Between 1500 and 1000 AC BCE, a number of related tribes of Indo-European pastoral nomads entered India from the north-west. They gradually moved east and ultimately settled in the Gangetic plain, which was subsequently known as Āryavarta (Aryan homeland), because these people called themselves Ārya (loyal or faithful). These tribes worshipped many gods, performed sacrifices and their priests composed beautiful hymns in praise of their gods.

It is necessary at the outset to mention that the word Hindu was coined by foreigners. The river Sindhu which flowed into the Arabian sea and formed a part of the western boundary of India was called 'Hindu' erroneously by the ancient Persians. The Greeks corrupted it to 'Indos' which was later converted into Indus by the British. The Greeks called the country east of the 'Indos' by the name of India. Its inhabitants became known as Hindus through the Persian mispronunciation, and their religion was called Hinduism.

It is believed that the original home of these tribes was the region between Central Asia and Eastern Europe. From this region, they migrated to the various parts of Asia and Eruope, some of them coming to India. The Aryans spoke an Indo-European language sometimes called the Vedic language from which have descended Sanskrit and other Indic languages. A brief description of the Indo-European family of languages would be instructive.

Indo-European Languages

a. *Indo–Iranian - Indic:* The oldest documents are in Sanskrit. Prakrit was a group of variants which developed alongside Sanskrit. Pali and Ardhamagdhi belong to a later period in which the Buddhist and Jain scriptures were written. The languages which descended from Sanskrit/Prakrit are Bengali, Hindi, Marathi, Gujarati etc. Iranian - Old Persian and Avestan, now modern Persian.

b. *Hellenic:* Ancient and modern Greek dialects, Albenian.
c. *Italic:* Latin and its descendents, Italian, French, etc.
d. *Balto-Slavic*
e. *Germanic:* East, North (Danish, Swedish), West (Modern English, High German, Low German)
f. *Celtic:* Irish.

This classification helps us relate Sanskrit to other Indo-European languages.

It is interesting to find that some of the common words in different Indo-European languages resemble each other to a great extent. For example; father (English), Vater (German), pere (French), padre (Spanish), pater (Latin), pater (Greek), pitṛ (Sanskrit); mother (English), mere (French), madre (Spanish), mater (Latin), mātṛ (Sanskrit). Incidentally the common initial 'm' also has another significance connected with mantras, and will be discussed later.

The Aryans who settled in India interacted with the local inhabitants and borrowed from them a number of words and sounds, for example some retroflex sounds pronounced with the tip of the tongue curled back. These sounds cannot be traced to other Indo-European languages.

1.2 The Vedas

The Vedas (From 'vid' to know) or the sacred books of hymns were composed dating from 1500 BCE, and are four in number; Rig (Ṛg), Yajur, Sāma and Atharva. The Rig Veda is the oldest and is believed to be the original Veda from which the Yajur and Sāma have been derived. The Atharva was added later. The Rig Veda has 1028 sūktas or hymns which are arranged in eight *aṣṭakas* (octaves) or *khaṇḍas* (sections), which are in turn subdivided into as many *adhyāyas* (chapters), 2006 *vargas* (classes), 10417 *mantras* (verses) and 153826 *pādas* or words. There is another subdivision into ten *maṇḍalas* (circles) and 85 *anuvākas* (sections). Both classifications yield the same number of hymns. It is believed that the hymns of the tenth *maṇḍala* were incorporated at a later period.

Many gods are mentioned in the Rig Veda. Most of them are personifications of the powers of nature. They were called devas, a word related to Latin 'deus'. The root 'div' implies brightness and radiance. Hence the devas are those who shine brightly. The most important gods were Agni, Indra, Sūrya and Varuṇa.

Agni means fire, the word is cognate with Latin *'ignis'*. More hymns have been addressed to this fire-god than any other god, and the hymns pertain to sacrifice. Agni was also a god of mysticism and an intermediary between humans and other gods. He consumed the sacrifices and transported them to other deities. The ancient Persians, the closest relatives of Indian Aryans, too, were fire worshippers. While fire is not worshipped directly in modern Hinduism, *Agni* is invoked on important occasions such as marriage, and cremation symbolizing sacrifices. The Ṛig Veda at some places wonders whether there is one *Agni* or more *Agnis*. According to Basham, this speculative stage is the precursor of monism.[1]

Aryans were warriors, and had an important warrior god, Indra, who was also a weather- god. He rode in a golden car drawn by two horses. In some respects he had the characteristics of the Greek Zeus and German Thor, and possessed a thunderbolt called *Vajra*, but also used arrows.

Sūrya or the sun is an important god because he provides heat and light. He is sometimes identified with other gods like Sāvitrī and Āditya. According to Dowson, the references to him are more poetical than precise[2]. Sūrya had many wives, and he travelled through the sky in a chariot driven by seven horses.

Varuṇa ('all-embracer') was regarded as the king of the universe, gods and men. He also possessed infinite knowledge. He was also known as Asura, a term applied to lesser gods and later to demons. He seems to have a connection with the Zoroastrian god of light *Ahura* Mazda, and was possibly the common god of Indo-Iranians before the migration of Aryans to India. Varuṇa was also the guardian of *Ṛta*, the cosmic order. Among all gods he seems to possess the highest ethical standards.

Soma was a god of a distinct genre. Soma was actually a plant from which a potent and possibly hallucinogenic drink was extracted. The beverage was drunk at the time of sacrifices. The ancient Persians had a similar plant called *haoma*. The soma juice is depicted in the Rig Veda as an exhilarating drink enjoyed by men as well as gods. Soma was raised to the position of deity who is omnipotent, the lord of gods and who could bestow riches. This perception was probably due to its hallucinogenic effect on those who drank it. An entire maṇḍala is devotated in his praise, and he is even identified with the Supreme Being.

There were also other gods and a few goddesses. Aśvins, two sons of the sun or sky, young and handsome who drove in a horse-driven car, and were harbingers of goddess Uṣas, the dawn; Aditi, 'free unbounded' or the infinite expanse; Pṛthvī, 'the broad one' or the earth; and Maruts the storm gods who were friends of Indra. Rudra was the howling or roaring god, Yama ('restrained'), the god of death, and Vāyu, the wind-god usually associated with Indra. Viśvadevas were a class of intermediate deities; Gandharvas were divine musicians and Apsarās were the beautiful women who might become mistresses of gods and men.

The second Veda, the Yajur Veda consists of hymns borrowed from he Rig with some modifications. It also has prose portions not found in the Rig Veda. It contains the rules prescribed for the performance of sacrifices, and was considered the priest's manual. It has many *śākhās* or schools and two *saṃhitās*, Taittirīya and Vājasaneyī. The Taittirīya is called the Black Yajur and is more ancient. The other is known as the White Yajur which is more systematic. Though both saṃhitās contain more or less the same material, the White Yajur includes a few texts not found in other.

The Taittirīya contains 7 *kāṇḍas* (books) 44 *praśnas* or Chapters, 651 *anuvākas* (sections), and 2198 *kaṇḍikāṣ* or pieces.

The Sāma Veda contains 1549 verses most of them from the Rig. The verses are tuned to music and are chanted at sacrifices and offerings. Most of them are addressed to Soma, Indra and Agni.

Each Veda had its own priest. *Hotṛ* (Hotā) recited the Rig, and was expected to know the entire Veda. Adhvaryu 'muttered' the formulas from the Yajur, and Udgātṛ (Udgātā) chanted the mantras from *Sāman*.

The Atharva Veda belongs to a later period dating from time when the tenth maṇḍala of the Rig was composed. The Atharva has about 760 hymns and 6000 mantras, some of them in prose. About one sixth of the Atharva is found in the Rig, mostly in the tenth maṇḍala. Its spirit generally differs from that of the other Vedas in that the earlier three Vedas depict gods as friendly willing to bestow bounties. The gods of the Atharva are a source of terror. Mantras are used not for devotion but as spells, charms and as exorcising chants. Their incantations are performed either by the sorcerer or the person himself who wants to benefit from them.

The Vedic society did not know writing and the mantras were handed down from one generation to the next by word of mouth. Hindus revere the Vedas and believe that they reveal the highest truth. If these scriptures have come down to us undistorted, it is because the teachers laid great emphasis on pronunciation and intonation of each word. There were also mnemonic aids to ensure the correctness of the verses, which will be mentioned later.

The Vedas are believed to deal with two goals which the human mind tries to achieve; material happiness here and hereafter (abhyudaya), and the highest good (nihśreyasa). The first is sought to be achieved through observation of worldly duties and propitiation of gods through sacrifices and offerings. The highest goal on the other hand, is attained through self- knowledge. Accordingly, the Vedas are sometimes divided into two parts, Karmakāṇḍa which deals with rituals and jñānakāṇḍa which teaches wisdom:

According to the orthodox Vedic scholars the Vedas consist of Mantras and Brāhmaṇas. Mantras, which also include saṃhitās deal with ritual and sacrifice. The Brāhmaṇas specify the rules for use of hymns stating their origin, and contain legends and illustrations. The Brāhmaṇas include Āraṇyakas which were studied by forest-dwellers, and deal mainly with symbolic representation of the sacrifices. The Upaniṣads form the concluding portions of the Āraṇyakas. The Vedas usually have their respective sections of Saṃhitās, Brāhmaṇas, Āraṇyakas and Upaniṣads, with a few exceptions.

The Western scholars who studied the Vedas had preconceived ideas about the 'primitive societies' and 'religion'. Many of them called the Vedic poetry primitive, and its religion polythesim because many gods were mentioned. The Vedic Aryans were certainly not advanced materially or technologically. There are many Indians who see hidden science in the Vedic verses, which undoubtedly reflects their glorification of the past. The Western interpreters seem to take the other extreme position in equating Vedic civilization with such primitive societies as those which existed in Polynesia. No one who reads the following verse would call the intellect of the poet 'primitive'

Thought was the pillow of her couch
Sight was the unguent of her eyes

(RV 10-85-7)

A number of gods were mentioned earlier. But we also find a mysterious entity " One" or "Brahman''. We also perceive a particular cult: the divinity is treated as " one in many and many in one". One god is identified with another or many gods are indentified with one.

Moreover, The lesser gods are identified with the mysterious *"Ekam"* (the One), or *"Tat Sat"* (That Being). Hindus interpret this being as the Ultimate Reality or the Supreme Being of which the other gods are mere manifestations. The following verses should convey to you a vague meaning of this entity:

They speak of Indra, Mitra, Varuṇa, Agni, and there is Suparṇa of divine wings.
The one Being the wise call by various names such as Agni, Yama, Mātariśvān.

(RV 1-164-46, AV 9-10-28)

In the following verse 'That' in the neuter is believed to mean the Ultimate Reality:

Agni is That, Āditya is That
Vāyu is That, Candramās is That
The bright one is That
Āpaḥ are Those, Prajāpati is He.

(YV 32-1)

Āpaḥ means waters and Prajāpati is the lord of creation
Again,
Thou art woman, thou art man
Thou art boy, thou art maiden
Thou art the old man doddering with the staff
Thou existest in all forms

(AV 10-8-27)

All these hymns appear to portray the idea of the omnipotent and omnipresent Being. This Being is identified with the self in such verses as

The Spirit (Puruṣa) that is the sun, the
Spirit am I
Om, the eternal Brahman

(YV VS 40-17)

Many Hindus interpret the idea of 'One' as reflecting *'advaitism'* or non-dualism which was later expounded by the Vedānta philosophy. However, many Western scholars seem to be reluctant to see any lofty philosophical conceptions in the Vedic verses.[3]

1.3 Religion and Dharma

Hinduism has descended from the Vedic 'religion'. However, Hindusim is not a religion in the sense in which Christianity or Islam is. The Western concept of religion has three ingredients; the Book, the founder, and the doctrine. The Vedas are revered by the Hindus, but they do not enjoy the status of the Bible or Quran. Many Hindus consider the *Bhagavad Gītā* more sacred than the Vedas; but even this work cannot be treated as 'the Book'. Hinduism has no founder, nor is there a single doctrine. A Hindu may be a polytheist, a monist, an agnostic or even an atheist. Hinduism is called a way of life.

The cornerstone of the conventional Hinduism is *dharma*. Dharma roughly means 'property' or 'form', but also implies the right way of life. The word appears as *'dharman'* in the Vedic religion.

The six principles of *dharma* are: truth (*satya*), order(*ṛta*), consecration(*dīkṣā*), austerity (*tapas*), Brahman (prayer) and ritual (*yajña*) According to the The Atharva Veda, "Truth, eternal order, that is magnificent and stern, consecration, austerity, prayer and ritual – these uphold the earth" (12-1-1)

The Vedas consider truth as the essence of divinity. "The Deity has truth as the law of His being" (AV 7-24-1). Truth in ethical sense indicates truthfulness and integrity, in metaphysical sense it signifies reality. "Lead me from unreality (*asat*) to reality" says Bṛhad-āraṇyaka.

The second aspect of dharma is *ṛta*, the 'eternal order' which keeps the universe in equilibrium or in order. *Ṛta* antedates men and gods. In ethical sense *ṛta* is more than truth; it connotes justice and goodness. It destroys evil without mercy. As cosmic order, it offers an explanation of natural phenomena including the creation and organization of the universe. *Ṛta* sometimes implies ritual and it is believed that if rituals are not properly performed the universe may collapse. At social level *ṛta* means social order. Gods such as Mitra and Varuṇa are depicted as the guardians of *ṛta*. These gods are role models for earthly kings whose job it is to maintain law and order. The cosmic order also has an esthetic aspect which incorporates beauty and symmetry.

Ṛta is not dependent on gods (though some gods are described as its guardians), and hence it resembles in some respects the Greek concept of Fate. However, Fate has a dark import which leads to the famous concept of Greek tragedy. In *ṛta*, eternal justice implies "a man reaps as he sows". This leads to the doctrines of *karma* and *rebirth*. Every man (soul) is born with a residue of *karma* of previous births which contributed to happiness or misery of the present life according to the eternal law of *ṛta*.

Dīkṣā and *tapas* are primarily meant to realize the Ultimate Reality. Dīkṣā is more than a formal initiation; it connotes a deep rapport between the teacher and the pupil. The importance of the teacher in the Vedic religion can be partly ascribed to the absence of writing, which made the teacher indispensable.

Great stress was laid in the Vedas on work. According to Rig veda (4-3-11), "Gods befriend none but him who has toiled". *Tapas* means strenuous effort and infinite perseverance in attaining higher knowledge. A singular example of *tapas* is toiling of the student *brahmacārin* who studied at his teacher's house where he also had to work and keep his teacher (*guru*) in good humor. His life was austere, and he had to practice celibacy.

Basically Brahman means prayer. It also means the Vedas. *Brahmancarya* is the discipline needed for mastering the Vedas. Brahman also means the Ultimate Reality which the *brahmacārī* seeks through the Vedas.

The Vedic ritual is called *yajña* and consists of offering libation or oblation on the sacrificial fire. *Soma* libation was very common though clarified butter (*ghee*), and animals, too, were offered. Rituals and mantras are discussed in detail in the next chapter.

1.4 Varṇa and Caste

The Vedas describe the division of society into four classes (*varṇas*). According to the Rig Vedic hymn (10-90) called Puruṣa Sūkta, Puruṣa or the primeval man existed before the universe was created. Gods sacrificed Puruṣa to himself and the universe came into being. The hymn mentions that the Brahmins came from his mouth, warriors from his arms, *vaiśyas* from his thighs, and śūdras from his feet.

Brahmins belonged to the highest class, and were sometimes regarded as divinity in human form. Their duty was to learn, teach, sacrifice, and give and receive gifts. Some Buddhist sources mention two types of brahmins; the learned who performed rites, and the village brahmins who lived as fortunetellers and sorcerers.

Immediately below brahmins were the fighters who were called kṣatriyas. Their duty was to protect society, but they also studied and performed sacrifices. Because of the power they wielded, they sometimes claimed precedence over brahmins. It is not improbable that when the king did not show sufficient respect to brahmins as enjoined by *dharma*, a covert struggle for ascendancy ensued between *brahmins* and *kṣatriyas*.

Vaiśyas formed the third class who also studied and sacrificed, but whose main duty was to trade and breed cattle. They also engaged in money-lending. Though the Brāhmaṇa literature depicts vaiśyas as the oppressed class, the later Buddhist and Jain sources mention many wealthy vaiśyas living in luxury. It is believed that vaiśyas played an important role in promoting Buddhism and Jainism. They were very influential in some part of India on account of their wealth.

Śūdras supplied labour, and were expected to serve other three classes. There appear to be two kinds of sudras, pure or non-excluded (*anirvāsita*), and excluded (*nirvāsita.*) The former formed the lowest rung of society, while the latter, like the fifth class mentioned below, were beyond the pale of society. The life of a śūdra had little value. A brahmin who killed a śūdra had to perform the same penance he did for killing a cat or a dog. Śūdras could not learn the Vedas but they could read other literature, such as Purāṇas.

There was a class below śūdras, the fifth class (pañcama) whose members were subsequently called untouchables, outcastes or scheduled castes and possibly contained the 'excluded' *nirvāsita* mentioned above.[4] Many scholars refused to give them a place in the social boundary. Many of them were probably non-Aryans, some belonging to aboriginal tribes. There were *caṇḍālas* who cremated corpses, *niśādas* who hunted and *kārāvaras*, the leather workers. A distinct subclass of the untouchables consisted of *mlecchas* or *barbarians* who had migrated to India from outside.

It would be worthwhile to quote from the *Bhagavad Gītā*. (XVIII 42-44)

Control of mind and senses, austerity, cleanliness forbearance, uprightness, knowledge, realization and faith—these are the duties of a brahmin born of his own nature. Heroism, high spirit firmness, resourcefulness, fearlessness in battle, generosity and soveregnty–these are the duties of a kṣatriya born of his won nature. Farming, cattle-rearing and trade are the duties of a vaiśya born of his own nature. The duty of a śūdra born of his nature is action consisting of service."

It would be also instructive to know what the Law-giver Manu thought about the varṇas. "It is better to do one's own duty badly than to perform someone else's duty well"

It is necessary to mention that while all Aryans belonged to some *varṇa*, ascetics, children and widows were excluded from the class system.

Some Indian scholars believe that the class system was flexible in ancient India, and it was the quality rather than the birth that determined a person's *varṇa*. Notice the words "born of his own nature" in the passage from the *Bhagavad Gītā* quoted above. According to Basham while there was no social mobility for the individual in the class system, it was possible for an entire group to move upwards over some generations by following orthodox rules prescribed in texts called *smṛtis* which belong to the post-Vedic period.

The word 'caste' is erroneously used to designate varṇa. The Portuguese introduced the word '*casṭa*' to designate the tribes, societies and families into which the Indian Society appeared to be divided. Caste roughly means a cohesive group bigger than a family whose common bond is a trade or profession, and which practices endogamy (marriage within the group). There are hundreds of castes which seem to have evolved later, while the varṇa system is more ancient.

Two examples will elucidate the difference between the concepts of varṇa and caste (jāti). Brahmins are distinguished by their *gotras*. *Gotras* are exogamous i.e. the marriage within the same gotra is prohibited. Brahmins belonging to the some *gotra* are found in many castes.[5]

In South India *śūdras* who constituted a large percentage of the population were divided into two major castes: left hand and right hand. In the first group were castes of craftsmen such as weavers, cowherds and a few peasants. In the 'right hand' were traders, potters, barbers etc.

1.5 The Stages of Life

The life of an ancient male Hindu was divided into four stages. A male child became a full member of society only, when he underwent an initiation ceremony called *upanayana*. He was invested with a sacred thread, and became a *brahmacārin*. Only the boys from the first three varṇas were entitled to *upanayana*, at which time they were 're-born'. The *brahmacārin* then went to his teachers home where he studied the Vedas. He practiced celibacy and lived with his teacher away from the attractons of the town. He also did such chores for his teacher as grazing his cattle and chopping wood for sacrificial fire.

After returning from his studies, he married and became a householder (*gṛhastha*). As a householder his duties included performance of various sacrifices and rituals mentioned in the saṃhitās and Brāhmaṇas.

As the person became older he retreated to the forest (*araṇya*), sometimes with his wife, leaving his children in charge of his property. This stage is called *vānaprastha*. Though technically not a *gṛhastha*, he had to perform certain obligatory rituals. However, since he could not procure the material for yajña, he had the freedom to perform symbolic worship. The Āraṇyakas describe the symbolic mode of worship.

When the person became very old, he entered the last stage called *saṃnyāsa* or monastic life. He renounced all types of sacrifices and rituals. The *saṃnyāsins* searched for truth and became wandering monks. They studied the Upaniṣads, the concluding part of the Vedas, which deal with the Ultimate Reality. It is interesting to see how the different stages of life correlated with the various sources of knowledge The *brahmacārins* read the Vedas, the *gṛhastha* followed the Brāhmaṇas, the forest-dwellers were guided by the Āraṇykas, and the *saṃnyāsins* profited from the Upaniṣads.

However, these four stages merely indicate the ideal pattern. In practice men must have dropped out at various points. On the other hand, a *brahmacārin* could straightaway jump to the last stage and become a monk.

It is belived by some scholars that this four-stage system was evolved as a reaction to the asceticism of Buddhism and Jainism. It was expected to inculcate in the minds of young boys a love for family life.

1.6 Later Gods

The Vedic pantheon did not remain static. During the last two thousand years many gods have lost their pre-eminence, some have been modified, and some have disappeared. New gods have been added especially from Dravidian sources. Many gods must have emerged purely from human imagination; for, since God is omnipresent he can be found anywhere, in humans, animals and even in stones.

Brahmā is the active creator of the universe, mentioned as *Prajāpati* and *Hiraṇyagarbha* in the Vedas.

Viṣṇu has grown in importance since the Vedic times. He sustains the universe, and when the evil on the earth exceeds a certain tolerance limit, he descends on the earth as an *avatāra* or incarnation. Rāma and Kṛṣṇa are the avataras worshipped widely. Buddha is believed to be Viṣṇu's ninth incarnation. The tenth *avatāra*, Kalkin is yet to descend.

Śiva is as popular as Viṣṇu and has evolved from the Vedic Ṛudra. He has contrasting qualities, creation and destruction. In the latter aspect, he is the god of death. He is an ascetic, and lives in the Himālayas. He has matted hair through which flows the river Ganges, and where the crescent moon is stationed. More often than not he is engaged in meditation. His third eye on the forehead symbolizes his inward vision, but can also be used as a weapon of destruction. He is worshipped symbolically as phallus (*liṅga*), and is thus a god of fertility.

Brahmā the creator, Viṣṇu the preserver and Śiva the destroyer form the Hindu trinity or *Trimūrti* who is widely worshipped in some parts of India.

The worship of Mother Goddess can be traced to pre-Aryan civilizations in India. She is worshipped as *Śakti* or power. She also appears in different forms. As Pārvatī the wife of Śiva she is of benevolent disposition; as *Durgā* ('Inaccessible'), *Kālī* (the Black) and Caṇḍī (the Fierce) she is a terrible goddess who destroys demons. She is symbolically worshipped as the goddess of fertility in the form of *yoni* the female counterpart of the *liṇga*.

Gaṇeśa, the elephant-headed god is the son of Śiva and Pārvatī. He has assumed considerable importance after the Middle Ages. He is the god of wisdom and the remover of obstacles. He is invoked and propitiated at the beginning of important ceremonies.

Skanda, the war-god, who is also called Subramaṇya or Kārtikeya is the elder brother of Gaṇeśa, who is widely worshipped in South India.

Rāma, an avatāra of Viśṇu is the hero of the epic Rāmāyaṇa. He is the upholder of ethical code or dharma, and in fact symbolizes everything that is virtuous. His wife Sītā is also worshipped as a symbol of virtue and womanhood.

Kṛṣṇa is the eighth incarnation of Viṣṇu and a king whose amorous adventures have been depicted in the epic *Mahābhārata*, but which have been interpreted as symbolic love between the god and his devotees. The *Bhagavad Gītā* is part of *Mahābhārata*, and contains his discourse to Arjuna on the battle field. Both Rama and Kṛṣṇa are very popular.

The celibate Hanumān, the devotee and loyal servant of Rāma is a monkey god who is worshipped all over India.

Lakṣmī, Viṣṇu's wife is the goddess of wealth and prosperity. Sarasvatī is the wife of Brahmā, and the goddess of learning.

While the Vedic gods like Indra, Soma, Varuṇa and Agni are not worshipped separately, they still retain ritualistic importance. In domestic rites and yajñas they are invoked and propitiated. However, they do not occupy a high place in idol worship.

It is necessary to make a few comments on the identity of gods. One god is often identified with another. Gods appearing in different works do not form a consistent system. This creates two problems for the scholars of religion. The first problem relates to individuation, since the identity of a god becomes obscure. The second pertains to the establishment of a coherent correspondence between gods on the one hand and qualities or legends on the other hand. This also seems to be the problem of other polytheistic religions. However, in India the ambiguity and contradictions have been interpreted as the very essence of its religion: one god in many gods, and many gods in one, which ultimately leads to monism or non dualism.

1.7 The Schools of Philosophy

The Indian concept of philosophy is much broader than its Western counterpart. It is called *darśana* or 'direct vision', and it not a mere theoretical system. It has a practical aspect which seeks the Ultimate Reality that is usually attained through transcendental insight.

There are six traditional systems which treat the Vedas as their sources. They are Nyāya, Vaiśeṣika, Sāṃkhya, Yoga, Mīmāṃsā and Vedānta.

Nyāya ('Analysis') was founded by Akṣapāda Gautama (between 3rd century BCE and 1st century (CE), and mainly deals with logic which is extensively used by other schools. It has also made important contributions to the theory of knowledge. It considers perception, inference, comparison and testimony as the sources of knowledge. It believes in the individual soul and posits that a person is liberated when he attains valid knowledge or *tattvajñāna* of the soul. For acquiring this knowledge a three stage path is prescribed. It regards God as the maker of the universe out of eternal atoms of space, time mind and soul.

Vaiśeṣika resembles Nyāya and was founded by Ulūka Kaṇāda (1st century CE). It divides Reality into seven categories (*padārthas*) : nine substances (*dravyas*), twenty-four qualities (*guṇas*), action (*karma*), generality (*sāmānya*), uniqueness (*viśeṣa*), inherence (*samavāya*) and non-existence (*abhāva*). The system is called Vaiśeṣika because it considers uniqueness as a separate category of reality. According to this school the substances air, fire, water and earth consist of *paramāṇus* or indivisible smallest parts of the particular substance. These atoms are eternal, and so are the non-atomic five substances, ether(space), time, direction, soul and mind. The other aspects represent the changeable nature of the cosmos. Like Nyāya, it treats the universe as a conscious construction of atoms by God. Its conception of God, soul and liberation is similar to that of Nyāya. It emphasizes the role of *dharma* as a means to achieve the highest goal in life.

Sāṃkhya is perhaps the oldest orthodox *darśana*. Founded by Kapila, it is a dualistic philosophy having two categories *Puruṣa* and *Prakṛti*. *Prakṛti* is the unconscious principles which has three *guṇas* or qualities; virtue (*sattva*), passion (*rajas*) and dullness (*tamas*) Puruṣa is the conscious principle which interacts with Prakṛti to produce the universe. The system mentions twenty-three evolutes which include *mahat* or *buddhi* (intellect), ahaṃkāra (ego) and *manas* (mind). There are, of course, many Puruṣas (*jīvas*) each eternal and intelligent. The earlier scriptures did not mention God because *Puruṣa* (the Father principle) and *Prakṛti* (the Mother principle) are sufficient to crate the universe. However, later writings, under the influence of monism and theism seem to have incorporated the concept of God. The *Bhagavad Gītā* says that the evolution of the universe is guided by God. Since pain and pleasure are transmitted by body, mind, ego and intellect to *Puruṣa* (self), there is a false identification between the senses and the self. However, when we learn to discriminate between the two, we acquire correct knowledge and the path of liberation (salvation) is opened.[6]

Yoga is the fourth system. The word is derived from the root 'yuj' (to unite.) and means a way of expanding the individual's consciousness to make it merge with the universal consciousness. Patañjalis Yoga Sūtra (2nd century CE) is the important text for this school. Yoga contemplates a rigorous training of the body and mind, which consists of eight stages; self—control *(yama)*, observance of rules (*niyama*), right posture(*āsana*), control of breath (*prāṇāyāma*), restraint (*pratyāhāra*) or withdrawal of senses, steadying of mind (*dhāraṇā*) or concentration, and the final stage called *samādhi* or spiritual absorption in which the individual consciousness merges with the super-conscionsness. Unlike the original *Sāṃkhya*, Yoga believes in the existence of God. (*Īśvara*). Like Sāṃkhya it is, however, a dualistic philosophy and is similar to it in many respects.

Patañjali's yoga is also called *aṣṭāṅga yoga* (*aṣṭāṅga*, for eight limbs) or rājayoga. There are many other yogas which have the same goal viz. liberation. These are discussed in Chapter 3.

Mīmāṃsā ("Enquiry") is the fifth school and is also called Pūrva Mīmāṃsā. It regards the entire life as a grand ritual, and provides a rationale for ritualistic worship. Mīmāṃsā is discussed at length in the next chapter.

The Sixth system is Vedānta, which is allied to Mīmāṃsā. Vedānta means the end of the Vedas, and its philosophy is rooted in Upaniṣads and Vyāsa's Brahma Sūtras which are an orderly assemblage of Upaniṣadic principles. While there are a number of sub-schools in Vedānta, the advaita ('allowing no second',) Vedānta of Śaṅkara (788-820) is the most influential. Advaita is the philosophy of monism or non-dualism according to which there is only one Ultimate Reality called Brahman which is all pervading pure consciousness.. Brahman is not other than *Ātman* (self). The universe and its phenomena are mere projections of its power called māyā. Māyā is also called *avidyā* (ignorance) because it veils Brahman and creates an illusion of multiplicity. We can get rid of this illusion through contemplation and meditation, and see the Ultimate Reality. This gradual process of realization is encapsulated in four 'great statements' or mahāvākyas of the Upaniṣads. They are:

1. Brahman alone is real, the universe is unreal.
2. There is only one Brahman.
3. I am Brahman.
4. The whole universe is Brahman.

THE DEVEANĀGARĪ (SANSKRIT) ALPHABET

Phonetic Notation	Devanāgarī Letters	Phonetic Notation	Devanāgarī Letters	Phonetic Notation	Devanāgarī Letters
A		**C**		**F**	
a	अ	c	च	p	प
ā	आ	ch	छ	ph	फ
i	इ	j	ज	b	ब
ī	ई	jñ	ज्ञ	bh	भ
u	उ	jh	झ	m	म
ū	ऊ	ñ	ञ		
ṛ	ऋ	**D**		**G**	
ṝ	ॠ	ṭ	ट	y	य
ḷ	ऌ	ṭh	ठ	r	र
ḹ	ॡ	ḍ	ड	l	ल
e	ए	ḍh	ढ	v	व
ai	ऐ	ṇ	ण		
o	ओ			**H**	
au	औ	**E**		ś	श
aṃ	अं	t	त	ṣ	ष
aḥ	अ:	tr	त्र	s	स
		th	थ		
B		d	द	**I**	
k (ka)	क	dh	ध	h	ह
kh	ख	n	न	kṣ	क्ष
g	ग				
gh	घ				
ṅ	ङ				

2

RITUALS AND MANTRAS

2.1 The Alphabet

Before we study mantras, it is necessary to familiarize ourselves with the sounds and the alphabet used in Sanskrit and other Indic languages. The English orthography (system of spelling) is not adequate to represent these sounds for two reasons. First, it is not phonetic. An orthography is phonetic when a letter or a group of letters always has the same sound. This does not happen in English – 'u' in 'put' has a sound different from the 'u' in 'but' or 'a' is pronounced differently in 'rat' and 'rate'. This is, however, not the defect of the Roman script which English uses, for French and Spanish use the same alphabet but their orthography is more or less phonetic: once you understand the basic rules of pronunciation, your can usually pronounce any word though you may not understand its meaning. The second reason is that certain sounds used in Indic languages are not used by the speaker of English.

Sanskrit uses the *Devanāgarī* script and it would be ideal if we could use it but unfortunately, it is not a common script even in India and not all Indians know it. It is therefore, necessary to phoneticize the Roman alphabet to facilitate pronunciation of Indian words. The Sanskrit alphabet is given on the opposite page along with its phonetic notations. The pronunciation of these notations is explained at the beginning of the book. It is not necessary to remember *the Devanāgarī* script, but its inclusion would help you identify the letters used in yantras in tantric rituals.

You will notice that the letters of the alphabet are arranged in a most scientific manner. In the first group (A) are the vowels (svaras). Groups B through F contain consonants called *vyañjanas*. In group B are dorso-velar (*kaṇṭhya*) sounds, which are pronounced when the back of the tongue (dorsum) touches the velum. In group C are *tālavya* consonants in which the position of the tongue shifts forward. Group D consonants are called *mūrdhanya* which are retroflex in which the tip of the tongue is curled back. Group E contains the dantya or dental consonants where the tip of the tongue touches the teeth. In F are bi-labial (*oṣṭhya*) sounds where both lips touch each other. In each of these groups, the consonants are arranged in a systematic sequence: voiceless, voiceless aspirated, voiced, voiced aspirated, nasal voiced. For example, k, kh, g, gh, ṅ.

Group G sounds are called antastha *varṇa* and those in H are called *uṣmavarṇa*. The consonant h is called *mahāprāṇoccārya* Observe also that the sounds in H and the first three in G have a correspondence;

y, ś, are *tālavya*
r, ṣ, are *mūrdhanya*
l, s are *dantya*

In the systematic representation of the alphabet, one can see the seeds of the science of linguistics which was born in India subsequently.

2.2 Religious Rituals

Religious rituals can be broadly divided into four categories; worship rituals, rites of passage, festive rituals, and sacraments. Rites of passage are the rituals performed when there is a transition in life from one stage to another. Birth, initiation and marriage are the occasions when these rites are conducted. Worship rituals may be performed at home, in temples or at public places where a large number of people may assemble to worship the gods. Festive rituals are undertaken to celebrate the birthdays of prophets and gods such as *Rāma* and *Kṛṣṇa*, but they may also be related to seasons or agricultural activities such as harvesting. An example of sacramental rituals is the ordination of the head of a monastery (*maṭhādhipati*). However these divisions are not water tight compartments, and there is considerable overlapping. The sacramental rituals are usually connected with the rites of passage, and worship rituals are present as subordinate rituals in most non-worship types.

Some of the words used in connection with rites and ritual need clarification. We shall use the words rite and ritual interchangeably to indicate all procedures and acts including utterances called mantras. When we want to distinguish between non-verbal acts and utterances, we shall use the words 'ritual acts' and 'mantras' as the case may be. The context should make the meaning clear in most cases. The word oblation will be used to indicate any thing that is offered to gods and also the act of offering. The word sacrifice appears ambiguous, but will be used to indicate ritual killing or the act of offering as well as the thing that is offered in sacrifice.

Staal distinguishes Vedic rituals form non-vedic rituals.[1] He regards the former as more elaborate and exotic which needed the services of many expert priests who were Brahmins. These rituals continued till c 500 BCE when they began to decline. The rituals of Hinduism and Buddhism belong to a different age. It must be mentioned that there are many Vedic elements present in the contemporary rituals. Moreover, both Vedic and *Purāṇic* (form *Purāṇas*) mantras are used optionally, though the trend towards the use of the latter is increasing.

The Vedic ritual can again be divided into *śrauta* and *gṛhya* rituals. The former are 'traditional', 'public' or 'solemn' in which gods Agni and Soma are usually invoked and propitiated with clarified butter (*ghee*) and soma juice. These oblations are thrown into the sacrificial fire. The word mantra in case of the Vedic ritual is confined to those portions or the bits of sentences lifted from, the Vedas and recited or chanted in conjunction, with the ritual acts. The *Śrauta* rites were conducted in accordance with the *Śrauta Sūtra*. Gṛhya rituals are domestic rites or the rites of passage for which *Gṛhya Sūtra* serve as manuals.

One of the descriptions of a ritual in the *Śrauta Sūtras* is that it consists of three elements, the thing (*dravya*) that is offered in oblation, *devatā* or the god to whom the thing is offered, and *tyāga* or renunciation of the fruits of action. The first and the third element can lead to confusion because 'sacrifice' connotes both these elements.

Rituals are also divided into obligatory (*nitya*) and optional (*kāmya*) types. The word *ahnika* is used to denote the routine rites which are to be performed every day, from morning till night ('*aha*' means day). Sometimes the word '*nitya*' is used to indicate regular rituals in contrast to '*naimittika*' rituals performed on specific occasions like initiation and marriage.

The word *saṃskāras* is used to denote personal ceremonies which are almost synonymous with the rites of passage. '*Saṃskāras*' means 'polishing' or 'making perfect'. Just as the potter has to perform some acts to convert the raw material into useful pottery or the sculptor has to chisel the stones to give them different shapes, *saṃskāras* in the form of ritual and mantras are used to convert the 'human material' into a refined product.

Some forty ceremonies or *saṃskāras* are mentioned by scholars, to which eight are add by *Gautama Dharmaśāstra*. Of the rites of passage, only sixteen are followed today by the orthodox Brahmins and are called *ṣoḍaśa saṃskāras*.

2.3 Sixteen Saṃskāras

The rites of passage begin even before the child is born. The first rite is called *garbhādāna* which is a 'purification' ceremony paving the way for conception. This is followed by puṃsavana which takes place after conception with the intention to have a male child. The third ceremony is called *sīmantonnayana* which is performed to protect the child in the womb.

Jātakarma is the ceremony performed after the male child is born and before his umbilical cord is severed. The ritual is believed to destroy any pre-natal defects. When the father sees the son's face, he is 'discharged' from some obligations. Among the many ritual steps involved are: (1) putting the mixture of honey and yoghurt in the baby's mouth, (2) whispering specific mantras in his ears and (3) invoking *Aśvins* and Indra, and imploring them to bestow a healthy body and mind and prosperity on the child and the family.

The naming ceremony is called *nāmakaraṇa* in which blessings are given to the child for long life. The next ceremony is *sūryāvalokana* and *niṣkramaṇa* performed in the third month after the birth. The baby is 'shown' to the sun and taken out in a vehicle with the accompaniment of music. *Annaprāśana* is the next ceremony performed 6-8 months after birth which involves giving the baby curd, honey and *ghee* (clarified butter).

Caula or *Cuḍākarma* is the eighth ceremony performed when the child is between three and five. The boy's scalp is shaved and only a topknot is left.

Upanayana is the initiation ceremony performed at the age of eight if the boy is a *brahmin*, at eleven if he is a *kṣatriya* and at twelve if he is a *vaiśya*. '*Upa*' means 'near' and '*nayana*' means ' to take'. The word upanayana is interpreted to mean that the boy is now fit to be taken to the guru for learning *Gāyatrī* mantra. Every male except a *śūdra* becomes a *dvija* (twice-born) when he undergoes upanayana. The boy is invested with a sacred thread called *yojñopavīta* hung over his left shoulder and under the right hand, which he is supposed to wear throughout his life—the position of the thread has to be changed on certain occasions. The ceremony consists of many rites, the most important being the teaching of the sacred *Gāyatrī mantra* and asking the *batu* (initiate) to repeat it. Later the *acarya* (priest) explains him the code of conduct he has to follow, which includes the daily performance of rites such as sandhya. Many non-brahmins have discontinued the upanayana ceremony.

Four ceremonies called caturvedavrata (*mahānāmnivrata mahāvrata*, upaniṣad vrata and *godānavrata*) are performed when the boy is a student. The last is performed at the age of sixteen when the brahmacārin discards his moustache.

The ceremony samāvartana is performed when the boy returns home from his studies. The ceremony consists of many rites interspersed with mantras. At the end the *brahmacārin* becomes a snātaka (one who has had a special religions bath). The *snātaka* vows to follow a certain code of conduct.

Marriage is the sixteenth rite of passage. One of the objects of marriage is to be released from the obligations to devas and manes. A Hindu marriage is a sacrament and not a contract. After marriage the man is expected to perform some obligatory domestic sacrifices. Sexual enjoyment and progeny are also important goals. Progeny ensures a happy after-life for the ancestors.

The marriage ceremony consists of not less than nineteen subordinate ceremonies, each of them consisting of several rites. The most important rite is called saptapadi in which the bridegroom holds the bride by the hand, and the couple take seven steps around the sacred fire. There are seven heaps of rice. When the bride treads one heap in each round, the bridegroom recites a mantra, seven mantras in all. The last mantra is sakhāsaptapadibhava : "You have walked seven steps with me and our wedlock is solemnized." The modern Hindu law treats the 'saptapadi' as the test of marriage unless contrary customs prevail.

2.4 Sacrifice

A ritual sacrifice is also called yajña. During the Vedic period Agni and Soma were the most important gods of sacrifice. Agni also appears in the form of sacrificial fire. Soma has the triple function : he is a god, a libation and a drink with which one can get intoxicated at the time of sacrifice. Two Rig Veda verses are worth quoting. "I pray to Agni, the household priest who is the god of sacrifice, the one who chants and invokes and brings most treasure." (RV 1-1-1)

In RV 8-79-1, Soma is described as restless—"You try to grab him, but he breaks away and overpowers everything". This certainly is the projection of the poet's own mind which is intoxicated with the soma juice.

Agni and Soma are thus gods as well as facilitators who help you establish contact with the gods in heaven.

Like Soma, butter is also offered as an oblation. In one hymn (RV 4-58) the butter is visualized as actual butter used as an offering, as the soma juice and as perfected speech in the heart of the poet.

The horse was not only revered in the Vedic period it was also offered as a sacrificial animal. Rig Vedic Hymns (1-162) and (1-163) describe the horse sacrifice in some detail. In hymn (10-56) he is given the funerary farewell. It is worth mentioning that the 'devatā' (god) associated with the first two hymns is '*aśva*' (horse); each hymn has its own ṛṣi, god and meter. Such fusion of the object of worship and sacrificial object is not confined to the Vedic rites. In fact, the idea of "sacrificing god to himself" has prevailed also in other primitive societies. James Frazer has discussed this cult at length in his book, *The Golden Bough.*[2]

There were a few grand yajñas performed by kings. Rājasūya yajña was performed when a new king was installed. Vājapeya was a yajña performed for the rejuvenation of a middle-aged king, which also elevated him from the status of an ordinary raja to that of a samrāṭ,a complete monarch. The most famous sacrifice was Aśvamedha performed by a king who desired offspring. The yajña involved the sacrifice of a horse and it was believed that this entitled the king to overthrow Indra and become the lord of the universe and gods.

Though many of the *yajñas* have disappeared, some have remained as domestic rites. The most important among them are *yajña*-homa and pancamahāyajña.

Yajña-homa or sthalipāka is performed to keep gods happy and gain their favor. Inflammable substances like ghee (clarified butter) are offered to the sacrificial fire with Vedic mantras. The homa is also performed as an ancillary ritual at the time of many ceremonies such as initiation and marriage.

Pañca *Mahāyajña* consists of 'five great sacrifices' to be performed as obligatory rites.

1. *Brahmayajña* is also called sandhyā and was performed thrice a day by every male who has been initiated, but is now restricted to two worships.

2. Devayajña is the worship of gods. It also purifies water, air and flora. It is also called agnihotra.
3. Pitṛyajña consists of paying homage to the elders like living parents and teachers.
4. Bhūtayajña is a sacrifice performed before lunch and consists of offerings of food to birds, animals and the men of very low status.
5. Atithiyajña is the worship of guests (*atithi*) who are offered a ritual meal.

It is necessary to mention that in most higher religions the word sacrifice has acquired a solemn meaning. The slaughter of animals has been replaced by more civilized ways of offering, and as societies progressed further, the physical oblations have been replaced by the ideas of self-abnegation and renunciation; and the performance of duty without attachment. A couplet from the *Bhagavad Gītā* is illuminating.

> "The world is bound by actions other than those performed for the purpose of yajña. Hence, O son of Kunti, perform action for yajña alone, free from attachment."
>
> (BG III 9)

Another stanza says:

> "Yet others offer wealth, austerity and yoga as sacrifice, while still others, of self-denial and extreme vows, offer sacred study and knowledge, as sacrifice."
>
> (BG IV 28)

2.5 Funeral Rites

Most Hindus cremate the bodies of the dead. The last rites which form a complex system of rituals continue for thirteen days after cremation, and the eldest son has the most important role in the process. Gifts (*dāna*) are given on eleventh and thirteenth day.

Periodic *śrāddhas* are continued to be performed even after thirteen days. A *śrāddha* is the rite of commemorating ancestors, at which rice balls or *piṇḍas* are offered. Sons, grandsons and great-grand sons of the deceased participate in the ceremony. It is believed that three generations of the dead also join the ceremony, creating a link between the living and the dead of the same family. The word sapiṇḍa is used to denote those who are entitled to participate in the *śrāddha*, and thus defines the 'family' of the dead.

Māsika *śrāddha* is performed every month for sixteen months after death. Sāṃvastarika *śrāddha* is to be performed once every year on the death anniversary of one's father, but it is also addressed to grandfather and great-grandfather. Mahāyajña *śrāddha* is performed for the benefit of all manes (deceased ancestors.) once a year on the day of the new moon in a certain month. Tīrthaśrāddha is a *śrāddha* performed in memory of ancestors at a holy place of pilgrimage. Akṣayyatṛtīyā is a *śrāddha* performed for the benefit of manes on a certain day of the Vaiśākha month of the Hindu calendar.

2.6 *Mīmāṃsā*

Mīmāṃsā or Purva *Mīmāṃsā* is one of the six orthodox systems of Indian philosophy. It was founded by Jaimini (c200BCE) whose *Mīmāṃsā Sūtra* is the most important text of the school. Śabara wrote a commentary on these sūtras, Kumārila and Prabhākara (7th century) further explained the tenets, but in the process created two sub-divisions of the system.

Mīmāṃsā provides a method of interpreting the Vedas. According to it, the apparent contradictions in the Vedic verses can be resolved through their correct interpretation. The Vedas employed three types of sentences : imperative (*vidhi*), negative (*niṣedha*), and praise (*stuti*). The last mode reflected an exaggeration deliberately used as a device to create confidence among the populace in the teachings of the scripture. Hence, the Vedic sentences should not be interpreted literally. The imperative expression should be accepted as the guide and applied in practice. The stuti sentences should be analyzed further for correct interpretation. The interpretative technique is elucidated by Maṇḍana Miśra in his *Mīmāṃsā Anukramaṇikā*.

We have already mentioned that *Mīmāṃsā* provides a rationale for ritual. According to its tenets the performance of ritual is man's highest duty or dharma. It regards those activities as dharma which do not obstruct the activities of others. Our activities which interfere with others' activities constitute adharma. However, since the doctrine of dharma implies a hierachy of duties, in case of conflict we have to choose the right duty at the right time. The Veda explicitly says that one should follow its advice "which is good and beneficial".

Mīmāṃsā interprets this proviso to mean that we should not follow the actions blindly in a stereotyped manner, but only such actions which are dictated by our conscience need to be followed.

As we mentioned in the last chapter, *Mīmāṃsā* treats the entire life as a grand ritual. The ritual, however, does not mean a routine stylized behavior, it has a spiritual dimension. Our routine activities such as brushing the teeth, eating, bathing and working, when treated as ritual need to be spiritualized, so that we enjoy these activities and do not look upon them as tedium. Rituals are not the outward appearance such as burning incense, offering oblations, praying etc., they "provide a context in which one receives full opportunity to understand the value of action"[3]

Mīmāṃsā teaches us to perform selfless action. According Maṇḍana Miśra knowledge which liberates us from all bonds is closely connected with such actions performed without attachment. The concept of ritual is thus connected with a sense of renunciation of the fruits of action. The element of non-attachment is manifest in a ritual act. The yajamāna holds a thing to be offered (rice pudding, clarified butter etc.) and says that the oblation is offered to the deity and renounces its ownership. The offering to the sacrificial fires is believed to symbolize renunciation. It is believed that when a ritual is performed selflessly as a duty, the karmic debts accumulated in the past lives can be cancelled and the path towards liberation is opened. The Mīmāṃsā philosophy is also called the yoga of action.

It must, however, be mentioned that like many theories which are propounded to justify the already well-established practices, *Mimāṃsā* has to use interpretative techniques to reconcile contradictions. This problem will be discussed when we examine the meaning of ritual in Part III.

Mīmāṃsā also developed a theory of sound which can be used to explain the efficacy of rituals and mantras. Mantras in this context mean all the verses in the Vedas

According to *Mīmāṃsā* sound is eternal though its perception is momentary. In Sanskrit '*vāk*' literally means sound or speech but conveys a much broader implication, thought followed by expression. Vāk śakti is the power of sound which is operative even before a person utters a word when he wants to communicate with another.

Mīmāṃsā analyzes *vāk śakti* in detail and perceives four levels; vaikharī, madhyamā paśyantī and parā.

Vaikharī is the lowest level where sound appears in its grossest or verbal and audible form. The next higher level of *vāk* is *madhyamā* (middle) in which the *vāk śakti* has already formed a thought pattern about to be expressed verbally. The third stage is called paśyanti (" one who sees") which is the unmanifest śakṭi. Tigunait calls it the language of silence or a universal language which is believed to be the source of language and speech.

This is a transcendental state which can be identified with the Ultimate Reality or Supreme Consciousness or Brahman of the Vedānta. Parā vāk is the highest state of perfection – it is primordial sound identified again with the Supreme Consciousness. This stage may be called 'dormant' paśyanti, because in paśyanti, the supreme consciousness "sees the entire universe in its primeval state''.[4]

Thus the vāk śakti may be said to flow from parā to paśyanti to madhyamā and ultimately to vaikharī where it becomes manifest.

Mīmāṃsā also posits that a manifestation is a complex of two inseparable parts, *śabda* (sound) and *artha* or the object (form) indicated by the sound. The forms are the deities while the sound patterns are mantras. The deity and its mantra are thus two sides of the same reality. A logical consequence of this theory is that a mantra or a sequence of vibration can be materialized into a specific deity and the deity can be dematerialized into a vibration pattern. The adherents of *Mīmāṃsā*, however, point out that the plethora of gods corresponding to different vibrational patterns, are only various manifestations of the same Supreme Reality.

Mīmāṃsā also believes that universal forces can be harnessed by using appropriate sound patterns or mantras and through the manipulation of physical objects in ritual. The use of physical objects emphasizes the belief that divinity pervades the physical world. These thoughts ultimately lead to the philosophy of Vedānta or *Uttara Mīmāṃsā* which conceives the all pervading Ultimate Reality or *Brahman*.

2.7 Mantras

Mantras are sacred utterances. They are recited or chanted when rites are performed. They may also be uttered without ritual acts. Etymologically, 'mantra' means an 'instrument to think'. It is usually regarded as the utterance which has the power to protect. Some mantras appear meaningless and are believed to be effective because of the hidden power or vākśakti contained in them. Mantras perform two functions; fulfilment of a wish and avoidance of injury.

The notion of the sacred word seems to prevail in many cultures.

In the Bible one finds the passage "In the beginning was the word and word was with God, and the word was God..." (John 1:1,14). This concept of identification of the word with God is similar to the mantra-deity unity of *Mīmāṃsā* mentioned above.

While the Vedas are the first source of mantras, there are also mantras in Purāṇas and tantra. Mantras have also been composed subsequently in Indian languages, whose status depends on the faith a person has in them.

Along with the concept of the (divine) word a parallel concept of the divine light exists in some religions. To the person who sees this divine light, the totality of knowledge is revealed. According to the Vedic and tantric tradition the sages called *ṛṣis* were the 'seers' of mantras who simultaneously experienced the divine light and sound. We have already seen that below parā there are three descending stages of sound, *paśyanti*, *madhyamā* and *vaikharī*. The sages received the Vedic knowledge when they were in samādhi directly at the paśyanti stage. Corresponding to the three stages of sound there are also three stages of the divine light, prajñā, pratibhā and medhā. Prajñā the highest stage is one where the knower and the knowledge are one. Pratibhā is the stage of intellectual clarity and medhā is the stage where the retentive power comes into play. The divine light is revealed to the ṛṣi directly at the stage of prajñā.

The teacher-student relationship is very important in the transmission of mantras. The teacher teaches a mantra to this student in the vaikharī form. Through meditation, the student reaches the higher stages of madhyamā and paśyanti and attains the level of his teacher (*guru*). But the guru himself had undergone these stages when he was trained by his own guru. According to tradition one can truly gain from mantras only if this 'śisya-guru' chain can be traced to the original ṛṣi to whom knowledge was directly revealed.

2.8 Types of Mantras

Traditionally, every letter in the Vedas is considered sacred and all its verses are Vedic mantras. We have already mentioned the epics called Purāṇas which are an important source of mantras in modern rituals. Tantras are considered later in detail and constitute another major repository of mantras.

Brahmāṇḍa Purāṇa (33-34) lists nine methods or vidhis relating to Vedic mantras. It also mentions twenty-four kinds such as praise (*stuti*), criticism (*nindā*), *praśna* (question), *yajña* etc.

Meditative mantras are those which the practitioner repeats and meditates upon. These are the mantras he has received from his teacher (*guru*). Guru is not just an ordinary instructor, he is the person who "dispels the darkness of ignorance". Those spiritual traditions which trace their origin to the Vedas permit the teacher to impart the mantras of this categories as 'guru mantras' to his disciple. Under the guidance of teacher, the practitioner may see the Ultimate Reality. Such a person who is liberated during his own life-time merges with the mantra *śakti* (power) after death.

Mahā vākyas, some of which we have already considered, are terse maxims from the Upaniṣads[5]. These are contemplative mantras linked with the philosophy of Vedānta or *Jñāna yoga*—the path of liberation through knowledge. The student has to study the relevant philosophy under a teacher and is expected to have already acquired such qualities as self-control and forbearance. It is only when he shows a strong motivation for being liberated that the teacher will initiate him into the depths of these mantras. Those who wish to use these mantras are expected to have complete understanding of the meaning of the mantras. It is the concentration on meaning rather than sound which is the key to success. A well-known mantra in this class is *so'ham* which is discussed later with 'om'.

Mahā mantras (great mantras) or mahā vidyās are those potent mantras which are secret mantras not found in scriptures. These are jealously guarded by the few who know them. Those who wish to practice this *vidyā* (knowledge) must be prepared to train their bodies through haṭha yoga. They also have to pass through several stages before they acquire self-realization. The first step consists of acquiring a thorough mastery over the theory on which this method is based. This involves the study of scriptures and Sanskrit without the help of any teacher. At this stage the teacher gives the student a guru mantra. It is only when the student acquires sufficient physical and mental prowess, that the guru initiates him to the mahā mantra. Finally, he is introduced to ritual worship. Mahāvidyā brings about a harmony between the physical and mental powers with cosmic forces and thus helps the seeker to achieve self-realization.

'Āpta mantras' cannot be easily identified as mantras. They appear as ordinary words uttered by saints, which conceal great powers. However, since they are not formally handed down as mantras, they are of no use unless the person for whose benefit they are uttered has a great faith in the person who utters them.

Some mantras are used to acquire extraordinary and supernatural powers. They are called siddha mantras, and the various powers the practitioners possess are called siddhis which may include curing diseases, mind-reading, forecasting and performing miracles. Tantra texts describe many such mantras. A person can be successful only if he is initiated by a guru and follows the teacher's instructions meticulously. Moreover, these mantras unleash tremendous energy which may harm the aspirant if he uses them prematurely. It is only when he acquires a state of tranquility that he can start using them. Most spiritual seekers consider siddhis as only a spin-off of the spiritual quest whose goal is self-realization, and are loath to use them for publicity.

Śabar means a barbarian or a bhil but the appellation is also used for god Śiva who is believed to have created śabar mantras for the benefit of ordinary people, at the request of his consort Pārvatī. These mantras are non-traditional and eclectic and borrow from numerous sources, and may incorporate words and concepts from Arabic and Islam. They appear strange and unintelligible and are used by ordinary people in India, South East Asia, China and Tibet for earthly gains and curing diseases.

Mantras have also been classified according to their 'gender'. Masculine mantras are those which end with 'vaṣaṭ ' or 'phaṭ '. Those which end with voṣaṭ and svāhā are feminine and the mantras ending with namaḥ have neuter gender.

2.9 Bīja Mantras

Mantras have also been classified according to the number of syllables they contain. According to Nitya Tantra, those mantras which contain upto ten syllables are called mūlamantras or bījamantras,those having twenty syllables are called kartrarī mantras and those having in excess of twenty syllables are known as mālā mantras.[6]

Most bījas are one-syllable mantras in which nasalizastion is usually involved. Bīja mantras are also called preparatory mantras which the teacher usually gives to the student in the beginning.

Bīja means seed, and all bijas are believed to convey some meaning or are associated with some deities or qualities. Some bījas along with their significance are given below.

Om (*praṇava*, Supreme Being), *eṃ* (speech), *iṃ* (Gāyatrī), *klīṃ* (māyā, *śakti*, passion), *hauṃ* (Śiva), *gaṃ* (*Gaṇapati*), *glouṃ* (earth), *rhīṃ (Girijā), svāhā (Agni), sau (Goddess, Varuṇa), strīṃ (bride).*

It is interesting to note that, nasalization of all the letters of the Devanāgarī script yields bīja mantras. When the letters are nasalized and re-written they appears as follows :

aṃ, āṃ, iṃ, īṃ, uṃ, ūṃ, ṛṃ, ṝṃ, īṃ, ḷṃ, eṃ, aiṃ, oṃ, auṃ, aṃ
kaṃ, khaṃ, gaṃ, ghaṃ, naṃ,
caṃ, chaṃ, jaṃ, jhaṃ, ñaṃ,
ṭaṃ, ṭhaṃ, ḍaṃ, ḍhaṃ, ṇaṃ,
ṭaṃ, ṭhaṃ, ḍaṃ, ḍhaṃ, ṇaṃ,
paṃ, phaṃ, baṃ, bhaṃ, maṃ,
yaṃ, raṃ, laṃ, vaṃ, śaṃ, ṣaṃ, saṃ, haṃ, kṣaṃ.

Almost every monosyllable listed above is a bīja mantra. This is a peculiar structural aspect which I have called "pattern completion" and which is discussed at length later. Traditionally each of these mantras has a special significance or association which we need not consider.

Bījamantras are also said to possess distinctive powers. A mantra ending with vauṣaṭ can be used to influence people ; *hamphaṭ* protects a mantra, *phaṭ* destroys an enemy, *huṃ* generates jealousy, *kheṃ* can be used in black magic to injure someone and namaḥ is used for gaining god's favour. For acquiring wealth you can use *vauṣaṭ*.

Bījamantras are sometimes classified according to the varṇa of the practitioner For example, *rhīṃ* is to be used by brahmins, *srīṃ* by kṣatriyas, *klīṃ* by vaiśyas and *eṃ* by śūdras.

In one classification the bījas are linked with the zodiac signs. Those who worship goddess Śabari use the bījas associated with the sign under which they are born.

Aries (*Meṣa*)	:	*om, aiṃ, klīṃ, sauṃ*
Taurus (*Vṛṣabha*)	:	*om hrīṃ, klīṃ, srīṃ*
Gemini (*Mithuna*)	:	*om srīṃ, aiṃ, sau*
Cancer (*Karka*)	:	*ōm aiṃ, klīm, srim*
Leo (*Siṃha*)	:	*om hrīṃ, srīṃ, sau*
Virgo (*Kanyā*)	:	*om srīṃ, aīṃ, sau*
Libra (*Tulā*)	:	*om hrīṃ, klīṃ, srīṃ*
Scorpio (*Vṛścika*)	:	*om aiṃ, klīṃ, sau*
Sagittarius (*Dhanu*)	:	*om hrīṃ, klīṃ, sau*
Capricorn (*Makara*)	:	*om aiṃ, klīṃ, hrīṃ, srīṃ, sau*

Aquarius (*Kumbha*)	:	*om hrīṃ, aiṃ, klīṃ, srīṃ*
Pisces (*Mīna*)	:	*om hrīṃ, klīṃ, sau*

Just as saṃskāras are performed on persons to make them fit for the next stage of life, mantras too are subjected to certain *saṃskāras*. In case of Vedic mantras, *Nityotsava* text mentions ten rituals necessary to 'activate' the mantras. They are considered in detail later as they provide fascinating structural patterns. As a preview, consider the sixth ceremony called *jīvanam*, Let us symbolically denote the mantra to be activated by A. A new mantra is created by prefixing and suffixing A with two bīja mantras *vaṣaṭ* and *svadhā*. The new mantra will appear as

Svadhā vaṣaṭ A vaṣaṭ svadhā or CBABC

where B and C indicate the bīja mantras. You will observe that the above symbolic expression contains a symmetry : it appears as if the right side is the mirror reflection of the left side. Such a structures is called palindrome.

It is also believed that the Vedic mantras have been 'cursed' by the previous practitioners, Brahmā and some ṛṣis. In order to 'extricate' these mantras and make them useful a ceremony called *utikīlana* is performed.

All śabar mantras are believed to be under the curse of some deities and similar rituals are conducted in order to make these mantras 'curse-free' and active.

The Meru Tantra text also prescribes a procedure for 'awakening' the mantras, which is to be performed by the guru.

2.10 Om and So'ham

Om (*praṇava*) is one of the most sacred bījas, and certainly the most popular mantra. It is the seed mantra of the Supreme Consciousness and is considered important both in the Yoga and Upaniṣads.

In Upaniṣads it is identified with Brahman, the Ultimate Reality. According to the *Māṇḍūkyopaniṣad*, its real structure is *a-u-m* which consists of three *mātrās* (letters) followed by silence, which corresponds to half a *mātrā*. The sound 'a' bestows wish-fulfilment, 'u' leads to progress and acquisition of knowledge and 'm' gives correct knowledge of space, time and substance. The first three letters also indicate the states of waking, dreaming and deep sleep. The fourth half-mātrā or silence is the highest stage when māyā is dispelled and you identify totally with the omnipresent, eternal Supreme Being.[7]

Om is also identified with the Vedas in the *Bhagavad Gītā*: "I (Brahman) am the syllable Om in all the Vedas" (VII-8). It also says "All the gates of the body shut, the mind concentrated on heart, fixing his life force in the head, engaged in firm yoga, uttering the monsyllable Om (Brahman), thinking of Me (Kṛṣṇa or Brahman), he who departs leaving the body attains the Supreme Goal (VIII 12, 13). According to Yogadarśana om symbolizes the highest point in any kind of worship (*sādhanā*). Scriptures have prescribed elaborate methods of the worship of om, or *praṇavasādhanā*. Gaṇeśa the son of Śiva who was mentioned earlier, is also identified with om. It will be recalled that Gaṇeśa is worshipped on most important occasions.

According to some scholars 'om' has been misused by the common man who seems to feel that the mantra should be used on every occasion. There is a facetious passage in the Chāndogya Upaniṣad which describes a vision of sage Vaka Dālbhya. In the scene, dogs move around each other, each dog holding in his mouth the tail of the predecessor, just as the priests to when they are about to sing praises, and then they sing "Om, let us eat! Om, let us drink! Om, may gods Varuṇa, Prajāpati and Savitṛ bring us food."[8]

Soham is another bīja which is considered sacred both by the Yoga science and the *Vedānta*. According to the Yoga, this mantra which eternally exists, causes the first breathing of the child just born. In a way the mantra is inherent in the human existence. However, our lifestyles create a discord with the natural rhythm of this universal sound. It is necessary, therefore, to practice the mantra so that the harmony is restored.

When you inhale, the life energy enters you and when you exhale, you expel only what is unnecessary. The sound 'so' occurring when you breath in means 'That' the supreme Being which enters you and becomes one with you. When you breath out, there is the sound 'ham' which is identified with 'I'. The repetition of soohmm, soohmm means "I am That", the realization that you are the Supreme Being. The continuous practice of soham brings tranquility to your mind and a peaceful identification with the whole universe.

We have already mentioned that "I am That" is one of the mahā vākyas of the Upaniṣads. The Vedāntic school emphasizes the contemplative aspect of soham. For total benefit of this mantra in relation to self-analysis, the guru's supervision is considered essential.

In North India, there is a religious sect (*pantha*) called Nātha which considers soham as equivalent to om. In s-o-h-a-m it sees the concealed om (o-a-m). According to *Gorakṣasaṃhitā* (1-41-44), soham liberates the yogis and has no parallel.[9]

On page 31 we mentioned that nasalization of the Sanskrit alphabet gives rise to many bījas. One of them is oṃ which is nasalization of 'o'. Oṃ has the same relationship to 'o' as aṃ has to a. In the *Devanāgarī* script it would appear as 'o' with a dot (*anusvāra.*) on the to top (Compare it with aṃ in the *Devanāgarī*). Many texts treat oṃ as distinct from *om* or *aum* (*praṇava*). The latter is the bīja *par excellence* associated with the Vedas and from which all other bījas have emanated. It has a unique symbol. ॐ *Oṃ* on the other hand is a bīja known as sadyojita bīja, Gāyatrī bīja, trayodaśī bīja etc. However, the distinction between these two bījas is often lost sight of in some contexts which leads to the merging of their identities.

In this book, as far as possible, we shall retain the individuality of these bījas. The *praṇava* will be indicated by om while oṃ will be reserved for the simple nasalization of 'o'.

3

TANTRA AND YOGA

3.1 Tantra

Tantra is an unorthodox method of acquiring spiritual power (*siddhi*) and liberation in life (*jīvanmukti*). It assumes that divinity is within us and can be realized through certain practices. Tantra literally means 'looms' or 'weaving'. It is believed that we are born with a pattern designed by Mother Nature, but our alienation from her occurs because of our defective lifestyle, which disturbs the original pattern. Tantra 'reweaves' the fabric of our life so that we are once again in harmony with the nature. Tantra has many schools and is practiced in Hinduism as well as Buddhism.

The tantric *sādhanā* (practice) incorporates diverse elements such as breathing exercises, meditation, hatha yoga, mantras, *yantras* (geometrical figures), *mudrās* (gestures) and *maṇḍalas* (circles). These different practices are believed to activate the dormant power (*śakti*) of the soul, which is then harnessed for different purposes. Apart from being a spiritual path which leads to liberation, it is also regarded as science inasmuch as its practice, when strictly followed, yields results whether you have faith in tantra or not.

Tantra regards the human body as a microcosm containing the diverse counterparts of the universal elements. With meditation, the student awakens the internal forces and polarizes them with the cosmic powers. It is, however, necessary that the student should be under the guidance of a teacher who initiates him to the right type of method, and supervises his progress.

Tantrics are the worshippers of goddess Śakti who is contrasted with Śiva the masculine universal consciousness. Mantras are treated as identical with various deities who are the manifestations of the primordial power. One of the tenets of tantrism is that only a god can worship a god, which means that the mantras divinize the worshippers who identify themselves with these deities.

Like mantras, tantras can be classified in many ways. In the past certain geographical regions have been associated with some predominant schools of tantra. Siddheśvara, Kalī tantra, nilā tantra, siddhiyāmala, yoginī tantra, kubjikā tantra, rudrayāmala and many others were practiced in what is now India. Śābar tantra, ḍāmar tantra, kuṇḍalinī tantra, etc. were prevalent in Afghanistan and Iran. Mahānirvāṇa, meru tantra, indrajāla etc. were practiced in China and Nepal. Guptadīkṣā, bhūtaśuddhi siddhamantra, līlāvatī tantra, etc. prevailed in Java (now in Indonesia)

Today most of the tantric sites in India are situated in the North and North-East with the exception of Kerala in the South where a shrine exists in Malabar Hills.[1]

Another broad classification of tantra is

1. Kaula, which can be practiced by householders,
2. Samaya, where meditation is considered important and
3. Miśra, which is a blend of the first two schools.

Before we consider the tantric schools it would be instructive to study the esoteric anatomy and physiology of the human body.

3.2 Anatomy and Physiology

As pointed out earlier the body is considered a microcosm. A correspondence exists between (1) the regions of the body, (2) mantras, (3) yantras and (4) the letters of the alphabet.

The currents of the energy in the body are called nāḍīs of which there are 72,000. A junction of two nāḍīs is called sandhi, an intersection of three nāḍīs is termed marma sthāna, and the point where more than three channels meet is a cakra. The center of each cakra is associated with a distinct sound.

The central channel of energy is called suṣumnā which passes through the center of the spinal cord, and connects the anus or the base of the spine with the crown of the head. The channel on the left of the suṣumnā is called *iḍā* and that on the right, *piṅgalā.* The energy in iḍa is called 'blue dot' (*asita bindu*) and that in *piṅgalā* 'red dot' (*rakta bindu*). Energies flowing through different channels interact with these bindus giving rise to innumerable patterns of vibrations.

The main cakras are located along the axis of the suṣumnā. They are mūlādhāra in the region of anus, svādhiṣṭhāna at the regenerative organs, maṇipūra at the navel, anāhata at the heart, viśuddha at the throat, and ājñā between the eyes. At the crown lies the thousand–petalled shasrāra.

Each cakra has a specific number of petals which are associated with definite bījas. Every cakra also has a bīja associated with its center. The following tables show several details.

Table 3.1

Cakra	*Number of petals*	*Central bīja*	*Tattva/Stimulation*
Mūlādhāra	4	laṃ	Earth, cohesion, sense of smell
Svādhiṣṭhāna	6	vaṃ	Water, contraction, sense of taste
Maṇipūra	10	raṃ	Brilliance; expansion, heat,sense of color and form
Anāhata	12	yaṃ	Air; movement, sense of touch
Viśuddha	16	haṃ	Ether; space, sense of hearing
Ājñā	2	oṃ	Mental faculties

Table 3.2

Cakra	*God*	*Goddess (śakti)*	*Liṅga and yoni*	*Maṅḍala*
Mūlādhāra	Bala Brahmā on Haṃsa	Dākinī	Svayambhū and Tripura trikoṇa	Square
Svādhiṣṭhāna	Viṣṇu on Garuḍa	Rākinī	—	Crescent
Maṇipūra	Rudra on a bull	Lākinī	—	Triangle
Anāhata	Pinākī	Kākinī	Baṇa and trikoṇa	Six-pointed hexagon
Viśuddha	Sadāśiva	Sākinī	—	Circle
Ājñā	Maheśvara	Hākinī	Itara and trikoṇa	—

Note that in Table 3.2 the gods and goddesses associated with the cakras are manifestations of the same God Śiva and Mother Śakti. Three cakras are associated with three forms of male and female reproductive organs. The cakras are looked upon as lotuses.

1. *Mūlādhāra*: This is the base or the foundation which supports

other cakras. Its petals are red and it has an unpleasant smell. In the lotus are the Śiva-liṅga called svayambhū and Tripura triangle or kāma yoni, where the sun resides. Around the liṅga is the serpent–like kunḍḍalinī (śakti) coiled three and a half times Under normal circumstances the kuṇḍalinī is dormant.

The cakra is also the abode of Gaṇeśa, the son of Divine Mother, the lord of gravitation, the god of intelligence, and the remover of obstacles. From here Gaṇeśa guides other cakras and turns the wheel of life. He is also an expert dancer and his cosmic dance symbolizes the awakening of the kuṇḍalinī śakti.

Four bīja sounds emerge from the petals (nāḍīs); (clockwise), vaṃ, śaṃ, ṣaṃ, saṃ

2. *Svādhiṣṭhāna*: The six bījas emerging from its petals are (clockwise) baṃ, bhaṃ, maṃ, yaṃ, raṃ, laṃ. The cakra is of vermillion colour and has a bad odor.
3. *Maṇipūra*: This lotus has a golden color. The emerging ten bījas are (clockwise) ḍaṃ, ḍhaṃ, ṇaṃ, taṃ, thaṃ, daṃ, dhaṃ, naṃ, paṃ, phaṃ.
4. *Anāhata*: This is the cakra of 'unstruck sound' identified with om. Its color is red and it smells like hot blood. Its twelve petals generate the bīja sounds as follows : (clockwise) kaṃ, khaṃ, gaṃ, ghaṃ, ṅam, caṃ, chaṃ, jaṃ, jhaṃ, naṃ, taṃ, thaṃ. It is believed to have a deep connection with breathing.
5. *Viśuddha*: This golden colored lotus generates sixteen bījas (clockwise) aṃ, āṃ, iṃ, īṃ, uṃ, ūṃ, ṛṃ, ṝṃ, ḷṃ, ḹṃ, eṃ, aiṃ, oṃ, auṃ, aṃ, aḥ,
6. *Ājñā*: This cakra is the abode of the mind. Its petal bījas are kṣaṃ and haṃ.

Sahasrāra: At the crown of the head is this lotus of thousand petals which is not usually regarded as a cakra. It is whiter than the full moon with its head turned downwards. Within the sahasrāra is the full moon which is cool and which sheds rays. Inside it is what is called A-ka-thādi triangle, in which is the Great Void or Para-bindu or śūnya. This sunya is well concealed, and is the root of liberation. Here is the god called Parama Śiva who is Brahman as well as the Atman of all.

Many authors are reluctant to describe the sahasrāra and contend that it is to be 'felt'. According to *Śiva Saṃhitā* a holier place than sahasrāra does not exist.

3.3 Kaula Tantra

The word kaula is a derivative of 'kula' which means family. Kaula practitioners believe that the entire universe is one divine family, the manifestation of the universal Mother (*Śrī Vidyā*).

There are two kaula stages : the right hand which is elementary, and the left hand which is more advanced. We have already mentioned that a mantra and a deity are two aspects, auditory and visual of the same entity. The kaula tries to realize oneness with Mother through this 1-1 correspondence. The right hand kaula begins with a preparatory mantra sādhanā which consists of two stages, *prāṇa pratiṣṭhā* and *nyāsa*.

Prāṇa pratiṣṭhā: This includes intense meditation which enables the practitioner to identify himself with the deity. In meditation the sādhaka concentrates on the anāhata cakra. A specific mantra is recited. The identification with the deity is consistent with the tantric principle, "Only a god can worship a god".

Nyāsa: This consists of synchronizing different parts of the mantra with different aspects of our body. For example, when goddess Gāyatrī is invoked the Gāyatrī mantra "*tat savituḥ vareṇyam bhargo devasya dhīmahi dhiyo yo naḥ pracodayāt*" is split into different segments.[2] They are then synchronized with the parts of the hand (*karanyāsa*) and then with the other parts of the body (*aṅganyāsa*) as follows:

Segments	Karanyāsa	Aṅganyāsa
tatsavituḥ	Thumb	Heart
vareṇyam	Index fingers	Head
bhargo devasya	Middle fingers	Crown and head
dhīmahi	Ring fingers	Chest and shoulders
dhiyo yo naḥ	Little fingers	Eyes
pracodayāt	Palm	Prāṇic body

In actual practice each of the Gāyatrī segments is prefixed and suffixed by '*om bhūr bhuvaḥ svaḥ*'. For example, the thumb synchronization would appear as: *om bhūr bhuvaḥ svaḥ tatsavituḥ/ om bhūr bhuvaḥ svaḥ aṅguṣṭhābhyām namaḥ. Aṅguṣṭhābhyām* relates to the thumbs.

The third nyāsa is *vyāpaka nyāsa* in which the aspirant meditates on the physical form of the deity occupying his body region and repeating the mantra. For example, if the deity is Gāyatrī, the mantra would be similar to the above in which aṅguṣṭhābhyām is replaced by other parts of the body.

This procedure leads to a fascinating structural pattern which is discussed later.

Japa: In the next step the student recites the entire mantra a certain number of times as directed by his guru. The entire japa may consist of over two million recitations. During the period the student observes certain austerities like abstaining from meat and liquor.

In the next stage the student makes oblations of some substances into fire, the number of propitiations depending on the quantum of japa he has already made. Sometimes the teacher may permit symbolic offerings in which the student meditates on the maṇipūra cakra.

The student is next introduced to the worship of yantra. It was mentioned earlier that a deity is associated with a mantra. In the same way a yantra, which is the visual dimension, is associated with a deity. There is thus a triad, deity – mantra- yantra which is ultimately identified with Divine Mother. Since śakti can take innumerable forms, there are countless triads.

First, the guru usually initiates the sādhaka to Gaṇeśa yantra and if the student shows sufficient progress, the doors of yantric worship are opened to him.

The Gaṇeśa yantra consists of three circuits and a central circle surrounded by a number of śaktis. Through meditation and mantras the student traverses the yantra from the outermost circuit to the center which is identified with mūlādhāra. We have already mentioned that this cakra is Gaṇeśa's abode. Gaṇeśa will help the sādhaka gain mastery over instincts and endow him with physical, emotional and intellectual strength. If he so desires, the sādhaka can now proceed to higher levels, through further sādhanā.

The student can now proceed to cakra pūjā which will acquaint him with the left-hand kaula (*vāma mārga*). The left hand path has an unconventional outlook. While the right-hand path, teaches austerity, the left-hand believes that we have to face our instincts boldly and not run away from them. Its practitioner try to enjoy the senses as their masters, they are not the slaves. They try to reach the stage where even while being involved with the sense objects, they are above them.

The student treats the body itself as the living yantra and meditates on its cakras, the centers of śakti.

We have already mentioned that the kuṇḍalinī lies dormant in the mūlādhāra. The goal of the practitioner is to awaken it. While many methods have been tried, cakra worship is considered the most successful method for awakening the serpent.

The pūjā is unconventional and uses the forbidden path in which the practitioner uses five 'M's; wine (*madya*), fish (*matsya*), meat (*māṃsa*). gestures (*mudrās*), and sex (*maithuna*), so that the gulf between the profane and the sacred is bridged.

The pūjā consist of the following rituals.

(1) The student accepts a cup of liquor from the guru and places it on a yantra. The liquor has already been subjected to certain saṃskāras by the guru. (2) The body, mind, breath and senses are purified with liquor (3) Gaṇeśa and other sages are invoked (4) The kuṇḍalinī is propitiated. The ritual consists of five rounds of meditation on Mother and other ancillary rituals including oblations of the liquor. If the pūjā is successful, the sādhaka merges with the supreme śakti and dissolves in Divine Mother.[3]

3.4 Samaya and Miśra Schools

The samaya school replaces external rituals by the meditation on the sahasrāra treating the body as yantra. The student meditates only on the *sahasrāra*. The school does not use the five 'M's mentioned above. Its goal is *mokṣa* or liberation unlike the left-hand kaula which seeks enjoyment and liberation.

The miśra school is a blend of both the systems mentioned above.

3.5 Kuṇḍalinī Dynamics

Those who believe in the kuṇḍalinī śakti offer several explanations of how the process of harnessing the power works. In what follows a brief version mentioned in the text *Ṣaṭ-cakra-nirūpaṇa* (description of the six centers) is given.

The student meditates on the cakras successively beginning from the mūlādhāra working his way up towards the sahasrāra. He not only meditates on the cakra but also on the deities, *liṅga*, *yoni* and other elements of the *cakra*.

Meditation on the first cakra *mūlādhāra* brings him learning, happiness, and makes him master of speech. He becomes a king and is free from all diseases.

Meditation on the svādhiṣṭhāna makes him the lord of the yogis.

By meditating on the maṇipūra he acquires the power to create and destroy the world.

When he meditates on the anāhata at the heart, he is able to protect and destroy the world. His mind is now engrossed in Brahman. He can enter someone else's body if he so wishes.

He has now acquired complete knowledge of Brahman, and he continues to meditate on the viśuddha lotus. He obtains complete peace of mind, is free from sorrow and disease, and can see the past, present and the future. He now practices kumbhaka or retention of breath while meditating. This gives him the ability to move the three worlds. Even Brahmā, Viṣṇu, Śiva, Sūrya and Gaṇeśa cannot counter his power.

He now meditates on the ājñā, and his self (Ātmā) becomes identical with his meditation. He can quickly enter another's body, acquires unknown powers, becomes the omniscient sage, and the most important, he realizes that Ātman (self) and Brahman are one and the same thing. He then makes such mudrās as the khecarī mudrā and yoni mudrā. He has such wonderful experiences as seeing the Light and Bhagavān (God). He blissfully places his breath here and enters the supreme, eternal primeval God, Brahman.

He then moves to the sahasrāra. Immersed in Brahman, he rouses Devī Kuṇḍalinī through 'humkāra'. The process of awakening the kuṇḍalinī has to be learnt from the guru. The Devī wakes up, passes upward piercing the cakras and three liṅgas and goes towards the shining Śiva producing the bliss of Liberation. The yogī is now ecstatic and should lead the kuṇḍalinī with Jīva to her Lord and should make all things absorb in her. When Devī Kuṇḍalinī reaches Śiva's abode she drinks the nectar issuing from Para-Śiva. She then returns to her original abode, namely, mūlādhāra. The yogi who is liberated is never born again in this world.

It must be reiterated that the practitioner can pass through different stages only with the help of his guru.

The various stages of the śakti arousal depend on the particular method used by the tantrik. The dynamics related above pertains to the specific method mentioned in the text, but it nevertheless gives us an insight into the general theory of the kuṇḍalinī śakti.

3.6 Yoga

Etymologically 'yoga' implies union, but the word is used to indicate any path which leads to liberation, even where the concept of union (with supreme consciousness) plays no role. For example, those who believe in monism (advaita), the self (Ātman) and the Ultimate Reality (Brahman) are not different, it is the māyā which creates the illusion of duality. Hence liberation merely implies realization that Ātman and Brahman are one : the question of union does not arise.

A brief survey of several yogas is made below.

1. *Jñāna yaga*: This is a path of acquiring self-realization through knowledge (jñāna). For monists, this means the realization that the self (Ātman) is the same thing at Brahman or the Ultimate Reality. In this connection, recall the four mahāvākyas from the Upaniṣads mentioned in Chapter 1.
2. *Sāṃkhya yaga*: This is similar to jñāna yoga, but relevant to those who believe in the dualistic philosophy of sāṃkhya. The path tells you to realize that the self (Ātman) is different from the body, senses, mind and intelligence. The self is indestructible. You should therefore learn to rise above the pairs of opposites such as hot and cold, pain and pleasure. When you are above the feelings of 'I and mine' you become a true *Brahmanjñānī*, and merge into Brahman. Chapter 2 of the *Bhagavad Gītā* discusses this yoga in detail.
3. *Karma yoga*: In this path you observe your duties without expecting any fruits of action. There is non-attachment to the objects of senses. The yoga is elaborated in chapter 3 of the *Bhagavad Gītā*, and has a close connection with the Mīmāṃsā philosophy. This yoga is particularly suitable for householders since it emphasizes the action (karma) connected with your duty.
4. *Japa yoga*: This method consists of repeating a mantra. The Vedic mantras such as 'om' and Gāyatrī mantra are considered sacred and particularly useful, while the mantras from the Purāṇas are considered less efficacious. However, according some sages like Swami Ramdas (17th century) even a simple mantra like 'Hare Rāma' is equally useful. Scriptures also mention different types of japas like *nityajapa*, *kāmyajapa* etc.
5. *Bhakti yoga*: This is the path of devotion (*bhakti*). There are

different methods of bhakti such as hearing god's glories (sravaṇa), remembering God (smaraṇa), praying (vandanā) etc. Chapter 12 of the *Bhagavad Gītā* deals with this yoga in which both the forms of worship, the worship of the manifest deity (saguṇa Brahman) and that of the unmanifest One or Brahman are described.

6. *Mantra yoga*: This is sometimes identified with japa yoga, but some scholars mention a sixteen-step yoga which includes bhakti, japa, mudrā, etc. in which sāmadhi is the last stage.
7. *Patañjali yoga*: This was briefly discussed in chapter 1. Something must be mentioned about its eight limbs. The five yamas or constraints are; non-violence (*ahiṃsā*), truthfulness (*satya*), non-stealing (*asteya*), celibacy and control of senses (*brahmacarya*), and non- possessiveness (*aparigraha*). Niyamas are the five observances one has to follow. They are, internal and external purity or cleanliness (*śauca*), contentment (*santoṣa*), austerity and perseverance (*tapas*), study of scriptures (*svādhyāya*), and dedication to God of one's actions and will (*Īśvara praṇidhāna*). The third limb is the posture (*āsana*). It is necessary to choose the right *āsana* suited to one's constitution. There are a number of *āsanas* such as *siddhāsana*, *vajrāsana, padmāsana* etc. The fourth limb is *prāṇāyāma* or the control of breath or vital force. There are ten different *prāṇas* of which inhaling (also called *prāṇa*) and exhaling (*apāna*) are important. The control of this force is central to the Patañjali yoga. The fifth stage is *pratyāhāra* or the withdrawal of sense objects. This is followed by concentration (*dhāraṇā*) on a suitable object. The seventh limb is meditation (*dhyāna*) in which the mind becomes one-pointed. The last stage is called samādhi a trance –like state. The first stage of samādhi is called seed (*sabīja*) samadhi in which the yogī still retains his individuality. The second stage takes him to seedless (*nirbīja*) samādhi which is a truly superconscious stage. While this yoga is a path of liberation, there are a few spin-offs. The yogī can acquire siddhis or extraordinary and supernatural powers. However, the guru unusually exhorts the student not to deviate from the primary goal of liberation, and be lured by siddhis. The true yogī uses his powers only sparingly for the benefit of others and not for publicity. *Saṃyama* is the word sometimes used to denote the

combination of *dhāraṇā*, *dhyāna* and *samādhi*.

Some of the siddhis found in Patañjali Sūtra are mentioned below:

Siddhis	*Sūtra*
Knowledge of earlier births	3-18
Knowledge of other people's transactions	3-19
Ability to make oneself invisible	3-21
Clairvoyance	3-25
Knowledge of the universe	3-26
Ability to enter someone else's body	3-38
Ability to walk on water or bog	3-39
Ability to fly	3-42

From the standpoint of science, the sūtras are important, and will be considered again later in chapter 15.

8. *Dhyāna yoga*: This path uses the dhyāna aspect of the Patañjali yoga and considers the dhyāna of 'om' and ajapā Gāyatrī as particularly effective.
9. *Tantra yoga*: A generic term used for any yoga which uses tantric methods.
10. *Kuṇḍalinī yoga*: A type of tantra yoga which seeks to awaken the kuṇḍalinī śakti, raise her to the sahasrāra and then restore her to her original place at mūlādhāra. This was discussed above under 'Kuṇḍalinī dynamics'. The yoga is also called 'bhūta - śuddhi' or the purification of the elements of the body.[4]
11. *Haṭha yoga*: This is the yoga of force (haṭha) which seeks liberation through the purification of body and consciousness. To attain this goal the practitioner seeks to create a 'divine body' through various practices. The yoga was developed by Nātha yogis between 9th and 11th centuries, and uses the first four limbs of the rāja yoga. In addition, it uses some purification methods like 'dhauti' which cleanses the stomach, neti which involves cleaning the nose with threads and kapala bhati which clears nasal passage and sinuses through proper breathing.

Haṭha yoga, lays great emphasis on the power of sperm (*bindu*). According to Gorakṣanātha, perhaps the most respected practitioner of the system, the loss of semen leads to death while its preservation is life. The natural movement of the *bindu, prāṇa* (breath) and kuṇḍalinī is downwards. With the appropriate techniques the yogī arrests the movement of the bindu and makes it ascend to the sahasrāra.

The ascent of the bindu plays an important role in elevating the kuṇḍalinī to the sahasrāra. He also uses the khecarī mudrā with the tongue, when the kuṇḍalinī reaches the sahasrāra and there is a shower of amṛta or nectar. The mudrā ensures that the drink does not pass downwards. This mudrā is so effective that it prevents the bindu from descending even if the yogī is embraced by a woman.

12. *Kriyā yoga*: This consists of the three of the niyamas of the Patañjali yoga, austerity, (*tapas*) study of scriptures (*svādhyāya*) and *Īśvara praṇidhāna* i.e. surrender to God.
13. *Laya yoga* or the yoga of dissolution: This yoga is mentioned in some texts such as Śaṅkara's *Yoga Tārāvalī*. The yogī trains himself to hear the anāhata sound emanating from the anāhata cakra. One of the prescribed methods is to use a posture called siddhāsana. With the vaisnavi mudra the yogī listens to this sound through the right ear, shutting off the external sounds. Gradually, he attains the state called turīya in which he dissolves into the superconsciousness.
14. *Surataśabda yoga*: This path believes that every person has two identities, the external or manifest and internal which is hidden. The practitioner tries to establish contact with his hidden self through the 'inner sound'. This has the effect of energizing various cakras, which ultimately helps the self to merge into the Supreme Being.
15. *Tāraka Yoga:* The method involves meditation on the center between the eyebrows. The student tries to see the hidden brilliance symbolizing the sun and the moon inside his head. This yoga is traced to *Tāraka Upaniṣad.*
16. *Sahaja Yoga*: This yoga has become popular in recent years, and involves awakening of the kuṇḍalinī. It is suitable for householders– 'sahaja' means easy. The student has to spend some time on dhyāna every day.

Certain concepts of tantric anatomy and physiology appear mystical: the cakras and suṣumnā do not exist as physical organs. However, this alone does not invalidate the entire yoga or kuṇḍalinī system. This will be discussed later; but it is pertinent to point out here that in science we do use certain artifices whose existential status is controversial. For example, we really cannot prove the existence of points, though the concept of points is important in geometry.

3.7 Yantras

It was mentioned earlier that countless triads, deity-mantra-yantra can emanate from the Supreme Being. Like mantras, yantras too are eternal and self existent. Hundreds of yantras are described in literature and are not only used in the kuṇḍalinī yoga, but also as vehicles of wish- fulfilment.

According to tantric texts the primordial sound (*nāda*) 'ekoham' gave rise the point (*bindu*) which is usually found at the center of many yantras. When it became the 'expanded point' (*vṛddha bindu*) it became circular. The point when viewed as the seed of a circle (cakra) is 'cakra sambhava' (potential of the circle). The first nāda was followed by another sound 'bahuśyāṃ' which created *paśyanti, madhyamā* and *vaikharī* elements within the circle. These elements are believed to have developed into cakras; *trailokyamohana cakra, sarvānandamaya cakra* etc. The goddess of these cakras is Tripurasundarī with whom the most renowned Śrī Yantra is associated.

Like the circle, the triangle is also believed to have developed from the bindu. (Fig 3.1)

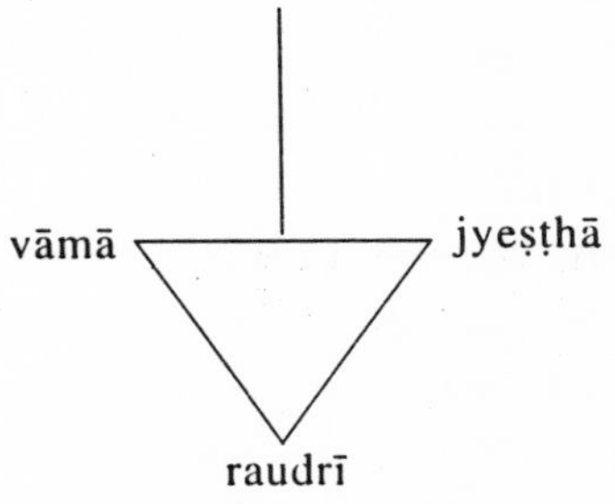

Fig 3.1 Śṛṅgāṭaka Trikoṇa

The bindu gave rise to a line. The vibrations of this line created two more points *vāmā* and *jyeṣṭhā*. The first is identified with Viṣṇu, sun and sattva (*guṇa*); the second represents *agni*, knowledge and tamas (*guṇa*). When these two bindu śaktis dissolved, a new śakti called *raudrī bindu* was formed which is associated with rajas (*guṇa*). The triangle formed by these points is called śṛṅgāṭaka trikoṇa. The whole triangle symbolizes the union of three characteristics; will, knowledge and action, and also light, life and love.

The point, triangle, circle square and petals are the most common components of a yantra and the following table shows their significance.

Table 3.3

Point	The superconscious state, Brahman, om, unity of Śiva and Śakti, Ultimate Reality sahsrāra.
Triangle	
1 Apex above base	Śiva
2 Apex below base	Śakti
Circle	Rhythmic vibrations (spandana)
Square	Earth, corners represent directions
Petals	Seat of Brahmā the creator, evolution of the universe
Mantric inscriptions	Corresponding deity. Corresponding region in the microcosm (body)

As mentioned earlier *Śrī Yantra*, the yantra of *Śrī Vidyā* also known as *Ṣoḍaṣī, Dakṣiṇākālī,* etc., is considered most important. It is believed to incorporate all other yantras.

There are three basic methods of *Śrī Vidyā* worship.

1. Kālikrama—associated with sattva-guṇa
2. Sundarīkrama—associated with rajas guṇa
3. Tārākrama—associated with tamas guṇa

The main sects who practice Śrī Vidyā are Ānandabhairava, Dakṣiṇāmūrti and Hayagriva. The mūla mantra of Śrī Vidyā is : *ka eī la hrīṃ, hrīṃ, ha sa ka ha la sa ka la hrīṃ*. It is also called pañcadāśī vidyā. (pañcadaśī means fifteen) because it contains 15 bījas.

The details about the construction of yantras are found in tantric texts such as Rudrayāmala, Gaurīyāmala and Tantric Upāsanā Darpaṇa.

For example, three types of Śrī Yantra have been mentioned: flat - surface (*bhūpṛṣṭha*), tortoise - surface (*kachacpṛṣṭha*) and mountain-surface (*meru-pṛṣṭha*). Gaurīyāmala text also mentions lotus surface (*Padmapṛṣṭha*) yantra. There are also a few injunctions specified in respect of the construction of Śrī Yantra: it should not be drawn on a wooden plank or wall. It is usually made of metals like gold, silver and copper.

Yantras have to be subjected to a ritual called *prāṇapratiṣṭhā* which 'activates' them.

The tantric doctrine of correspondence is very important. One component of the tantric triad mentioned earlier may emerge from another e.g. a yantra from a mantra or a god form a mantra.

Tantrics often warn against the use of the yantras sold in the market. They assert that only those yantras which are kept 'alive' through tradition and given by the guru to the student can have any effect. This also implies that the tantric sādhanā cannot be undertaken without the guidance of a teacher.

Yantras may be simple or complex and may have inscriptions of mantras, bījas and numerals. They may also be associated with specific deities or planets (regarded as gods)

Figures 3.2 through 3.6 show yantras with different degrees of geometrical complexity.

1. *Hanumāna yantra*: It is perhaps one of the simplest yantras, and is used as an antidote for ill health, loss of wealth or family feuds. It is to be installed in a particular manner and worshipped every day. Observe the bījas on it.(Fig 3.2)
2. *Dhana-yaśa-prāpti yantra*: The yantra is worshipped every day for prosperity, and is made of copper. A japa of a certain mantra is to be used in the worship. There are numerals instead of mantras on the yantra. (Fig. 3.3)
3. *Śrī Bagalāmukhī yantra* – Bagalāmukhī is a goddess. The yantra has a complex pattern and there are many allied types, of which one is shown here. It is made of copper and worshipped every day. It is used for inflicting injury (*māraṇa*), frustrating enemies (*uccāṭana*) propitiating planets, seduction (*vaśīkaraṇa*) and for many other purposes. (Fig 3.4)
4. *Śrī Yantra:* As mentioned earlier, this is the most revered yantra and is used for the prosperity of the family. It is worshipped along with mantras and auxiliary rituals. (Fig. 3.5)
5. *Śrī Mahāmṛtyuñjaya Yantra*: This is made of copper and used for curing diseases, for wealth and prosperity. (Fig. 3.6)

We recall that there is a correspondence between the microcosm (body) and the macrocosm(universe), and the human body itself is treated as yantra especially by those who follow the samaya school of tantra.

3.8 Yantras and symmetry

The most outstanding geometrical features of yantras is symmetry. This will be discussed in Parts II and III in depth, but a few preliminary remarks would be helpful. There are two kinds of symmetry, mirror and rotational.

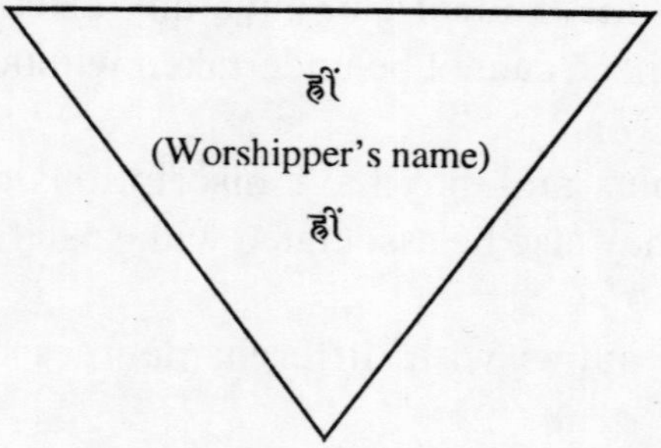

Fig. 3.2 Hanumāna Yantra

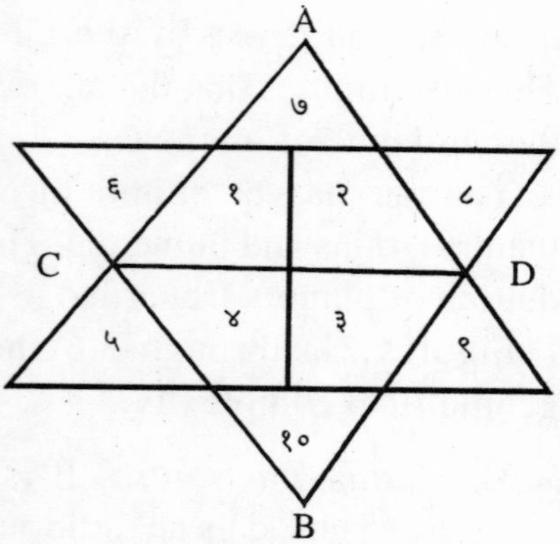

Fig. 3.3 Dhana-yaśa-prāpti Yantra

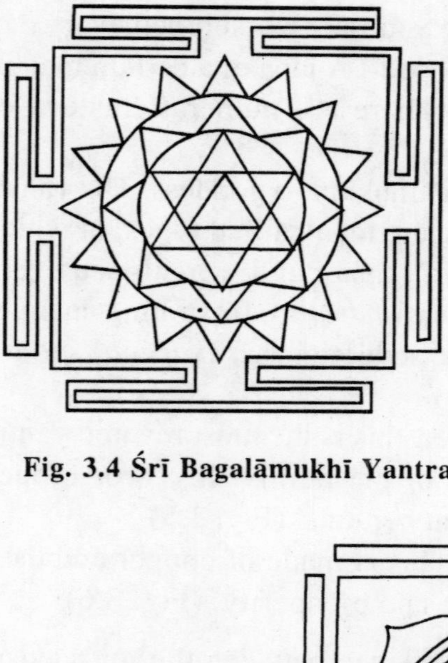

Fig. 3.4 Śrī Bagalāmukhī Yantra

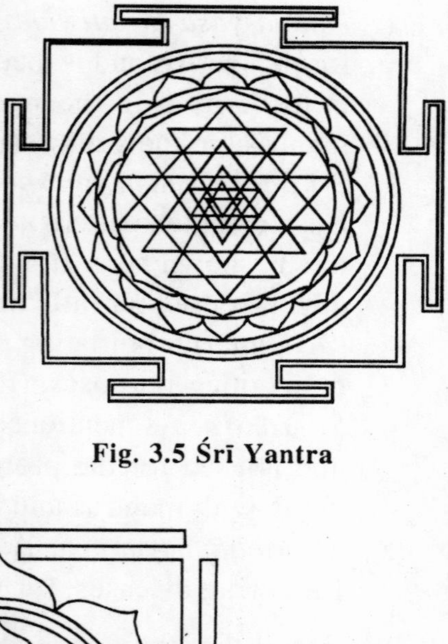

Fig. 3.5 Śrī Yantra

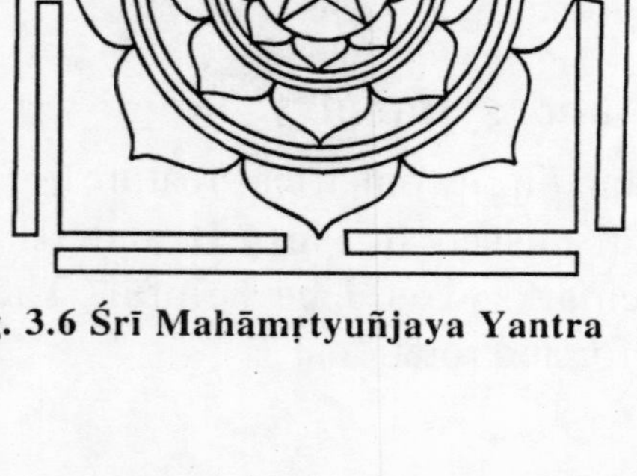

Fig. 3.6 Śrī Mahāmṛtyuñjaya Yantra

1. *Mirror symmetry*: You can observe that the right hand side of dhana-yaśa-prāpti yantra is the reflection of the left hand side (and vice versa) in the 'mirror' AB You can observe a similar symmetry below and above CD.
2. *Rotational Symmetry*: If mahāmṛtyuñjaya yantra is rotated about the axis perpendicular to the plane of the yantra through 90^0, 180^0 and 210^0 the yantra has the nearly same original appearance.

All the yantras shown here have both kinds of symmetry which you will be able to detect without any difficulty.

The yantras bearing numerical inscriptions have another kind of symmetry. Fig 3.7 shows a yantra used to propitiate nine planets. The yantra is used with ancillary rituals which include chanting of mantras. Observe that the sum of the numbers along each row, coloumn and diagonal is 45. The yantra is believed to have been introduced by a sect called 'Gosāvi'

Most yantras bearing 'numerical squares' would be a subject of recreational mathematics. Not only is there numerical symmetry, but one yantra can be obtained from another by the rotation of the whole yantra through a certain angle or by cyclic rotation of columns and rows. These aspects are discussed in chapter 7 on structure.

3.9 Mudrās

Mudrās ('seals') are gestures which are sometimes considered as important as yantras. While they are predominantly used by yogīs and tantrics, they are also employed in traditional worship such as japa and pūjā.

Different mudrās are used to gain favor of various gods. For example there are 29 mudrās used in the worship of Gāyatrī. There are mudrās to be performed before a pūjā, at the time of invocation and after the pūjā.

The most important mudrās for a pūjā are *surabhi* (fabulous cow of plenty) *jñānam* (wisdom, knowledge), *vairāgyam* (asceticism), *yoni* (female sex organ) *śaṅkha* (conch), *pankajam* (lotus), *liṅgam* (phallus) and *nirvāṇam* (liberation).

In yoga and tantra mudrās are used for specific results. For example when a yogī uses mahā mudrā or 'great mudrā' in the sitting posture the apertures at the top and bottom of the torsŏ are sealed. According to *Haṭha Yoga Pradīpikā* this mudrā cures leprosy, piles and many other ailments. It also destroys death and pain.

Khecarī mudrā ('roaming through space') is one of the most important mudrās in yoga and tantra and was mentioned earlier in passing. *Gheraṇḍa Saṁhitā* describes it at some length : The lower tendon of the tongue is cut, the tongue is moved constantly, and rubbed with fresh butter. It is drawn out with an iron instrument so that it is lengthened and is able to reach the space between the eyebrows. The yogī then turns the tongue backward to block the holes to the nostril opening into the mouth, which stops inspiration. He then gazes at the space between the eyebrows. This is khecarī mudrā. When practiced continuously the yogī conquers hunger, thirst, laziness, disease and even death.

As in yantras, symmetry abounds in mudrās. *Sumukham* (good mouth), *dvimukham* (double mouthed), *trimukham* (triple mouthed), *caturmukham* (four-mouthed), *pañcamukham* (five-mouthed), *ṣaṇmukhạm* (six-mouthed), *adhomukham* (mouth downwards), *yoni*, *liṅga*, and a host others show mirror symmetry. One reason for this is that the mudrās use both hands and symbolize human and animal anatomy which itself is symmetric.

3	2	8	5	4	9	1	6	7
5	4	9	1	6	7	3	2	8
1	6	7	3	2	8	5	4	9
8	3	2	9	5	4	7	1	6
9	5	4	7	1	6	8	3	2
7	1	6	8	3	2	9	5	4
2	8	3	4	9	5	6	7	1
4	9	5	6	7	1	2	8	3
6	7	1	2	8	3	4	9	5

Fig. 3.7 'Gosāvi' Yantra

Part II

ANALYTICAL TOOLS

4

KNOWLEDGE

4.1 Analytic-Synthetic Dichotomy

Everything we can learn about the nature is knowledge. This is a very wide definition about knowledge since 'nature' means the whole universe including our minds. We can, therefore, talk of the knowledge of art, science, mythology, religion, politics, sociology and so on.

Man acquires his knowledge through his senses including his mind. The branch of philosophy which discusses how knowledge is acquired is called epistemology or the theory of knowledge.

There is an unfortunate controversy between two schools of epistemologists – rationalists and empiricists. The former consider logic as the primary determinant of human knowledge while the latter feel that experience is the most important factor. These two aspects, rationalism and empirictisim have given rise to what is called analytic – synthetic dichotomy.

To understand this dichotomy consider the following statements.

I. 1 A. Since all cats are mammals and all mammals are mortal, all cats are mortal.

B. One of the following statements must be true – (i) The sun is a star (ii) The sun is not a star.

C. There cannot be a circular square.

D. A dog is a mammal. A parrot is not a mammal. Hence a parrot is not a dog.

E. If a, b, c are real numbers and $a < b$, $b < c$ then $a < c$

F. $a + b = b + a$ Where a and b are real numbers.

G. The sun rises in the East every morning.

H. Hydrogen is lighter than carbon dioxide.

I. Man cannot live for more than 200 years.

J. The height of Mt. Everest is 8872 meters.

We would certainly call all these statements true, but the statements A through F appear *obviously* true. If we define each constituent word and notation, the truth of these statements would automatically follow. Such truths are called analytic or logical and the knowledge is called a priori. The truth follows from the logical 'laws' which are innate to human mind. Such statements are also called tautological. The analytical statements belong to either logic (A-D) or mathematics (E-F), Bertrand Russel has conclusively shown that logic and mathematics are almost synonymous.[1]

The attitude of most philosophers towards analytic statements is reflected in Wittgenstein's statement in his famous work *Tractatus Logico-philosophicus*. "The propositions of logic all say the same thing." To understand what Wittgenstein means, let us re-write I. 1 A symbolically.

All cats are mammals can be written as " x is a cat implies x is a mammal" or a => b, where a is the proposition 'x is a cat,' => stands for 'implies' and b is the proposition 'x is a mammal'.[2]

Similarly, "all mammals are mortal" can be written as "x is a mammal implies x is mortal" or b => c

where c is the proposition ; 'x is mortal'. Our argument then means

If a => b and b => c then a => c..............1

a => b and b => c are called premises and a => c is the conclusion.

(1) is known as 'syllogism'. This argument is valid whatever the nature of a, b and c, i.e. it is not restricted to 'cats' 'mammals' and 'mortal'. To appreciate this consider a revised version of I. 1 A

All cats are mammals and all mammals are immortal. Hence all cats are immortal.

The argument is a valid syllogism. The conclusion "cats are immortal" is not true because our premise "mammals are immortal" is not true. A logical argument is valid or invalid, it is not concerned with the truth of the premises or conclusion. What it says is that if a => b and b => c are true then a => c will be true. For example if, mammals were immortal (b =>c), then, cats would be immortal (a => c)

While logical statements appear absolutely true, there is an element of uncertainty about the synthetic statements. (G-J) The height of Mt. Everest may vary from season to season, or we may not be able to measure it precisely. There may have been people who lived beyond

200 years, whose ages were not recorded, or in the future man may live for more than two centuries. Even the statement G may not be as certain as it appears to be. It is merely based on our observation from time immemorial. But there may be a celestial accident which could tear the earth away from the sun's orbit and we may (if we continue to exist) no more see the usual sunrises and sunsets.

There are philosophers like Ayan Rand who severely attack this logical-empirical dichotomy. According to them knowledge is acquired by the application of logic to experience. In fact the logic-experience split is treated as artificial by some thinkers. There is considerable substance in what these philosophers say. If we realize that our minds which are the source of logic, are part of the nature, the analytic-synthetic dichotomy becomes redundant.

However, from the standpoint of methodology it is sometimes useful to isolate logical (deductive) laws from other knowledge. Since these laws are absolutely certain, they can be used as irrefutable assumptions, when we discuss the credibility of any knowledge.

Deduction is a method of arriving at logical inference. There are many logical 'laws' which we use in our thinking, though we may not be aware of their technical names, such as syllogism (Ex.A) or the law of the excluded middle (B) or the law of contradiction (C). A characteristic of analytical statements is that they can be expressed in an abstract fashion. We have already shown that syllogism can be expressed this way. The law of the excluded middle appears as "Either A is B or not B" (there is no third alternative). The law of contradiction is "A cannot be both B and not B". We shall find later that such abstractions facilitate structural analysis of ritual.

While there are many logical laws, some can usually be derived from others. Logicians, therefore, treat some laws as axioms which are not demonstrable.

An analytical statement like (1) is always valid, whatever the 'contents' of a, b and c. It is necessary to remember that in analytical statements the conclusion does not provide any additional knowledge not already contained in the premises.

Sometimes a difference is made between 'a priori' statements and 'analytic' statements but we need not consider these nuances.

Statements G-J are called synthetic statements. While these are true, we feel that their truth depends upon our observation, and there is always an element of uncertainty.

How do we acquire knowledge though experience? Through our senses we perceive the world. A percept is a bundle of sensation retained by the brain. However, at the perceptual level the world is disjointed. It is through the two processes of 'differentiation' and 'integration' that a child reaches what is call the 'concuptual' stage. For example he will be able to distinguish between a table and a chair because their shapes are vastly different. He will soon integrate the essential characteristics of the chair, the most important being its use. The inessential characteristics of the chair : arms, cushion, colour etc. thus will have no place in his concept called 'chair'. In the process of learning, language serves as an important tool.

The concept formation is a hierarchical process. Simple concepts through further differentiation and integration give rise to more complex concepts. The process leads to greater abstraction and generalization.[3]

The fact that the process of learning has components other than logic (whose laws are certain) implies that there are other epistemological premises or postulates contained in "differentiation and integration of percepts". Some of them are induction, memory, testimony and analogy. Induction is making a general inference on the basic of limited number of observations. Induction is perhaps the most important principle for science. At the outset it must be pointed out that being non-logical all those principles contain a certain degree of uncertainty. Induction is not cent percent valid, memory may fail and the person who testifies may be a cheat. This raises an important question : How reliable is our knowledge? Or what is its "degree of credibility"? Fortunately, as science progressed, humankind's ability for accurate measurement also improved. Modern scientific instruments including computers have considerably reduced the margin of error. But what about the principle of induction itself?

4.2 Induction

Induction consists in making general inferences on the basis of a limited number of observations. Unlike deduction, inductive guesses are never cent percent correct. But all our knowledge of the external world is based on induction. The principle of induction cannot be proved, and it must be accepted as an epistemological premise. It must be observed that some philosophers use the term 'inductive logic' to distinguish it from 'deductive logic'. However, it is better to treat induction as outside the province of logic, the word we shall reserve for deduction. Sometimes the word induction is also employed to denote any process of inference other than deduction, and includes analogy, testimony etc. The following examples will indicate the scope of induction in the wider sense.

I. 2. A. A large container is full of beans of varieties, *A* and *B*. The beans are thoroughly mixed up and samples are taken from different parts of the container. In the resulting single sample obtained by mixing all these samples, it is found that 30% of the beans are of variety *A*, 70% of the variety *B*. It is concluded that the entire container has 30% type *A* beans and 70% type *B* beans.

B. A student of religion reads a certain chapter of a book of mantras and finds that every mantra in the chapter begins with 'Om'. He concludes that every mantra begins with 'Om'

C. In the wake of the atrocities perpetrated by the Nazis on Jews, it can be safely assumed that all Germans are cruel.

D. *X*, a famous actor asserts in a TV advertisement that a certain health drink of brand *A* can increase longevity. Within one month the sales of *A* double.

E. Quoting Einstein's theory it is asserted that "everything is relative."

F. Competent scientists opine that the efficiency of no machine can be 100%.

G. *X* is a renowned Indian physicist who believes that ancient Indians knew how to build an aeroplane (vimāna). He recites a few mantras which purport to describe the construction of a vimāna. His research students conclude that the vimānas did exist in ancient India.

H. Gregor Mendel who discovered some genetic laws was a monk.Most communists in 1930s rejected his theories as 'bourgois idealism.'

I. *A* and *B* are male twins who resemble each other to a great extent. Both are good sportsmen and have interest in movies, music, languages and enjoy reading. What's more, they are usually found together and are known to be in the same class, reading for a physics degree. We learn that *A* is the topper in the class. We guess that *B* must be one of the brightest students in his class, but later learn that he failed in the degree examination.

J. Franz Joseph Gall was an outstanding neuro-anatomist who distinguished between the grey and white matter of the brain, explained the role of the cerebral cortex and vindicated the Hippocrates' theory that the brain was the interpreter of consciousness. But he also created 'phrenology' a 'science' according to which it is possible to read a person's character by studying the external features of the cranium. Since he was regarded as a genius, his theory was accepted by many fellow-scientists as valid.

Ex. A through C are illustrations of induction in the narrower sense where inference about the population is made on the basis of the characteristics of its samples. When this method is used it is necessary to ensure that the sample is truly representative of the population, which implies that it should be (i) sufficiently large and (ii) not biased. These requirements unfortunately cannot be precisely defined and depend on the facts of each case. Attempts have been made to quantify the margin of error inherent in this kind of inference, but their utility is limited.

Ex. A is a case of 'strong induction' since the sample appears to be truly representative. The inference, therefore, is fairly sound. Ex.B is an example of insufficient statistics. One cannot make a general statement about mantras based solely on single chapter of one book. Ex.C uses an inference based on biased statistics. We cannot condemn the entire German race on the basis of the atrocities committed by Hitler and his lieutenants.

Ex. D thorough F involve "arguments from authority". Ex.D shows how the TV viewers are swayed by glamour, little realizing that the actor is not an authority on health. In Ex.E Einstein is misinterpreted. Einstein's relativity theory is confined to a restricted class of phenomena in physics. Ex.F is a case where all competent authorities are in agreement. The statement will have a very high degree of credibility. In Ex.G the gullible students are obviously under the influence of his research guide. The physicist has no evidence to prove his assertion. The only manner in which he can vindicate his claim is by engaging the students in a research project to build an aircraft according to the putative mantras and prove that the machine really flies. Ex.H illustrates the case of an 'argument against the man'. Just because a person is a monk it does not follow that he cannot make scientific discoveries.

Ex. I is a case showing how an analogy can fail. Ex.J again shows an instance of defective inference and how even learned men under the sway of a towering figure can accept his opinions blindly.

Memory plays an important role as a source of knowledge. However, it is not an original source; the original source is perception. Memory merely helps us pick the stored knowledge at the appropriate time. Thus objections can be raised against our dependence on memory.

The first objection comes from sceptics. An example based on Russel's oft-repeated illustration will elucidate the point. Suppose you recall that you met your friend yesterday at 5 p.m. I dispute this contention, I maintain that the entire world came into existence only today morning at 7 A.M. in the state in which it appeared at that time. Everything including human beings was born at that time in a 'ready-made fashion'. This means we were all born with our so-called memories. This implies that your belief of having met your friend yesterday is an illusion, because 'yesterday' did not exist. You might ring up your friend and 'confirm' your meeting. But since your friend too came into existence today at 7 A.M. with ready-made 'memories', his memory itself is an illusion, and his corroboration has no value. Such an argument is not illogical, but will not be accepted by most people because it can lead to extreme scepticism and one may doubt the existence of everthing except one's own mind.

The second objection has greater practical value and pertains to the fallibility of our memory. It is true that our memory fails on many occasions, and it can also be distorted. This is indeed a valid argument. However, memory can be corroborated by other evidence such as notings in the diary. Collective memory also enhances the credibility of the remembered event. If several people remember an event, the probability that the event did not occur is negligible. Though theoretically such a contingency can occur as a result of mass hallucination, the burden of proof that the event did not occur should lie on the person who contests it.

Testimony is another secondary source of knowledge. However, since it depends on the memory of the person who gives testimony, it can be fallible in the same way as our own memory. But testimony furnished by a number of people is usually accepted even in the court of law. Of course, the testimony can be fraudulent if the deponent has an ulterior motive in lying, but when it is apparent that the testifiers is disinterested, her testimony is accepted as a source of knowledge. An important kind of testimony involves the statements made by experts in the field of their specialization. Such statements, if they pertain to science, may be accepted by the common people, but the scientific community will usually insist on the appropriate evidence, which can be scrutinized by fellow-scientists.

It needs to be observed that the fallibility of memory and to some extent testimony has been considerably reduced because of the availability of modern instruments which can record acoustic and visual impressions.

4.3 Memory and Oral Tradition

It was mentioned earlier that the Vedic mantras were transmitted traditionally from one generation to another by word of mouth since writing was not known to ancient Indians. This raises an important question. How reliable are the Vedic mantras or what is the degree of distortion they may have undergone when they passed through several generations?

The first thing we have to remember is that the tradition emphasized the correct pronunciation of the mantras which were supposed to be learnt by heart. The meaning had either secondary importance or did not constitute an essential aspect of formal teaching.

Secondly, there were a few ingenious techniques devised to ensure that the original Vedas were transmitted without distortions. The continuous form of recitation which represents the normal flow of speech is called saṃhitāpāṭha. In Sanskrit when two words come together, they often form a compound word in which there are sound modifications. The process is called sandhi and there are many rules pertaining to it. If sandhis are disentangled from saṃhitāpāṭha the constituent words would appear separate. Consider the following example which is from the *Bhagavad Gītā* and not from the Vedas.

Imaṃ Vivasvate Yogaṃ Proktavānahamavyayam
Vivasvānmanave prāha Manurikṣvākavebravīt *(BG 4-1)*

(This imperishable yoga, I declared to Vivasvat, Vivasvat taught it to Manu. Manu told it to Ikṣvāku).

When the compound words are split, the lines would appear as :

Imam Vivasvate yogam pra-uktavān aham a-vi-ayam
Vivasvān manave pra-āha Manuḥ Ikṣvākave a-bravīt

When such a process is applied to saṃhitāpāṭha the text one gets is called padapāṭha. Each Vedic school had a prātiśakhya which not only taught how to derive saṃhitāpāṭha from padapāṭha but also introduced innovations which served as anti-distortion devices. To understand these aids, suppose that a given *padapāṭha* appears as :

a / b / c / d ... where a, b, c, d are separate words. This are now rearranged as (ab) (bc) (cd) ... The bracketed words are then compounded using sandhi rules.

These new sandhic combinations of the original sequence thus gives a new text called *Kramapāṭha* which was committed to memory. This introduces a double-check on the correctness of the original *saṃhitāpāṭha.*

There were also more intricate aids such as *jaṭāpāṭha* which has the arrangement (ab baab) (bccbbc)..., in which the bracketed units are compounded.[4] We thus have different combinations which when split, can provide us elements a, b, c,... from different sources. If all the sources give identical elements, there should not be any doubt about the correctness of these. If there is a discrepancy, it could be easily detected by a person who knows Sanskrit well.

4.4 The Postulates of Induction

We mentioned earlier that induction cannot be proved but must be assumed as a premise. However, since induction is a complex process, attempts have been made to search for simpler postulates which together constitute the basis for induction. Russel's contribution in this area has been truly singular and his five postulates can be considered adequate to validate a scientific method.[5]

We shall consider these postulates briefly. The importance of these postulates lies in the fact that they are a bridge between common sense and science. While the student of science may not be taught these epistemological premises science uses them implicitly. If any scientific theory violates them, in all probability it is invalid. This aspect will be recalled when we discuss science, pseudo-science and non-science. There are five postulates and they will be called the postulates of induction.

Modern scientists and philosophers prefer to replace the concept of substance by 'event'. One of the compelling reasons is that ever since the relativity theory was firmly established, the boundaries between matter and energy have become blurred, since under certain circumstances, one can be converted into the other.

An event may be defined as any happening which occurs at a certain place and time with respect to an observer. An explosion, lightening, an accident, watching a star are all events.

Suppose you are watching a cricket match and perceive a series of appearances which you interpret as the ball which is rolling on the ground after being hit by a batsman. Actually what you are seeing is a series of events e_1, e_2, e_3 ... At times t_1, t_2, t_3... What is the reason to believe that these events constitutes a "thing" or a ball? There is no logic behind it. The only reason is that from experience you have found it convenient to group a certain series of events into a thing, it fits admirably into the world in which you live. This principle is the postulate of semi- permanence which may be stated as follows. If there is an event *A*, it very frequently happens that there is another event close to *A* in time and space, very similar to *A*. A series of such similar events we call a thing. In the present case you call it the cricket ball which is rolling on the ground. However, once the identity of a thing is established, it is not necessary that the events characterizing the thing should all be close to one another. For example, you may recognize a friend even when you see him after many years.

The second postulate has to do with cause. The concept of cause is primitive and pre-scientific. You see a boy lift a brickbat and after a few moments receive a blow on the head. You conclude that the boy is the cause of the injury. You are a diabetic and need a daily injection of insulin. You forget to take the injection on three successive days. You feel uncomfortable and the blood test shows that the blood sugar has shot up. You attribute it to the missing injections.

The concept of cause, however, is an embarrassment to science. If an event of type *A* is always or usually followed by an event of another type *B*, we usually assume that it is the cause of *B*. But this may be misleading. If you find that your postman always delivers your letter at 5.30 p.m. and your husband returns home from office at 6 p.m., you do not conclude that the frail postman is causing the movements of your muscular husband.

There is also the problem of multiple causes. Suppose an intoxicated man jumps through the open window of his apartment on the first floor, falls on the ground and breaks his neck. What is the cause of his injury? Is it the open window, the liquor he has consumed or the gravitational force? In the next chapter we shall see how science tackles this problem. But at present we are concerned to find the broad premises for knowledge which can also be used by science.

The concept of cause is replaced by another and more satisfactory concept called causal line. The second postulate or the postulate of separable causal lines states that, it is very frequently possible to form a series of events such that, from a few members of the series, something can be inferred about other events in the series. A causal line is the series of the events connected in this way. What makes such an inference possible is called a causal law.

Let us go back to the cricket match you were watching. You identify the ball as the series of events e_1, e_2,... at times t_1,t_2...... From a few members of the e-series you can know something about other events. The e-events constitute the causal line. Two events in this line are related in such a way that the prior event can be called the cause of the later event. But the first event does not entirely determine the second, because there is also the effect of the environment — also of causal nature – on the causal line itself. To understand this, suppose a fielder is chasing the ball. His movements give rise to another causal line. When the fielder stops the ball, the two causal lines have interacted.

The second postulate involves separability of causal lines. A given event can be a member of two lines. For example, when you are watching the ball or the the series of e-events, the light ray (*AB*), consisting of photons from an event, say, e_2 reaches your eyes and causes, the perception of e_2 – *AB* and e-series are two causal lines, e_2 being the common member. *AB* itself consists of several closely separated events which are similar to each other. (see fig. 4.1)

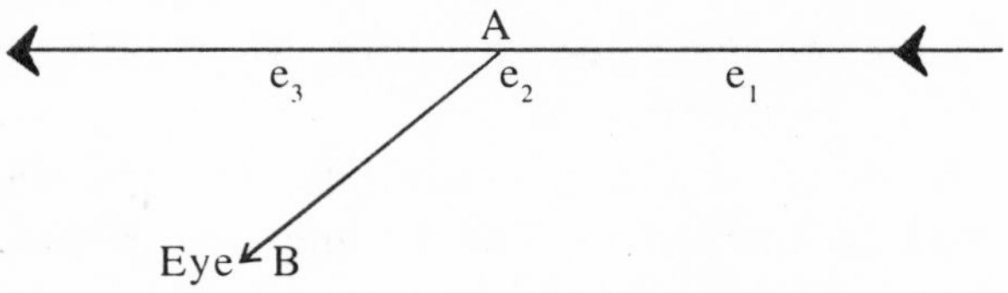

Fig. 4.1 Causal Lines

The second postulate implies that an event is frequently one of the series of events which has always an approximate law of persistence or change. The postulate is general and applies to other branches of knowledge as well as physics. For example, it implies that the cricket ball rolls on the ground preserving its shape and colour, a photon travels with the same velocity and direction, a mango seed when planted grows into a tree and yields mangos, and so on. The first law of motion in physics states that a body continues to be in the state of rest or uniform motion unless it is disturbed by outside causes. A little thought will convince you this is only one case of the postulate of separable causal lines. We must, however, mention that the postulate does not attempt mathematical precision, and leaves this question to the respective branches of science.

The concept of causal lines can however be valid only if it is assumed that space and time are continuous. This takes us to the third postulate or the postulate of spatio-temporal continuity. If we assert that there is a causal connection between two events *A* and *B*, there should be a continuous causal link between *A* and *B*. This postulate abolishes the notion of 'action at a distance' which at one time seriously blocked the progress of physics.

It must, however, be observed that this postulate can be used when a causal law is presupposed. For example, if you see *A* in London on a certain day, and another person resembling *A* in New York a week later, you cannot infer that *A* traveled to New York (as you did) unless you first verify that the person you saw in New York is really *A*.

The fourth postulate is called 'structural postulate.' Going back to the cricket match, there are thousands of spectators who are watching the match. They are located at different distances and in various directions with respect to the 'centre' where the match is being played. Their perceptions are similar, not identical. But we have no doubt that they are observing the same event. What this means is that the structures which reach these spectators have causal lines which have a single origin having the same structure. More will be said about this in the Chapter 7 on structure.

Our last postulate is the analogy postulate. All of us unconsciously use analogy to draw inferences. For instance, we believe that other people have minds on the evidence that they not only resemble us in anatomy and physiology, but also react to stimuli in the same way as we do. Analogy cannot be proved logically, but must be accepted as an epistemological premise, if we want to avoid the extreme skepticism which we mentioned in connection with the memory premise.

The analogy argument can be stated as below : If the objects of type *X* and *Y* have properties a, b, c, d and those of the type *X* are known to have property e, then the objects belonging to *Y* will have the property e.

Logicians often speak of 'relevant similarities' which can strengthen analogy. For example, biologists perform experiments on rats and the results are then used to draw analogous inferences in case of humans. While rats and humans may appear dissimilar they have some physiological similarities which can be considered as relevant.

In physics analogy has been instrumental in propounding new theories. When Huygens discovered similarities in the behaviour of sound and light he guessed that light could be of wave nature. It must, however, be remembered that analogical arguments do not provide proof, the theory suggested by analogy needs to be verified experimentally.

However, even when analogy appears 'strong', the inference may fail. I2(I) provides an example. This only shows the limitations of non-logical inferences which are only probabilistic.

We have already mentioned that these postulates, connect common sense to science. When science describes the behaviour of bodies in motion it is assuming the postulate of quasi-permenance. When astronomers tell us about different heaveny bodies, they have an implicit belief in separatable causal lines. When the TV companies installs telecasting stations they assume that audio-visual structures will be transmitted continuously through space and time. They are in fact assuming the postulate of spatio-temporal continuity. When a TV programme is watched by millions of viewers, the common people as well as scientists believe that all viewers are watching the same event, thus displaying their belief in the structural postulate. The fact that everyone assumes the existence of other peoples minds demonstrates the universal acceptance of the analogy postulate.

Since knowledge was defined in a wide sense, the question arises whether certain private experiences – superconscious states and other mystical experiences constitute knowledge. The problem with such knowledge is that it cannot be verbally communicated. Capra rightly points out that such knowledge cannot be obtained just by observation, but full participation of one's whole being is needed.[6] Neuroscientists try to glean something about such experiences through brain chemistry.

But such investigations can at best yield correlations between the states of the brain and consciousness, they cannot tell us what the experience feels.

Closely related to mystical experience is knowledge relating to supernatural and transcendental phenomena. Supernatural phenomena have non-physical explanations that lie beyond natural laws. Transcendental concepts include God, afterlife, heaven and hell. Strictly speaking transcendence implies that they are beyond human comprehension.

Paranormal phenomena such as clairvoyance (ability to see that which is beyond the eyeshot) and prognostication (prediction) are sometimes distinguished from the supernatural phenomena. It is believed that one may be able to explain the former scientifically when science has sufficiently developed. These phenomena will be briefly discussed in Chapter 15.

This takes us to metaphysics which is defined in several ways, but is usually concerned with the first principles of things, essence, being, existential status and so on. It discusses such questions as " Is there a deeper reality to the table you see?", "What is time?"

If such questions concerned only mystical experiences and personal knowledge, it would not create many problems for science. But two revolutionary theories – relativity theory and quantum theory propounded in the 20th century have shaken the very foundations of science. They have prompted physicists to change their fundamental concepts about space, time, mass, existence and even logic.

We normally distinguish between space and time as two different types of dimension and assume that there is a universal absolute time. Einstein firmly established that time measurement is as relative as space measurement. This means that in order to specify an event you not only require the corresponding space coordinates and time coordinate, but also need to know with respect to which observer the coordinates are measured. One of the strongest results of relativity theory is that two events may be simultaneous (i.e. occurring at the same time) with respect to one observer, though occurring at different times with respect to another. A corollary of the theory is that there is no sharp distinction between mass (m) and energy (E) and one can be converted into another under suitable conditions according to relationship $E = mc^2$ where c is the velocity of light which, incidentally, is constant for all observers whatever their location. Fortunately, the relativistic effects are perceptible only when the velocities are very high and are a matter of no interest in our daily life.

Quantum theory affects the world at the sub-atomic level. Light is a type of electro-magnetic radiation. It is found that light has a dual nature. It behaves like waves as well as a bundle of particles called photons. An offspin of this theory is Heisenberg's uncertainty principle according to which the position of a particle and its momentum (mass x velocity) cannot both be correctly determined. The more accurately we try to measure one, the greater error we make as regards the other. This is a fundamental law of nature and does not reflect the limitations of either the apparatus or human parception. Certain phenomena also lead scientists to an uncomfortable paradox: a photon can be at two place at the same time.[7] Scientists also believe that at the sub-atomic level an event cannot be specified independently of the observer. This has led many writers to link quantum theory with consciousness and mysticism.

5

SCIENCE

5.1 Knowledge and Science

The word science is derived from Latin 'scientia' (knowledge) and in its broadest sense connotes a body of knowledge about nature obtained through observation, experiment and deduction. In English it is usually restricted to 'natural sciences' which include physics, chemistry and biology, which are also sometimes called exact sciences. This reflects the influence of Rene Descartes (1596-1650) philosopher and mathematician who thought that all science is certain, evident knowledge. He rejected all knowledge that was merely probable. He seems to implicitly believe that all scientific phenomena should be mathematically expressed to be credible. However, we have seen that all knowledge of the external world is probabilistic. Incidentally, before Newton, the analytic-synthetic dichotomy was represented in science by Descartes and Francis Bacon (1561-1626), followers of deduction and induction respectively. It was Newton (1642-1727) who synthesized both these methods in his *Principia.*

In French the word *science* and in German its equivalent *Wissenschaft* are used in a broader sense than in English, and connote social sciences and even humanities. In Sanskrit and many Indian languages, the word śāstra can mean knowledge, science, precept, theory and even command, and would not fit into the Western concept of science. There are also other two words jñāna (knowledge) and *vijñāna* (knowledge, science) in Indian languages.

Interestingly while ancient Indians regarded linguistics as science in the modern sense, the West accepted it as such only recently. In India there was also a science of ritual. The Western science has yet to bestow that honour on the systematic study of mantras and ritual.

5.2 Characteristics of Science

Since science in the widest sense can mean almost any kind of knowledge and in its narrowest sense means exact sciences, we face a dilemma. Where do we draw the line? This is quite important when we are discussing the relevance of science to ritual. We saw in the last Chapter that certain types of knowledge involving personal experiences – heavenly bliss, religious ecstacy, samadhi etc. cannot be shared by the humankind in general. If we exclude such knowledge, what remains may be called social knowledge. It is from social knowledge that we have to create the category of science. I shall approximately follow Staal and consider science sufficiently wide to include social sciences and linguistics, but narrow enough to exclude history and literature. Instead of defining science rigorously we shall set up a broad criterial framework to decide what constitutes science. It will be assumed that a social knowledge can be called science if it has the following characteristics.

1. *Empirical Adequacy:* It consists of theories or models which describe the observed phenomena of the universe with a fair degree of accuracy. A model may consist of (a) an exhaustive list of rules or (b) mathematical/statistical equations correlating different observed phenomena or (c) when quantification is not possible, statements of cause-effect relationships. This requirement is concerned with empirical adequacy.

   In physics and to some extent in other natural sciences it is usually possible to provide a quantitative model. In social sciences one often uses statistical models or one may be content with statements showing cause-effect relationship. The mathematical theories, of course, can describe the world with greater precision than the statistical ones. This is why a science like physics is called 'exact science'. In a science like grammar a model may consist of a set of rules with exceptions to rules. The latter will reflect the inexactness of this science.

   A theory or model can be called scientific only if we can make definite predictions about the future. If it merely describes the results obtained before the model was set up, it cannot be called a scientific theory. Given the already obtained results, a trivial model can always be designed, say, by a simple enumeration. It is only in case of logic and pure mathematics, that a cent per cent accuracy can be achieved in prediction. Even in physics there is a margin of error attributable to the limitations of instruments and human perception. In social sciences, where human behaviour is involved, a greater deviation from the predicted results is usually permitted.

2. *Abstraction*: A theory may introduce entities which are either abstractions or whose existential status is debatable. Such entities with assigned properties do not invalidate the theory so long as it is internally consistent and constitute a system that can correctly describe the observed phenomena.
   Electrons and protons cannot be 'seen' and the nature of photons (light particles) is elusive, but they serve a useful purpose in describing the sub-atomic world. In geometry the existential status of points and lines is dubious. Nevertheless they play an important role as parameters in geometry.
   In Freudian Psychology the human mind is described in terms of the id (instinct), ego (self) and superego (conscience) which are abstractions. Freud freely borrows concepts from dynamics to describe psychological phenomena. So long as such entities and concepts form a consistent system and help us understand human behaviour, their indeterminate existential nature by itself should not detract psychoanalysis from being a science.
3. *Consistency:* A scientific theory which seeks to explain a phenomenon should be consistent. To explain what consistency means, we shall give an example from mathematics.
   The multiplicative inverse a^{-1} of number a is that number which satisfies the equation
   $a \times a^{-1} = a^{-1} \times a = 1$. Thus the inverse of 5 is 1/5. However, zero does not have an inverse. If possible, let a^{-1} be the inverse of 0 where $a = 0$.
   Let us follow the following argument:

$$0 = 0$$
$$5 \times 0 = 20 \times 0$$
$$5\,a = 20\,a \qquad (a = 0)$$
$$5\,a\,a^{-1} = 20\,a\,a^{-1} \qquad (\text{multiplying both sides by } a^{-1}.)$$
$$5\,(a\,a^{-1}) = 20\,(a\,a^{-1})$$
$$5 \times 1 = 20 \times 1 \qquad (\text{since } aa^{-1} = 1)$$

Hence 5 = 20 which is absurd. This shows that if we introduce an inverse of zero, an internal inconsistency appears.

You should observe that the (internal) consistency we are speaking of is inherent in the very mathematical apparatus we use for a theory and should not be confused with the consistency with experimental results, which is covered by the first requirement. Suppose you define 'mantrik' as a person who chants mantras. Subsequently a person tells you that he is a mantrik because he recites a few lines from the Vedas every day. You assert that he is not a mantrik because he does not practice sorcery though he may recite mantras. There is an inherent contradiction in your definitions which prevents us from testing whether a person is a mantrik or not. Such internal contradictions can be removed by redefining your concepts.

4. *Provisional Nature:* A scientific theory is always provisional. As the human ability for scientific observation, improves, the scientist may find evidence which contradicts her earlier theory. A new theory is then propounded which is a refinement of the old theory. Newtonian mechanics was found to be inadequate to accommodate the bodies moving with high velocities. The Newtorian theory is now superseded by Einstein's relativity theory. But the former can still be used when the velocities are not high.

   This characteristic of science, which involves a continuous appraisal of the old theories and the introduction of modified theories is sometimes expressed by the maxim, "science is progressive."

5. *Generalization:* In science there is what, Einstein calls "stratification of the scientific system".[1] As science progresses, there is a march from special laws to general laws. For example, the orbits of the planets can be understood with the help of Kepler's laws and the behaviour of falling bodies can be understood with the help of Galilio's experiments. But it was Newton's discovery of the gravitational law which incorporated both these theories and raised physics to a higher level. The planetary motion as well as the motion of the falling bodies thus could be derived from a single Newtonian theory.

   What this means is that there is a constant progress in which the number of primary concepts and relations is minimized and a logical unity is established.

In this context the principle called 'Occam's razor' may be mentioned. According to this "entities are not to be multiplied without necessity'. William Occam (1285-1349) was an English theologian.

Suppose we explain a group of interrelated phenomena in terms of n parameters $x_1, x_2, \ldots\ldots x_n$ and it is found that one of these, say, x_1 is completely determined by $x_2, x_3, \ldots. x_n$, then x_1 can dropped from the set of variables.

As explained earlier all scientific theories have only a probabilistic significance. The laws of physics enjoy the highest probability. Economic laws have a much lower credibility. In general, the laws of natural sciences have a greater probabilistic value than those of social sciences.

If we define science in the broadest sense and include logic and mathematics in it we should get a continuum with logic/mathematics at one end with probability one (certainty) followed by natural sciences which in turn will be followed by social sciences. If this spectrum is followed beyond science we will reach the end of zero probability where astrology and psychokinesis (ability to affect objects by mental efforts) would appear.

It is necessary to bear in mind that there can be more (valid) theories than one to explain the same phenomenon. For example, two different approaches, microscopic and macroscopic, can be used to describe the behaviour of gases. The various gas laws such as Boyle's law were first empirically established using temperature, pressure and volume of a gas. This is a macroscopic approach. In the 19th century the "Kinetic theory of gases" used the microscopic approach which considers the behaviour of individual molecules. Using statistical techniques, the theory derives the same gas laws which were established earlier.

A number of illustrations chosen from various fields are given below. We shall examine whether they can be called scientific statements, and assess their degree of credibility.

I.1. Since all cats are mammals and all mammals are mortal, it follows that all cats are mortal. This has already been mentioned in the last Chapter (I.1 A). However, we shall now view it as a scientific statement. The statement is a syllogism and as mentioned in Chapter 4, always valid. Since it has nothing to do with the truth of the premises or the conclusion, the question of experimentation does not arise.

I.2. The sum of the three angles of a triangle is 180^0.

We mentioned in the last chapter that logic and pure mathematics are almost synonymous. With about ten principles of deduction and ten other premises of a general logical nature, entire pure mathematics can be constructed. The statement made above is true in what is called the Euclidean space. If we define such terms as 'points', 'lines', 'triangle', 'parallel' etc. in a certain way, the above statements will follow as true. We do not have to draw a triangle to verify this statement, because it is a tautology. But if you draw triangles on flat surfaces you will find that the sum of their angles is really 180^0. What is the significance of this? It means that the surfaces on which you have drawn the triangles are Euclidean planes. A spherical triangle does not have this property because it is not in a Euclidean plane.

Theoretically we can have a number of geometries whose nature will depend on our definitions of points, lines etc. These are purely logical constructions. It may happen that one of such geometries – the Euclidean geometry – holds good for the space in which we live. This fact will have to be verified by experiments.

I.3. $7 + 5 = 5 + 7$

This again is an example from pure mathematics. The above law is called the commutative law of addition. Once the numbers, + and = are defined the above statement appears as a tautology.

I.4. A. The planets describe ellipses with the sun in a focus.

B. The areas described by the radii drawn from the sun to a planet are proportional to the times of describing them.

C. The squares of the periodic times are proportional to the cubes of the mean distances of the planets from the sun.

The laws relating to the planetary motion about the sun were enunciated by Johann Kepler (1571-1630) through observation. This is a simple scientific law which can be experimentally verified. As we observed earlier, scientific theories can undergo modifications. In fact, Kepler's laws were subsequently modified in the light of new evidence.

I.5. The universal gas law in physics is given by

$$\frac{PV}{T} = \text{constant}$$

Where P, V, T are pressure, volume and temperature of a given mass of a gas. The physicists realized that the law was only approximate since the equation assumed a gas to be 'ideal'. The law was later corrected by Van der Waal. Nevertheless, the original equation may be considered fairly accurate.

I.6. There was a time called 'big bang' when the universe was infinitesimally small and infinitely dense.

This is the well-known big bang theory.[2] The theory implies that the universe came into existence with a hypothetical explosion, and is based on Edwin Hubble's discovery of the expanding universe. Its greatest weakness is that it cannot be verified. It therefore uses analogy and employs extrapolation – or rather 'retropolation' – back in time. It tries to find out at what time the universe was 'a point'. Extrapolation may ensure mathematical precision, but it raises a question whether the method of such going back in time over 10-15 billion years is epistemologically sound. Suppose you observe the behaviour of a given quantity of water between, say, 30 – 90 degrees Celsius, it will tell you that it expands when it is heated. But can you glean from your experiment that the water freezes at 0^0 C or boils at 100^0C?

The big bang theory is beset with considerable uncertainty and its scientific credibility appears very low.

I.7. $2NaOH + H_2SO_4 = Na_2\ SO_4 + 2H_2O$

This is a well-known equation in chemistry explaining the reaction of sulphuric acid (H_2SO_4) with Sodium hydroxide (NaOH). The products are Sodium Sulphate (Na_2SO_4) and water (H_2O). Since this result has been confirmed innumerable times there should not be any doubt about its validity.

I.8. "The ghost of Banquo enters and sits in Macbeth's place" (*Macbeth*, Act III Scene IV)

What is peculiar about this statement is that it is not made by any character in the play. We may have great suspect for Shakespeare, but the sentence (whether it reflects the bard's personal belief or not) is not a scientific statement. We do not have an incontrovertible evidence of the existence of ghosts. A better approach to handle such statements will be found in Chapter 15.

I.9. In English orthography consonant 'q' is followed by the vowel 'u'.

This is a scientific statement of high credibility. There are only a few words used in English such as qintar, qanat and qwerty which do not obay this rule. They are so few that the above statement can be amended with a proviso : with a few exceptions. Incidentally this illustration shows that linguistics can be studied as a science.

I.10. MV = PT

This is the Fisher equation in economics where M is the amount of money, V the velocity of circulation, (the number of times each unit of money is spent during a given period.) P the price level and T is the volume of trade. Though economic laws have a lower degree of credibility than the laws of physics, Fisher equation is one of the exceptions. The reason is that it is a tautology since the two sides merely represent the same quantity in two different ways.

I.11. Hitler persecuted Jews.

This is a factual statement that can be verified from records. However, this is a historical and not a scientific statement, though it is true.

I.12. A society is stratified on the basis of education, profession, wealth and race.

This certainly is an empirical fact though it cannot be quantified. It should also be understood that there can be other important determinants of social strata, in some societies. For example, among Hindus caste system is still a major factor that determines one's social standing. As a scientific statement it has a fairly good credibility.

I.13. As the income of a community increases, the consumption increases, but the rate of increase with respect to income falls. What this means is that for every additional unit of income, the additional consumption falls.

These were the views of economist John Keynes (1883-1946), and were based on the behaviour of an individual family. This consumption pattern certainly holds good for a family – except perhaps in the range of very low income. You will agree with this view from your own experience. However, Keynes thought that the data about individuals could simply be aggregated to obtain the consumption pattern for the whole nation. Empirical studies contradict this hypothesis and suggest that the national consumption has approximately a linear relationship with income. i.e. for every successive unit increase of income, the additional consumption is the same.

This phenomenon can be satisfactorily explained, but its technicalities cannot be discussed here.[3] But the moral of this example is that we cannot rely totally on intuition and extrapolation, but must subject our theories to verification.

I.14. According to the tantric text Indrajāla you can convert a man into a monkey using the following mantra:[4]

om praphullita hunkāra jvale jala vikaṭa vānare svāhā.

The mantra is to be recited in a prescribed manner with some ancillary rituals.

This claim is verifiable. However, since no person claiming the power of this mantra has demonstrated its efficacy, it may be assumed that the mantra has no scientific validity.

I.15. Vedic rituals and mantras follow a certain structural pattern.

The statement does not claim any supernatural powers. If we are able to show that the rituals and mantras do have some structural patterns, we would be making a scientific statement. I. 14 and I. 15 make it clear in what sense we can associate science with ritual and mantras.

These illustrations should convinces you that one can conceive of a continuum in which knowledge and sciences are arranged in the credibility range from probability zero to probability one. It must however, be added that, within the same science there can be instances of 'laws' whose credibility may vary widely.

5.3 Hypothesis and Verification

How are scientific theories formed? There is no simple answer to this. The raw material a scientist has is the observational data and previous hypotheses, if any. There is no straightforward inductive method which can translate this information into a hypothesis. Scientists usually hit upon a hypothesis through intuition in a flash, though analogy may also help them. Superstition and even dreams sometimes lead to important theories. Fortunately most scientists believe that there is some order in the world phenomena which uniquely determines the theoretical system. Leibnitz called this a 'pre-established harmony.' Such belief enables scientists to work with infinite patience and perseverance. In his essay "What is the theory of relativity?" Einstein observes, " The state of mind which enables a mind to the work of this kind is akin to that of the religious worshipper or the lover; the daily effort comes from no deliberate intention or program, but straight from the heart.[5]

Sometimes the words 'hypothesis', 'law' and 'theory' are used in a technical sense to indicate slightly different connotations. We shall not observe such distinctions but use the term hypothesis to indicate a scientific assertion in general. When the other two terms are used, they may be considered equivalent to hypothesis.

The confirmation of a hypothesis is done by what is usually called the 'hypothetico-deductive method'. It consists of three stages: (1) setting up a hypothesis, (2) deducing its consequences by logic and mathematics, and (3) verifying if experimental observations agree with the predicted results. The deduction from hypothesis may be schematically shown as :

Hypothesis => observational predictions. (A)

As this stage the scientist may have some options. He may select a certain experiment for which the deductive argument will have to be set up.

Suppose the scientist makes a number of observations which agree with the theoretical prediction. Can he conclude that the hypothesis is confirmed? In fact what we are trying to assert is whether the following argument is valid.

Observations agree with predictions => Hypothesis is true (B)

Observe that (B) is the converse of (A) and the converse need not be true. But we have already seen that the knowledge of the external world can be gained only through induction and is always probabilistic. The conclusion we can draw from B stands amended as "the hypothesis is probably true". The degree of credibility will depend on a number of factors such as the number of observations and the extent of deviations if any. Since one of the characteristics of a scientific theory is that it is provisional, the established hypothesis may be used until it is superseded by a more accurate hypothesis which can take care of even minor deviations. This incidentally shows that the scientist may have to hunt for an alternate hypothesis or evaluate an already existing rival theory.

Sometimes scientists take into account what is called the 'prior probability' of the hypothesis as an additional evidence in assessing the hypothesis. The prior probability of a hypothesis is its perceived credibility independent of its experimental verification. ESP (extra-sensory perception) provides an example.

A person may claim that he can communicate with another person thousands of miles away instantaneously. Now, according to the relativity theory, the maximum velocity with which a signal can travel is the velocity of light, which rules out any instantaneous communication. This creates a low prior probability when a scientist wants to assess the hypothesis relating to telepathy.

It must be observed that the hypothesis may not be simple but may involve auxiliary hypothesis which have already been independently verified. For instance when a scientist conducts an experiment using an electron microscope to prove his main hypothesis, he is assuming the validity of electron microscopy. In other words he assumes that the wave theory of matter upon which the electron microscope is built.

The question of using induction arises only when observations fairly agree with theoretical predictions. What if they do not? The scientist may be tempted to reject the hypothesis as the easiest solution. However, if she is shrewd and finds that the deviations have a recognizable pattern she might wonder whether she has not made mistakes in the details of the hypothesis. Is it possible that she has not taken certain factors into considerations? Could it be that she has omitted certain initial conditions or less important 'causes' (variables) from the hypothesis? Sometimes it is possible to revise the hypothesis by adding a few conditions so that the experimental results agree with the amended hypothesis.

Before the planet Neptune was discovered, it was found that the orbit of Uranus differed from that predicted by Newton's theory. Adams and Laverrier conjectured that the perturbations of Uranus could be ascribed to the wrong initial conditions in the hypothesis. They thought there was another undiscovered planet in the sun's orbit. The postulate of this new planet Neptune led to the revision of the original initial conditions. The revised calculations correctly described the orbit of Uranus. This shows how the revision of the 'lost' hypothesis may lead to new discoveries. Incidentally Pluto was discovered in a similar manner.

A hypothesis should not be rejected merely because it has roots in superstition. Physicist Copurnicus was also an astrologer who believed that tides were influenced by the moon. The theory was derided by Galilio who held an erroneous view that the tides were caused by the earth's rotation around the Sun. Another illustration is related to John Good, another astrologer, who kept a thirty-year record of his observations in connection with the supposed planetary effect on weather and epidemics. The records led to the discovery that there was a seasonal variation of suicidal rates. This is a real sociological phenomenon, for which no satisfactory explanation has yet been provided.

It was mentioned in the last chapter that a 'cause' was an embarrassment to science because it is difficult to define and also because there may be innumerable causes. This is true because no phenomenon occurs in isolation and different events in the universe are interlocked to form very complex systems and sub-systems. Science speaks of a 'causal law' which correlates a number of interrelated variables. Since, in practice a phenomenon depends on a number of causes (variables) it is not always possible to incorporate all of them into a causal law. Fortunately not all causes are equally important. For example, many packaged liquid products are marked for volume. But the volume of a liquid changes slightly with the temperature. These changes are, however, considered insignificant and hence ignored.

Complex scientific laws usually develop gradually. Initially a hypothesis connecting most important causes may be propounded. As the observation proceeds, the other causal factors may be added which would entail a slight modification of the old theory.

Gas laws provide a good example. Suppose you are a scientist, and lived before the gas laws were discovered. You observe that a gas can easily charge its volume. You have some idea about the pressure of a gas from the appearance – slack or taut - of a bag or a ball in which a gas is enclosed. This gives you reason to believe that there must be a relationship between the volume of a given mass of gas and its pressure. You perform a number of experiments in which you maintain the temperature of the gas constant because you have a hunch that the temperature variation may upset the relationship between the pressure and volume. Your experiments convince you that the volume of a given mass of gas is inversely proportional to its pressure. If you double the pressure the volume is halved.

Now you wish to find out how the volume would change when you altered its temperature. Again, in order that the volume-temperature correlation should not be disturbed by extraneous factors, you decide to keep the pressure constant. A few experiments convince you that the volume of the gas increases by about 1/273 of its volume at 0^0 Celsius for every degree rise of temperature.

These two results which you obtained are precisely what Boyle (1627-1691) and Charles (1746-1823) found, and are known as the Boyle's law and Charles' law. If you are sufficiently talented you might be able to combine these laws and obtain the 'equation of state'

$$PV = RT$$

which we mentioned in I. 5.

Unfortunately the law was found to be only approximate. Physicist Regnault found that not only this was not strictly obeyed by all gases, but the deviations from the predicted results in case of certain gases (air, nitrogen and carbon dioxide) were opposite to those in case of others like hydrogen.

Boyle's law and Charles' law reflect the macroscopic approach to science. The scientists began to consider a microscopic approach when they asked themselves what was happening inside a gas. They now treated a gas as consisting of molecules in motion. They rightly believed that the pressure of the gas was caused by the impact of its molecules on the boundary (for example, the inner surface of the bag in which the gas is trapped.). This approach led to a new theory called the Kinetic theory of gases.

Bernoulli (1700-1782) was able to derive Boyles' law on the basis of the kinetic theory. However, it was soon realized that the equation of state was only approximate and was valid for a hypothetical 'perfect' gas, and assumed unrealistic assumptions such as (1) the molecules were infinitesimally small and (2) they had only kinetic energy and no potential energy. Van der Waal presented a revised equation for 'real' gases in 1873 which appears as

$$(P + a / V^2)\quad (V - b) = R\,T$$

where a, b are constants which have different values for different gases. But even this equation was subsequently found to be inadequate. More than fifty equations of state have been suggested incorporating 'causes' not hitherto taken into consideration.

This somewhat lengthy discussion on gas laws was undertaken purposely to demonstrate the scope of scientific hypothesis. The history of gas laws shows that as more and more variables are brought into the picture to accommodate the discrepancies, the laws undergo successive refinements, but one can never speak of the final result. As the investigations proceed, finer deviations from the predictions may be noticed and a search is made for new variables. The discovery of new variables leads to the revision of the hypothesis. The history also sheds light on how the same phenomena can be approached from different angles – microscopic and macroscopic in this case. It also demonstrates how two areas of science – in this case heat (Charles' law) and dynamics (kinetic theory) can be integrated. In fact it provides us an insight into the process of unification in science, mentioned earlier.

It was mentioned earlier that knowledge-science formed a continuum with scientific credibility ranging from zero to one. We now ask ourselves whether sciences defined in the broader sense can be categorized on a different basis. Logic and mathematics, it was observed, are almost synonymous and their laws are 'certain'. What's more unlike, say, physics, they have no causal connections. For example, when we say that the opposite sides of a parallelogram are equal, we are asserting a logical connection.

Causal connections are found in other sciences. : natural and social sciences are characterized by causal connections. However, in natural sciences, the casual connections are on a firmer footing and can be quantified. In social sciences they appear to somewhat loose, beset with uncertainties. One often uses statistical theories in these areas, for example, in economics. The presence of uncertainties can be traced to psychological elements. Of course uncertainty too has a place in modern science, for example, in quantum mechanics and genetics, where statistics may be used; but the instances are fewer.

How do we categorize a science like linguistics in terms of 'connections'? The apparent characteristics of linguistics are the set of rules and structural correlations. They are supported by causal as well logical connections. When we assert that the Norman conquest in 1066 C.E. introduced many French words in English, we can perceive the causal lines. Speaking and hearing are causally connected. On the other hand logic cannot be divorced from the structure of language. In fact, logic and mathematics are sometimes called quasi-linguistic systems.[6]

It was mentioned in the last chapter that many logical and non-logical postulates were necessary as premises in the theory of social knowledge, and hence in science. These premises sometimes appear as pedantic statements and it may be believed that the five postulates mentioned earlier apply only to natural sciences. In fact they are equally relevant to a science like linguistics, though their importance is not manifest. Linguists and even 'ritual scientists', if such a term can be used, use them implicitly. Those who study historical linguistics and phonology (linguistics related to sound) assume not only causal lines but also the postulate of spatio-temporal continuity. Analogy is used not only by linguists but also by common people to coin new words. When the linguist studies the history of a language or a word he has a belief in the postulate of semi-permanence. And without the structural postulate no two linguists would have a common ground of agreement in regard to utterances, script or even concepts.

6

MEANING AND INTERPRETATION

6.1 The Meaning of 'Meaning'

The word 'meaning' appears simple and we use it frequently in speech and writing, but if you try to find out what it really stands for, the meaning of 'meaning' will elude you.[1] One of the reasons for this uncertainty is that we use the word in different senses. The second reason is that philosophers, too, have tried to analyse this word which has not only made it profound, but added to it dimensions ordinary people will not think of. I can give the following list of its different connotations, but I am not sure it is exhaustive, and there is also some overlapping.

1. *Symbolic indication*: 'Man' written on this paper signifies a species of mammals, and not on ordered collection of letters m-a-n. Symbols are used to convey meaning; words in language, dots and dashes in the Morse and gestures in pantomime. We call the process translation in which a set of symbols is converted into another set of symbols having the same meaning. Thus a French text may be translated into Swahili, or an English novel into the Braille.

   The symbolic meaning consists of standard rules, so that communication is possible, between one person and another.

   Apart from the prescriptive symbols, it is also believed that there are universal symbols common to the whole humanity, but usually concealed in the unconscious mind. It looks as if symbolism is "an obsolete mode of expression of which different fragments have survived in different fields.[2] Symbolism finds an expression in such diverse fields as myths, fairy tales, popular sayings jokes, poetry and drama. Some of the more commonly occurring symbols are house (human form) emperor and empress (parents), sacred number three, reptiles, *liṅga* (male sex), *yoni* (female sex), and vessel (woman). Symbolism plays an important role in interpreting mythology and art. Freudian psycho-analysis uses symbolism extensively in interpretating dreams and neurotic symptoms. In religion, symbolism is believed to provide deep insights and truths.

2. *Instinct and meaning*: When a cat 'smells' a mouse, it becomes alert and expectant and would not be surprised if the mouse soon appeared before it. To the cat the smell 'means' the presence of a mouse. This sense involves a causal connection instinctually determined and different from the normative symbolism in which the connection is conventional.
3. *Association and meaning*: Pavlov conditioned his dog to salivate in response to a stimulus. If we find that the appearance of an object *A* is invariably followed by the appearance of *B*, we are conditioned to expect *B* when we see *A*. In case of animals, who cannot analyse the situation as man does, the appearance of *A* would 'mean' *B*. The causal connection inherent in this process is of 'association' and not instinctual.
4. *Function and Meaning*: If you see a person wearing an amulet you might ask him what does this mean. He might answer you that the talisman is 'meant' to ward off the evil. The 'meaning' of an object in this case is the function it is believed to perform. A closely associated with this sense is an attribute of an object. When a poet says "this is heaven" he is using a metaphor to indicate his feelings in response to his environment.
5. *Surprise and Meaning:* Suppose you are expecting a friend for dinner. The door bell rings at the appointed time. You open the door and find to your horror a lion cub accompanying your friend. Pointing at the quadruped you ask your friend "What is the meaning of this?". You are not only expressing astonishment but demanding an explanation of your friend's abnormal behaviour.
6. *Gestalt and Meaning*: A gestalt is a perceptual structure conceived as something more than an assemblige of its parts. Suppose you know two persons *A* and *B* individually. One day you learn that they are brothers. The complex (*A,B*) based on the relationship between *A* and *B* provides an additional

dimension to your knowledge. Complexes whether geometrical (spatial) or temporal (in which the components are related in time), convey a meaning which transcends the meaning revealed by its components. It may be mentioned that what gives a meaning to the gestalt is the interrelations among its constituents. This aspect is discussed in Chapter 7 on structures.

7. *Cause and Meaning*: When an animal is hurt it may whine, grunt or make weird movements. When the baby is hungry it cries. We may say that the cause of the whining, grunting or crying is the meaning of the sounds or the movements.
8. *Teleology and Meaning*: When we ask "What is the meaning of life?" or "Where do we fit into the scheme of the universe?", we are consciously or unconsciously wondering whether there is any design, purpose or goal behind our lives or the unfolding of the universe. Those who believe in teleology on a grand scale usually believe that there is a prime mover, generally called God who is planning everything. Of course, teleology when referred to isolated processes may mean a plan designed by someone other than God.

Suppose you are visiting a foreign country. You come across a strange object surrounded by a group of people. You ask "What does this mean?" You may get several answers

"This is Amoo".
"Amoo will bring us luck".
"We display this object every year in the first week of January".
"This was brought by our forebears when they migrated to this place".
"Don't worry, it will not attack you."
"Nothing, we are just enjoying ourselves".

None of these answers can be said to be irrelevant to your question which seeks meaning. It is for you to pick up the right answer. Incidentally, your question and the several answers show that an entire philosophy can be built around an innocuous looking word meaning. One can see almost every department of philosophy – logic, epistemology, metaphysics (The view about reality) and even esthetics.

We can see that there can be either causal or logical connections involved in the meaning of meaning. When we tell a Frenchman that

" I hold" means "Je tien" we are specifying a conventional linguistic equivalence which is logical. But when we say that a nuclear war will mean total destruction, we are thinking of a causal connection.

But what do philosophers think about meaning? Some of them refuse to define it at the outset but develop the notion gradually. For example, Russel defines proposition as "all the sentences which have the same meaning" without defining meaning.[3]

Some philosophers like G. E. Moore (1873-1958) go to ordinary people like us to find from their usage what 'meaning' really means. According to them the common sense provides us reliable knowledge which contains unanalyzed truths. It is the business of philosophy to find out the meaning of these truths. Thus for Moore, the philosopher goes to the common people to understand the truth and not discover them. Incidentally it may be noticed that 'truth' is another idea which philosophers are loath to define. A few words about truth will be said later.

Ludwig Wittgenstein (1889-1951) appreciated multiple uses of ordinary language, and asserted that instead of being obsessed with the object of determining the meaning of a statement, we should try to find out the different ways in which language functions. For him, when one analyses a statement, one is trying to find out how the statement is contextually used rather than what it 'means'. He typifies the ordinary language philosopher who warns against dogmatically labeling a statement meaningless merely because it does not meet the criteria of 'meaning' prescribed by a given school. What the philosophers like Wittgenstein want to say is that each statement has its 'own logic'.

It would be instructive to briefly discuss what is called the verifiability theory of meaning which was authored by Moritz Schlick (1882-1936).who is generally regarded as the father of logical positivism. The theory has been a topic of fierce debate among philosophers.

According to this theory the meaning of a proposition is the method of its verification. The theory looks simple in some cases. If I assert that the length of this room is 20ft., the meaning of the statement lies in measuring the length. If the room is really 20ft. long, the statement is true, otherwise it is false. In any case it does have a meaning However, some statements such as "Jupitor has a core of gold" appear uzzling. How can we actually verify it? Schzick concludes that it is ot necessary for us to actually verify. What he implies is 'verifiability' ot actual verification. A statement is verifiable if there is no logical npossibility of verification. To understand this distination, consider he following examples:

(a) The lady wore a dark dress which was bright yellow.
(b) The child is naked and wears a long white gown.

Both these statements according to Schlick are meaningless because hey are logically impossible. In fact they violate the law of contradiction mentioned earlier.

Consider, however, the following famous example:

What is the other side of the moon like?

When this question was raised, man had no knowledge of the other side since artificial satellites were not invented. According to Schlick the sentence is meaningful because, given the above question we know exactly how to verify an answer like 'the other side of the moon is made of gold'. It is not necessary for us wait till man explores the other side to find out its truth. The fact that man has knowledge of the other side does not in any way add to the meaningfulness of either the question or the answer, though it may tell us whether the answer is true or false.

Consider now an example which philosophers regard as metaphysical and prefer to remain silent.

Do we continue to live after we are dead?

According to Schlick such a question is meaningful. He contends that he can imagine witnessing the funeral of his body and continue to exist without body since there is no logical contradiction in the question.[4] In fact he goes to the extent of asserting that this is not a metaphysical statement, but the immortality (afterlife)conceived as above is an empirical hypothesis which is verifiable. However, immortality in the sense of 'living for ever in some form' according to him is not verifiable because it involves the notion of infinity.

The meaning of 'meaning' will be relevant when we try to find out whether ritual and mantras have any meaning (Chapter 14). You will do well to remember that 'meaning' has a number of senses which are contextually determined. In other words you will have to remember what the common language philosophy says.

6.2 Truth

Truth like meaning is difficult to define. Broadly, two types of trutl are distinguished, epistemological and metaphysical. In the forme there is some correspondence between a concept or an assertion anc the reality it seeks to describe. In the words of Kant truth is "th conformity of our concepts with the object". Metaphysical o existential or ontological truth relates to the underlying reality o things.

According to Russel truth is primarily a property of belief and derivatively of sentences which express beliefs.[5] Truth according to him consists of a certain relation between a belief and some facts outside the belief.

Suppose we always find two things or circumstances *A* and *B* together. Then the moment we see *A* we would react as if *B*, too, was present. It may be said that the presence of *A* makes us 'believe' *B* to be in the environment. If someone shouts 'fire' you are likely to believe that there is fire in the neighbourhood. Your belief will be true if the fire really exists and false if it does not. The 'fire' is the verifier of the truth, and may be beyond the experience of the believer. For example, in the present case truth of there being fire does not depend upon your seeing it.

According to Russel, every belief is in the nature of a picture combined with a yes-feeling or a no-feeling. (1) In case of a yes-feeling it is true if a fact exists which has to the picture the same kind of similarity that a prototype has to an image (2) In case of a no-feeling the belief is true if no such fact exists. (3) The belief is false if it is not true. Suppose you are a New Yorker and are told that a yogi has demonstrated the feat of levitation in Mumbai before the audience of 20,000 people. You believe in supernatural phenomena while your wife is a materialist. On hearing the news you will have a yes-feeling while your wife will have a no-feeling. Subsequently, it is confirmed that levitation did take place. Then your belief happened to be true while your wife's belief was false. On the other hand if you subsequently come to know that levitation failed, your belief was false while your wife had a true belief.

The fact which makes a belief true needs to be described. Consider the question whether a certain woman is married. If she is married we can indicate her husband by description, " *X* who studied with ou in college". This is a verifier which makes the statement "the 'oman is married" true. Of course there may be more ways than one) establish truth. But if no description is possible, the woman is a pinster.

The philosophy of pragmatism bases the value of knowledge by s utility. For most pragmatists the truth of a hypothesis is no more ıan the success in solving a problem which occasioned the hypothesis. uch a utilitarian definition of truth creates many inconsistencies in ıe theory of knowledge. It also makes a mockery of the common ıan's concept of truth. William James (1842-1910) one of the earliest ragmatists resolves this dilemma by treating "success in solving the roblem" a relative concept. For example in experimental science, true ideas are those that we can assimilate, validate, corroborate and erify. False ideas are these which we can not".[6] The standard of 'uth in this case is certainly different from that involved in such uestions as reality of God. In the latter case, "the true is the name of 'hatever proves itself to be good in the way of belief, and good, too, or definite assignable reasons".[7]

The concept of truth in pragmatism appears to be highly flexible ut is justified on the ground that the criterion for truth cannot be ıdependent of the purpose for which the truth is tested.

Another concept of truth is due to Reichenbach, which is based on ıe degree of credibility or the probability of the occurrence of an vent. Since, as described in Chapter 4, in empirical science, there is lways an element of uncertainty, Reichenbach's concept of robability as replacement of truth suits it very well.

Metaphysical or existential truth relates to the underlying reality of ıings. Eternal goodness, God, being, Brahman are some of the topics n which metaphysical truth has relevance.

Religions are mainly concerned with existential truths, though they nay sometimes discuss epistemological truths to justify their doctrines. A person is established in truth when he has complete rapport with God and expresses his involvement in His existence. In the Old 'estament the expressions like "to do the truth" means to live in .ccordance with God's will, while in the New Testament the raditional view of truth, Christ appears to be at its center. "Christ is he way, the truth and life." (John 14-6)

In Vedānta philosophy the ultimate truth is Brahman "which is neither being (*sat*) nor non-being (*asat*)" (BG XIII 12). A perso who realizes this truth ceases to distinguish between the individu soul (Ātman) and the Oversoul (Brahman). Brahman is believed be above the pairs of opposites – good and bad, honest and dishones hot and cold and so on. This aspect shows how metaphysical trut radically differes from the concept of epislemological truth. Evidentl there is no place for metaphysical truth in science.

6.3 Interpretation

The word 'interpretation' is roughly equivalent to 'meaning' bu usually covers a much wider field.

It may mean proper explanation or signification of somethin translation of a book or a speech, or the technique of obtainin significant information from an action. In creative works it ha acquired a wider dimension. The rendition of Mozart's *Eine klein Nachtmusik* by well known musicians may be called the 'interpretatio of the maestro's original piece. The Western musicians using the instruments may interpret 'Bhairava' a well-known rāga of the classic Indian music. In both the cases by interpretation we mean the stylisti representation of Mozart or 'Bhairava' as the case may be by th concerned musicians according their understanding of the grea composer or the rāga. Leonardo's 'Mona Lisa' can be similarl interpreted by a modern painter.

In fact, a creative work can be interpreted in different ways b different people : by the audience, by psychologists, art critics and s on. What's more, the work of a great master is interpreted and re interpreted by several generations.

However, it sometimes happens, usually in logic and mathematic that a certain statement appears to be true, but it can be interpreted i several ways. In this case the different interpretations are not vagu or subjective depending upon one's taste, as in the case of arts. Th truth in this case admits of several true interpretations. This may soun improbable to you, but consider the following illustration :

I.1. Suppose you are provided with the following data :

a) o, a, b, c,... are some entities forming a set S

b) a + b = b + a for every a, b of S

c) a + (b + c) = (a + b) + c for every a, b, c of S.

d) a + o = a for every a.

How would you interpret the data? Most of us who have not studied advanced mathematics would identify o with zero, + with addition, and= with arithmetical equality. However, in fact there are many interpretations, which are equally valid as can be seen from the following table:

Table 6.1

Symbols	A	B	C	D	E	F
a,b etc	Natural numbers	Rational numbers	Real numbers	Complex numbers	Vectors	Matrices of the same order
O	Zero	Zero	Zero	Zero	Zero vector	Zero matrix
+	Addition	Addition	Addition	Addition	Vector addition	Matrix addition
=	Equality	Equality	Equality	Equality	Vector equality	Matrix equality.

In fact the number of interpretations is infinite. For example, 'real numbers' can be replaced by 'even numbers' or "three times the intergers" and so on. It is the context that will tell us which interpretation fits the case. This illustration consists of entities that have logical connection. An example containing parameters having causal connections may be provided.

I.2. The share price index at a certain Asian stock exchange falls by 3% in a week. Different analysts offer the following numerous interpretations:

a) The variation is too small to warrant any explanation, and should be attributed to statistical fluctuations.
b) The weightage given to IT and pharmaceutical shares in the index is about 80%. The fall in index can be attributed to the speculators keeping away from these stocks.
c) It is a reaction to the movement of Dow Jones average which fell by 4% during the same period.
d) The bears were more active than the bulls.
e) The propospects of an armed conflict between two neighbouring countries made the speculaters panicky.
f) There are rumours that corporate taxes will be hiked soon.
g) An oil depot with huge oil stocks in a West Asian country caught fire and was totally gutted.

This example shows how vast is the scope of interpretations of the data from social sciences. What's more, some of the interpretations can never be proved. In this respect they differ from I.1 where only logical connections are present and all interpretations are equally true with absolute certainty – it was the context that decided which interpretation was the relevant one. A social scientist or an expert can take you for a ride. For example, D above is no more than a tautology. When experts cannot find a proper explanation for a phenomenon they usually use an interpretation couched in technical jargon.

6.4 Hermeneutics

Hermeneutics or the 'science' of interpretation first appeared in the Hellenic period in connection with the study of classical texts. It was later used in biblical interpretations. The interpretations are believed to have two aspects. The objective side deals with the grammatical meanings and their historical variations, while the subjective approach tries to understand the author's intention.

The 19th century saw what is sometimes called 'free' hermeneutics which could be used to handle almost every subject including esthetics, social sciences, literary theory and even natural science.

Friedrich Schleirmarcher delivered a series of lectures in 1819 in which he developed a theory of 'general hermeneutics'. According to him in order to understand the meaning of the part of a linguistic whole, we must perceive the structure with a prior sense of the meaning of the whole; but we can know the meaning of the whole only by knowing the parts. For example, if I say "my existence cannot be doubted", you can understand the word 'existence' fully only when you keep in mind what the sentence means. On the other hand you cannot understand what the sentence means unless you know what existence stands for. To us this might appear circular reasoning, but philosopher Wilhelm Dilthy (1833-1911) did not consider this as logical flaw. On the other hand, he thought it was not a viscious circle. He christened this innovative device 'hermenuetic circle'. According to him, any interpretation is achieved through an interplay between our understanding of the parts and an evolving sense of the whole. He added a historical dimension to hermenuetics Dilthy's philosophy centred around the idea of a living spirit which develops in historical forms. According to him hermenuetics is a bridge between philosophy and history. He thought that the life of the society could be understood only through the intentions of the historical figures.

E.D. Hirsch, a follower of Dilthy, asserts that 'a text means what its author meant'. According to him, if a text is read without reference to the author's intentions, it remains incomplete, but if it is read with reference to the evidence such as the cultural milieu in which it was written, or any other evidence concerning "relevant aspects in the author's outlook" or "horizon" its meaning can become determinate. If such internal and external evidence is not taken into consideration, the text could have innumerable interpretations. He calls this determinate meaning, which is to be fixed by experts, or the meaning intended by the author 'verbal meaning'. For him the 'significance' of the text is the relation of the verbal meaning to the reader's beliefs and his cultural milieu. What this means is that the verbal meaning is stable while the cultural meaning is variable. In a nutshell, innumerable meanings are converted into a definite meaning by the "experts". It is then allowed to have innumerable significances according to the readers' situations.

Existentialists have made their own contribution to hermeneutics. Existential philosophy emphasizes the limitations of rationalism. Our awareness is a transrational act and feelings are more important than abstract intellectual thinking. Each man is unique. Edmund Heidegger (1859-1938) uses the word *Dasein* to indicate the proper mode of human existence – the mode in which man is responsibly creating himself through choice. It is only when we are deeply engaged in the world that Desein reveals itself. Beyond Dasein we can glean *being* itself of the common ground of all modes of being – human being is only one such mode. An authentic man is one who responsibly acts on his own without the instruments of social conventions or intellectualism. For existentialisıs freedom means that man should not be moulded by social forces, he must shape himself or create himself by each of his acts. This highly individualistic philosophy means that no two existentialists may have identical views. Most existentialists agree that their philosophy is closer to art and literature than to science.

To Heidegger the process of understanding is a part of individual's being. Haus Georg Gadamer, Heidegger's student, adapted existentialism to Dilthy's 'hermeneutic circle' and Hirsch's 'horizon' (author's outlook). Gadamer conceives of readers' horizons. He exhorts the reader to engage in a dialogue with the author's text. The reader can, thus bring to the text a 'pre-understanding' which is determined by his own unique place – his temperament, milieu and other 'horizons'. The meaning of the text which is finally understood by the reader is the fusion of the horizons brought together by the text – the author's outlook and the reader's 'pre-understanding'.

Gadamer is fully aware that the fusion of horizons can create innumerable possibilities or interpretations. This is probably why he thinks that normative concepts such as the author's intention are no more than empty slots which can be filled by *Verstehen*.[8] 'Verstehen' in German means "to understand, agree, consent to". For Gadamer it includes emotion, feeling and intuition.

The consequences of Gadamer's philosophical hermeneutics can be illustrated by an example. Consider the injunction of a religious leader "You will not lie". Two experts *A* and *B* fathom the intention of the author. According to *A* it means "you will not lie under any circumstances". According to *B* it is "You will not lie except under extenuating circumstances". Because it is the experts who determine the author's intention, there are two determinate interpretations in this case. Only a few saints and neurotics persecuted by their own conscience will accept *A*'s interpretations. *B*'s interpretation, in contrast, is widely accepted. But different people bring their own 'horizons' to fuse with the author's horizon as perceived by *B*. This results in different interpretations of 'extenuating circumstances'. The fiat ultimately means "you may lie when you want to save someone's life", "you may lie to your enemies", "you may lie to criminals" and so on. It may also throw up an interesting situation. *A* as expert believes that "you will not lie under any circumstances" is the author's intention. However, as a human being, he brings his own horizons. He may believe that *B* is a better expert than himself and interpret the message as "you may lie if such a lie helps a sick man to recover". The net result of the determinate intention as perceived by *B* is, if one may be permitted to be facetious, "you may lie if it suits you."

An excellent example of interpretation is provided by psychoanalysis. Sigmund Freud, its founder, developed a theory of the 'dream work'. Dreams appear to us bizarre, but according to Freud it is possible to interpret the manifest contents of the dream and fathom its hidden meaning.

According to him a dream appears strange because the latent thoughts are distorted on account of two major factors. First, the material which our conscience would consider objectionable is censored in several ways. Second, there is a symbolic representation of the latent contents. The psychoaualyst uses the technique of 'free association'. When the patient is relaxed she is, it is believed, able to give uninhibited expression to ideas that enter her consciousness during the analysis. The trained mind of the analyst is assumed to be able to decode the dream.

This technique closely resembles hermeneutics. At every step in his search for the latent content the analyst sees a number of ways from which he has to select the 'right way'.

The criticism leveled against this procedure by W.H.R. River appears quite pertinent. It was Freud's rule that only the analyst who studied the dream has the final authority to decide how a symbol in the dream should be interpreted. And a symbol sometimes could have two diametrically opposite meanings. "Such a method", writes Rivers, "would reduce any other science to absurdity".[9]

Following is a dream analysed by Freud himself.

A young woman was averse to the idea of spending summer holidays near her mother-in-law. She avoided this possibility by booking a room for herself in a distant resort. Later Freud explained to the patient that dreams were wish-fulfilments. Soon after she acquired this knowledge, the patient dreamt it that she was traveling with her mother-in-law to a holiday resort. Did the dream mean that she wished to be near her mother-in-law? This patently contradicted Freud's hypothesis that a dream was a wish-fulfilment. Freud began to doubt his own theory. However, he soon found a solution. He writes, "No doubt it was only necessary to follow the dream's logical consequences in order to arrive at its interpretations. The dream showed that I was wrong. Thus it was her wish that I might be wrong, and, her dream showed that wish fulfilled.[10]

The interpretation clearly shows how pliable hermenuetics can be.

Interpretation, as we shall see in Chapter 15, is one of the sources of pseudo-science. While interpretative techniques can have profound implications for social sciences, they can also be used to 'detect' modern scientific theories in scriptures. A number of Indian intellectuals believe that behind the symbolism and metaphors of the Vedic hymns are hidden the scientific theories discovered by the West only recently.

Nāsadīya or the hymn of creation consists of some of the most provocative stanzas in the Rigveda. Its poetic excellence and metaphysical profundity cannot be doubted. The hymn as translated by O'Flaherty along with other interpretations by other writers is given below.:[11]

1. There was neither non-existence nor existence then; there was neither the realm of space nor the sky which is beyond. What stirred?' Where? In whose protection? Was there water, bottomlessly deep?
2. There was neither death nor immortality then. There was no distinguishing sign of night nor of day. That one breathed, windless, by its own impulse. Other than that there was nothing beyond.
3. Darkness was hidden by darkness in the beginning; with no distinguishing sign, all this was water. The life force that was covered with emptiness, that one arose through the power of heat.
4. Desire came upon that one in the beginning; that was the first seed of mind. Poets seeking in their heart with wisdom found the bond of existence in non-existence.
5. Their cord was extended across. Was there below? Was there above? There were seed-placers; there were powers. There was impulse beneath; there was giving-forth above.
6. Who really knows? Who will here proclaim it? Whence was it produced? Whence is this creation? The gods came afterwards, with the creation of this universe. Who then knows whence it has arisen?
7. Whence this creation has arisen - perhaps it formed itself, or perhaps it did not – the one who looks down on it, in the highest heaven, only he knows – or perhaps he does not know.

a) Bose interprets "What stirred" as "what lay covered."
b) Despande interprets 'breathing without air' to mean vibrating naturally (in contrast with vibrating under force.)
c) Acharya treats 'life force' and 'that one' as Brahman. According to Deshpande the word 'salila' should not be translated as 'water' since the description pertains to the pre-creation stage. It should be interpretated as 'soft', referring the matter-energy-sky mixture which existed as a potentiality before the creation.

d) The cord refers to the word raśmi; which is also interpreted as light. According to Deshpande it is indicative of the big bang.

In this verse Acharya sees the creation of man and then women.

Deshpande differs radically from other writers whose interpretations deviate only slightly from O'Flaherty's translation. According to Deshpande the hymn is the description of the big bang theory mentioned in I.6 Chapter 5 (Science). The 'One' is the pre-existing unmanitest stage of the mixture of matter, energy and sky, "squeezed into the highest density, a kind of cosmic egg". It was vibrating with its own energy. This generated tremendous heat followed by the big bang which gave birth to the universe. The unmanifest elements became manifest and were scattered in all directions.

However, the hymn has an unmistakable mark of pre-scientific metaphysics. The poet's source of knowledge is plain and the metaphors are too transparent to need any decoding. In the origin of the universe, the poet perceives a biological birth.

It is difficult to believe that there can be a 'science' of interpretation. The fact that a text can be interpreted in diverse ways implies that its meaning is derived, to a large extent, from sophistical arguments. It, however, does not mean that hermenuetics in its broadest sense has not played any useful role in society. It has made us realize that since human thoughts and actions cannot be expressed in terms of rigid formulas; social sciences differ a great deal from material sciences, especially physics.

We live in a world of contradictions. On the one hand, we worship our past and revere our scriptures. On the other hand, we also accept the world of science based on reason. We face a dilemma when there is a conflict between scriptures and modern life. Should we believe in the biblical version of creation? Should we accept the supernatural powers of mantras and rituals? Here hermeneutics steps in and interprets our scripteres in a convenient way so that we continue to live in the world of science without totally abandoning our past. This also ensures that society gradually progresses from the pre-scientific stage to the industrial era without any shocks.

Hermeneutics also helps people of different faiths to live together amicably. One can see how scholars of different religions have tried to reconcile apparently diverse philosophies and religious tenets. Many times these attempts appear intellectually dishonest, but they do serve the purpose of creating 'unity in diversity'. This is especially relevant to multi-religious and multiethenic societies like the U.S.A. and India.

What is true of the texts and mantras is also true of rituals which admit of different interpretations. Myths and symbols still play a major role in the study of religion. Since a symbol can have more meanings than one, there is ample scope for interpretative maneuvers in mythology. As Daniel Ingalls rightly observes, "One can prove almost anything of the nature of myths if one selects only a part of the data and refuses to look at the context".[12]

Scholars have therefore wondered whether there can be a non-semantic (not relating to meaning.) approach to ritual. It was indicated earlier in passing that ritual and mantras demonstrate certain characteristic structures. Could we profit from a structural approach to ritual? This means whether we can have a syntactic analysis of ritual and mantras. Syntax deals with the relations (in abstraction) between different elements of a set, and will be discussed in Chapter 7. It will be shown that relations and structures can be mentioned in an abstract sense independent of meaning. I1 also showed that syntactically identical statements can have different semantic implications depending upon the context.

It is necessary to point out that we may wrongly interpret the meaning of a system, or a system may have no meaning; but we can hardly make any mistakes about its structure.

7

STRUCTURE

7.1 Introduction

Before we consider the patterns of the rituals and mantras, it would be instructive to say something about the general nature of what is called structure.

Most of us know intuitively what structure means. We would say, for instance, that the structure of a triangle has to do with its sides and the included angles, or that the structure of a circle is 'fixed' when we specify its radius. We also have some idea of structural similarity. Different circles are similar though they differ in size. Two human beings appear structurally similar and so do two animals of the same species. Sometimes we perceive the degree of similarity: there is some similarity between a cat and a dog, but we can discern a greater degree of similarity between a cat and a tiger. However, some similarities are not obvious.

For example, we would be reluctant to admit that a disc has a structure similar to the music it plays.

To understand structure and structural similarity in an abstract sense, we need to know a concept called relations.

7.2 Relations

A collection of things is called a set. If we say that a set S consists of three elements or objects a, b, c, we are merely mentioning an aggregate of three things. But if we add that a, b, c are human beings and a is the father of b, and b is the father of c, we have provided an information pertaining to a *binary* or dyadic relation "is father of". This relation may be symbolically denoted by R and we can write aRb and bRc. This relation makes the set structured.

I.1. Consider a set of letters a, x, b, e, m, arranged as below

x a b e m

If we define a relation R "is immediately to the left of" we shall have xRa, aRb, bRe, eRm. A relation closely related to R is the relation R_1
("is to the left of"). Thus x R_1 a, x R_1 m, b R_1 m etc. Other connected relations are "is immediately to the right of" and "is to the right of".

Some relations are *triadic* which require three elements to be specified. For example, "a is between x and b" specifies one such relation in the above illustration.

A relation R is called *reflexive* if for every element a of the set we have aRa. "Is equal to"is a reflexive relation in the set of real number. R is called *symmetric* if aRb implies bRa. In the set of lines the relation "is parallel to" is symmetric. The relation "is the brother of" is not symmetric, for if aRb, b may be a female in which case bRa does not hold good. R is called *transitive* if aRb, bRc implies aRc. In I1 'above "to the left of b" and "to the right of" are transitive relations, but "immediately to the left" and "immediately to the right"are not. The relation "is the descendent of" is transitive but "is the son of" is not.

A relation R is *asymmetric* if aRb implies bRa is not true. The relation "is the son of" is asymmetric, but the relation "is the brother of" is not. All relations mentioned in I1 are asymmetric.

A set will be called 'totally ordered' if there is a relation R such that (1) R is asymmetric and transitive (2) between any two distinct elements a and b either aRb or bRa. Thus in I1 "to the left of" and "to the right of"are total order relations. The set of real numbers is totally ordered with respect to "is greater than" and "is less than". There are also other types of orders, but for rituals the total order is the most important.

I.2. Five events occur at times mentioned as follows : A (7 A.M.), B (5 P.M.),
C (11 A.M.), D (7 P.M.), E (11 A.M.). We can introduce relations like "occurs before", and "occurs after" which are asymmetric and transitive. However, there is no total order because C and E occur simultaneously.

7.3 Structural Similarity

An important concept in philosophy is structural identity which is based on another concept called similarity of relations. The flowing example will explain these concepts.

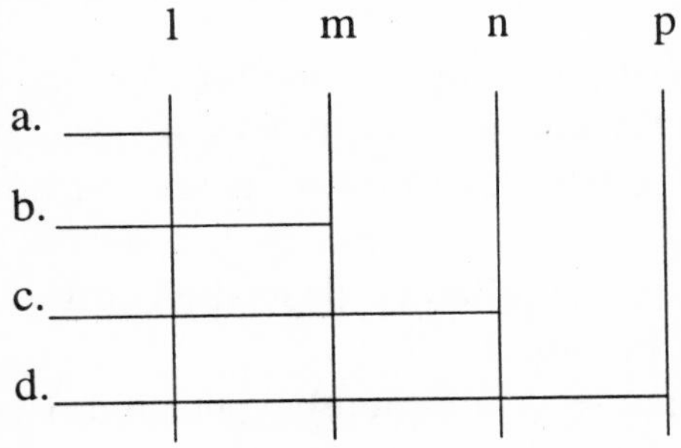

Fig. 7.1 Similar Relations

X is the set of points a,b, c, d, and l, m, n,p are parallel lines constituting set Y as shown in the figure 7.1. In X we define the relation R "is above" and in Y the relation S "is to the left of". For example aRb, bRd, lSp, nSp etc. Note that there are as many points as there are lines. Let us pair the elements, one from X and one from Y : a↔l, b↔m, c↔n, d↔p such pairing is called 1-1 correspondence. Such correspondence allows us to say that R and S are similar and X and Y are structurally identical.

A more formal approach to structural identity can now be made.

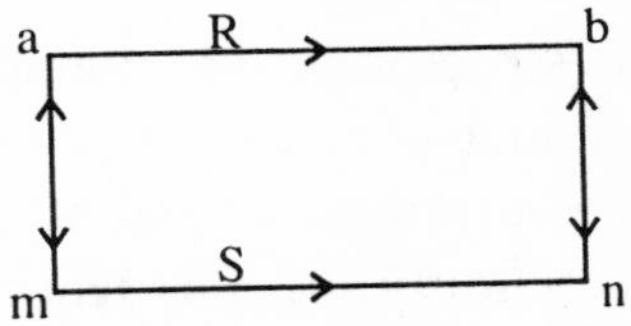

Fig. 7.2 Structural Identity

Suppose we have two sets X and Y (fig. 7.2) in which relation R and S are defined. Let a,b be any two terms of X such that aRb. If it is possible for us to find elements m, n in Y such that mSn, we can have the correspondence a↔m and b↔n. If this holds good for every pair a,b of X, we shall say that R and S are similar and that X and Y have identical structures. It is then possible to think of an abstract structure in which the nature of its terms is immaterial.

The abstract nature of structural identity will be clear if we consider two very dissimilar sets. One consists of father (A), son (B) and grandson (C), the other consists of numbers 7, 8, 9. The first is totally ordered with respect to "ancester of" and the second set with respect to "less than". The 1-1 correspondence A-7, B-8, and C-9 establishes the similarity of relations and shows that the two sets have identical structures.

In practice, structures are much more complex than those we have just considered, and they may involve more relations than one. The one-relation structures, however, enable us to have an idea of how structures can be abstracted.

Sometimes, a structure may be completely described without explicitly specifying the relations involved.

In the figure 7.3 below the structure is completely specified if we describe it as follows:

1. ABCD is a square of length l.
2. A circle circumscribes ABCD.
3. ODC is a triangle where O is the center of the circle.

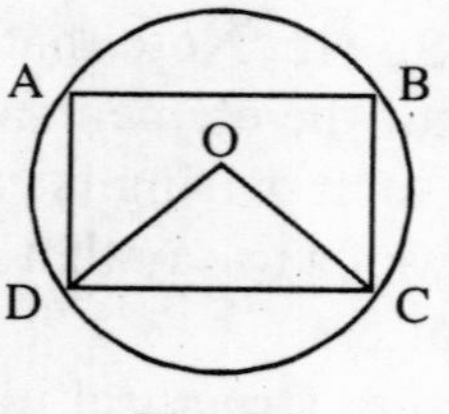

Fig. 7.3

When we speak of the structure of an object or an event, we imply that the object or event consists of smaller components. To know its structure is to know the interrelations of its constituents. When a medical student studies anatomy she may learn the names and shapes of different bones and their location in the skeleton. This gives her the structure of the skeleton in which bones are the components. However, bones can be further analysed: they are made of molecules which in turn are composed of atoms. These atoms have a complex structure, the nucleus at the center consisting of protons and neutrons, and the electrons around the nucleus. Where should the analysis stop? It depends on the purpose for which the analysis is undertaken. If you are a furniture maker assembling chairs and tables from the designs supplied to you, you are only interested in ensuring that the different parts are fixed in relation to each other according to the design. You will not worry about the molecular structure of these components. However, if you are a physicist or a philosopher you might go right up to the elementary particles – electrons, protons and so on.

In practice we may not encounter identical structures, but structures vhich are almost identical. Suppose there is a map of a country to cale, which marks towns, roads, rivers and so on. With each item on nap, there is a 1-1 correspondence with an object of the country. Vhat's more, any two objects in the country have a spatial relation vhich is translated into another spatial relation in the map. There is hus a structural identity as far as the surface distances are concerned. Iowever, the heights of the mountains and the depths of the lakes ind rivers cannot be indicated because the map is two – dimensional, hough this object may be partly achieved by using different colors on the map. This is a case of structural similarity and not identity.

A three dimensional model of a building if made according to scale affords an example of structural identity.

It would be erroneous to believe that structurally similar complexes have similar appearances. Consider a piece of music played by a record, a cassette or a CD. The musical piece has several distinguishing characteristics - pitch and intensity of notes, pace, etc. All these characteristics are duplicated by the playing device. It is reasonable to assume that such a device has structure identical to the structure of the musical piece. In this case there is no need to analyse the structures. The very fact that a device duplicates the original sound is a sufficient ground to believe that it has a structure identical or it least similar to the acoustic structure it reproduces. It must, however, be pointed out that the reproduction of music provides an example of multiple relations involving the various facets of music.

Before we proceed we may consider a few illustrations.

I.3. Suppose a, b, c, d, e are employees of a small organization having different ages, earning different salaries, differing in their efficiency and having different heights. We can define four relations within the set itself : "is older than", "earns more than", "is more efficient than" and "is taller than". Suppose the first and the second relations are R and S and we have the pattern aRb, bRd, dRe, eRc ; bSc, cSa, aSe, eSd

R	a	b	d	e	c
	↕	↕	↕	↕	↕
S	b	c	a	e	d

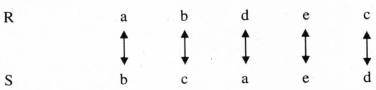

The set is ordered in two ways - with respect to R and S. The relations are similar and hence the structure is identical. However, the corresponding elements are not identical; only e is paired with itself.

I.4. A ritual consists of seven acts in the sequence a_1, a_2,............ a_7. A mantra is chanted after each act except a_7. Let the mantras be m_1, m_2,.................... m_6

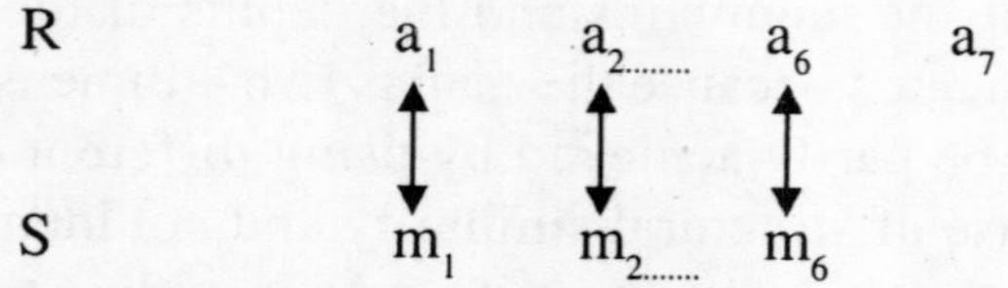

Among the acts we can define a relation R "occurs before" and among mantras a relation S "is chanted before". These relations make the acts and mantras ordered. The 1-1 correspondence is shown in the figure. Since there is no mantras corresponding to a_7, the structures are not identical. Nevertheless, since this is only a minor deviation, we might say that the acts and mantras have similar, though not identical, structures. Incidentally you may have noticed that in order that two sets should be structurally identical they must have the same number of elements.

7.4 Transmission of Structures

Suppose you are looking at a table from a certain distance. The reflected light rays from the table strike your eyes, and an image is formed on the retina, which through nerve impulses is then transmitted to your brain. The visual center in the brain enables you to see the table. Let us assume the causal connection between the table and your perception of it. The source (table) and the perception are similar in two respects (1) quality and (2) structure. However, in the causal chain that links the table to the perception, the message is transmitted through various modes, electromagnetic waves, nerve impulses and so on. The structures emanating from the table may undergo outward changes in form but their similarity is preserved till you see the table.

The structural similarity is preserved during transmission not only through space but also through time. Suppose you are watching a play. At a given instant certain audio-visual structures emanate from the stage. As the play progress different structures are given out continuously and perceived by you in the same temporal order in which the play is staged. The structural similarity is thus preserved not only spatially but also temporally.

We shall now deal with the structural postulate which was mentioned in chapter 4. In the previous illustration, there are a number of viewers who are watching the play along with you. They are not only located in different directions with respect to the center (stage) but also at different distances from it. The visual and acoustical impressions received by the audience are bound to vary to some extent from place to place. But you will not have the slightest doubt that all the people are watching the same play. The fact is there are several different causal lines which radiate in different directions from the common source, but all these lines preserve the original structure or rather a sequence of structures.

The assumption that the structurally similar complex events located about a center are usually caused by an event of the same structure at the center is called the structural postulate. Of course, the inference inherent in the postulate is only probable, but it has an exceedingly high degree of creditability especially when the surrounding events are not widely separated and when the number of such events is very large, for instance when millions of viewers are watching the President's address to the nation.

This postulate is not only used in science, but also in law courts. Its may also help us in making useful inferences. For example, if several persons are listening to a humorous speech and only one of them feels that the speaker has a gun with which he is about to shoot the entire audience, we may safely assume that the frightened listener is hallucinating, and requires medical attention.

7.5 Symmetry

Symmetry in a wider sense means harmony of parts, pleasing proportion of the components etc. There are however a few restricted senses which are of interest to us.

Consider the following figures :

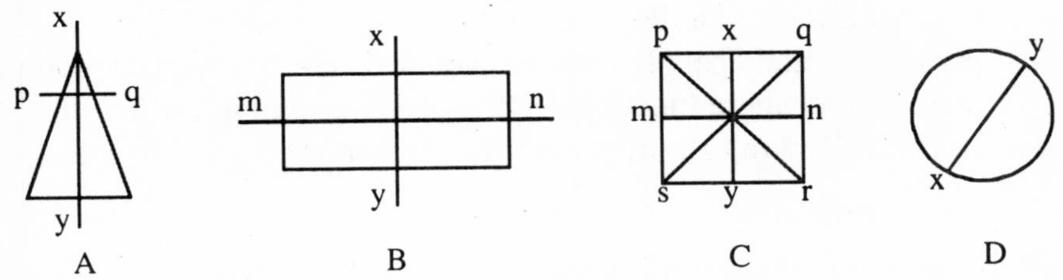

Fig 7.4 Mirror Symmetry

Fig A is an isosceles triangle which appears symmetrical about the line XY. What this actually means is that the part on the left of XY is a mirror image of the part on the right side, and vice versa. XY, the imaginary mirror is called the axis of symmetry. Fig B shows a rectangle which has two axes of symmetry XY and MN. Fig C shows a square having four axes of symmetry XY, MN, PR and QS. The circle in fig D has infinite number of symmetries – any diameter XY is an axis of symmetry.

Rotation, like mirror reflection can also give rise to symmetry. For example in fig 7.5,

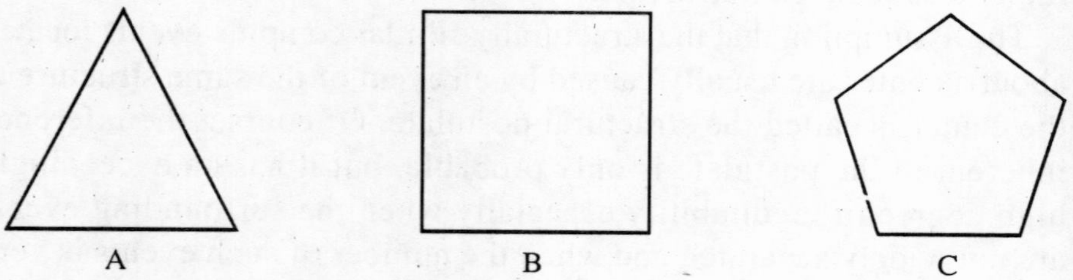

Fig 7.5 Rotational Symmetry

The diagrams A (equilateral triangle), B(square), C (regular pentagon) will look the same if they are rotated through (120^0, 240^0, 360^0), (90^0, 180^0, 270^0, 360^0,) and (72^0, 144^0.....360^0) respectively.

Symmetry has an esthetic appeal. An intricately woven carpet depicts a number of figures symmetrically arranged and its beauty can be partly ascribed to the symmetrical patterns.

Symmetry abounds not only in man-made objects but also in nature as the following illustrations will show.

I.5. Structural symmetry is quite evident in biology and can be observed in the flora and fauna. Our own body is an instance of symmetry about a central vertical plane. A characteristic of this symmetry is that when an animal has an even number of organs – eyes, hands etc. they are symmetrically placed. Even abnormalities usually appear pair-wise; we find short-legged people but rarely people with only one leg short. The butterfly affords an example where functional symmetry is combined with esthetics.

I.6. In the following popular mantra the symmetry is obvious.

om namaḥ śivāya \ śivāya namaḥ om

I.7. Acoustical symmetry is mentioned in Wordsworth's following lines from "The Cuckoo Again"

Yes it was the mountain echo
Solitary, clear profound
Answering to the shouting Cuckoo
Giving to her sound for sound

I.8. In particle physics symmetries other than reflection and rotation are also observed. Mesons are subatomic particles of which there are eight types. With each of these two variables (quantum numbers) called isospin and hypercharge are associated as follows:

Mesons

Particle		Antiparticle
Pion	π^+ (π^0) π^-	
Kaon	K^+ K^0	$\bar{K}^0$ K^-
Eta	(η)	

An antiparticle has the same mass but opposite charge with respect to its particle.

Particle	*Hypercharge*	*Isospin*
π^+	0	1
Π^0	0	0
Π^-	0	-1
K^+	1	$^1/_2$
K^0	1	$-^1/_2$
$\bar{K}^0$	-1	$^1/_2$
K^-	-1	$-^1/_2$
η	0	0

When these values are plotted with isospin along the X axis and hypercharge along Y the axis the pattern appears as in fig 7.6

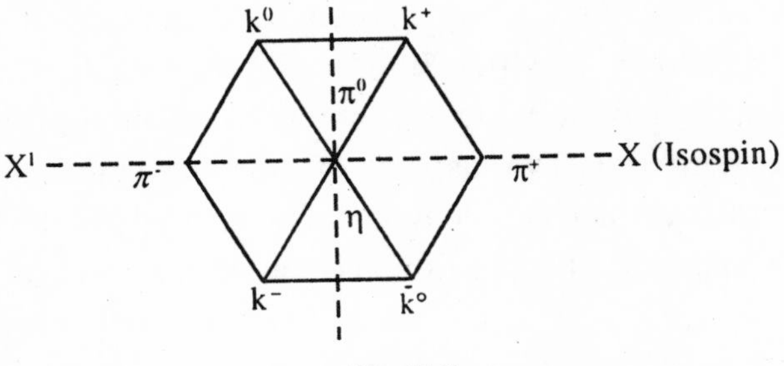

Fig 7.6

The hexagonal symmetry is quite evident. Particles and antiparticles occupy diametrically opposite positions. At the center are π^0, η which are their own antiparticles. This symmetry is called the meson octet.[1]

I.9. The fifth cakra of Śrī yantra is shown in fig 7.7

Fig 7.7

It is easy to observe that there are two axis of symmetry. Moreover, there is also a rotation symmetry: the figure is unchanged when rotated through 180^0.

The significance of the symmetrical relation can now be explained. Consider figure A of the isosceles triangle in fig 7.4 Among its points we can define a relation R "is a reflection of..... in XY" which gives us PRQ and QRP showing that R is symmetric. All points on ABC can thus be paired except the apex of the triangle which is the reflection of itself. The rotational symmetry can be similarly explained by introducing a slightly complicated relation.

7.6 Recursion

We now introduce a very important concept of recursion which has relevance in ritual structure.

Consider the following passage : There was a town called A in which lived a boy named B. B narrates a story : There was a town called A in which lived a boy named B. B narrates a story. There was a town called A in which lived a boy named B ... ...

This apparently frivolous story contains a profound principle used in logic and mathematics. Two aspects of the story stand out. First there is a hidden formula which is used repeatedly. Second the story never ends.

This is an instance of recursion. To understand it, consider the set of numbers 0, 1,2, ... Let us call the number which follows a giver number n, its 'successor' denoted by s (n) Thus s(0) = 1, s(1) =

2, s(2) = 3 and so on. We start with s(0)=1 and apply this formula repeatedly. The process can be described as

0	→	1
1	→	2
2	→	3 etc.

Starting with the single number 0 we can generate the entire set of whole numbers 1,2,3.. by using the formula successively. Such a process is called recursive. In the above example the various members are s(0), s(s(0)), s(s(s(0)))...

Recursive rules are important in modern mathematics. An arrangement of the type

a_1, a_2, a_3, ... is called a sequence. Some examples of the sequence are

A 1, 5, 7, 0, 3 ... ...
B 5, 1, 5, 1, 5, ...
C 0, 0, 0 ... ...

It is possible to express a sequence recursively using what are called 'recursive theorems'. While a sequence is endless, some of its terms may be repeated. In A above the number of terms involved is infinite while in B and C the number is two (1,5) and one (0) respectively.

However, a recursive process need not lead to an endless sequence. Suppose we want to find the highest common factor (HCF) of two numbers say 1925 and 300 using Euler's algorithm. The first step is to divide 1925 by 300. The remainder is 125. in the next step the divisior 300 becomes the dividend and the remainder 125 becomes the divisor. The steps are show below

Dividend	*Divisor*	*Quotient*	*Remainder*
1925	300	6	125
300	125	2	50
125	50	2	25
50	25	2	-

The recursive formula is divisor → dividend and remainder → divisor in the successive steps. When the remainder is 0, the process stops. The last divisor 25 is the HCF, which you may verify.

The word algorithm comes from the name of the Persian mathematician Abu Ja'far Mohammad ibn Musa al-khowarizm, and means a well defined sequence of operations. It is extensively used in computer science.

The most striking feature of recursion is that a finite number of instructions can create an infinite number of elements. Suppose our instructions are $n \rightarrow 2n$, $n=1$. Then $1 \rightarrow 2$, $2 \rightarrow 4$, ... Which gives the sequence 2, 4, 8, 16 ... ...

In some cases the recursive formula may generate an infinite sequence but contain only a finite number of elements. Suppose five persons are seated as shown in fig. 7.8

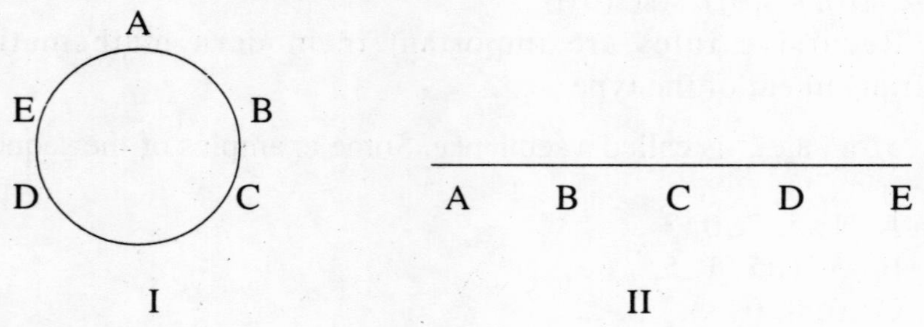

Fig 7.8

Starting with A an object is passed to the person seated "next to next", in the clockwise manner. The sequence is ACEBDA... Though the process is never ending it involves only five elements. In fig II, the same persons are seated in a line and the object is passed to the person seated next to next, starting from A. with only two passes the process would end : A→C→E

We shall now consider two recursive rules some of which will be mentioned again in connection with ritual structure

1. A→BAB
   in which A is successively replaced by BAB. We get the following sequence of structures
   A→BAB→BBABB→BBBABBB...
3. A→ABA which gives
   A→ABA→ABABABA→ABABABABABABABA......
4. A→BA which gives A→BA→BBA→BBBA.....

7.7 Permutation and Combination

It will be shown in chapter 8 that one of the characteristics of ritual is 'pattern completion' which inter alia involves permutation and combination. To understand their meaning consider two letters A and B. In how may way can be arranged? There are two ways viz. AB and BA. If we have three letters, there would be six different arrangements: ABC, ACB, BAC, BCA, CBA, CAB.

These arrangements are called the permutation of the given set. Thus we have 2 permutations in the first case, and six in the second. We will write them as P(2) = 2, P(3) = 6. You may try the permutations for four elements and you will find P(4) = 4 × 3 × 2 × 1=24. In general if we have a set consisting of m objects, there are P(m) arrangements given by:

$$P(m) = m \times (m - 1) \ldots\ldots\ldots\ldots \times 2 \times 1$$

Sometimes out of m objects r objects are arranged at a time. The number of such permutations will be denoted by P(m,r). For example, three objects arranged two at a time give the following permutations:

AB, BA, AC, CA, BC, CB

The formula for P(m, r) is complicated, and need not be discussed.

The concept of combination is slightly different and we shall discuss two main types.: (1) Suppose there are three letters (or any other objects). How many pairs can be made from this set? There are three pairs, namely AB, AC, BC. We shall write this as

$$C(3, 2) = 3$$

Observe that AB and BA are the same pair because, unlike in permutations, order is of no relevance in combination. If you try to make distinct pairs from four objects, you will find that there are six pairs :

AB, AC, AD, BC, BD, CD

That is, C(4, 2) = 6. In general if from we m objects we form distinct sets each containing r objects, the combination is C(m, r). We need not discuss the formula but you will appreciate that P(m, r) is usually greater than C(m, r) because in the former order does count, while in the latter it is ignored.

(2) Another types of combination that should interest us involves two different sets. Suppose (A,B,C) and (a, b, c) are two sets. How many pairs can be made if we choose one from objects from the first and one from the second? There are six (3x2).

(Aa, Ab, Ba, Bb, Ca, Cc)

In general if the first set has m objects and second set has n, the number of combinations or pairs is m x n.

I.10. Examples of combinations of the second type abound in ritual. In many worship rituals there is a subordinate ritual called Upāṅga-devatā-sthāpanam pūjanam (Chapter 12) in which 21 deities other than the main deities are worshipped. Let us call these deities D_1, D_2, ... D_{21}. Each of them is saluted (mamaḥ) and invited (āvahayāmi). These two 'acts' can be called A_1, A_2. We find that there are 42 mantras (21 x 2) giving the combinations

D_1A_1, D_2A_1 ... D_2A_1; D_1A_2, D_2A_2, ... $D_{21}A_2$

7.8 Geometrical Transformations

We have seen that yantras are used in tantric worship. Yantras not only display symmetry but are related with one another through permutation, magnification, rotation, reflection and (rarely) translation, the last four modifications are called transformations of geometrical figures.

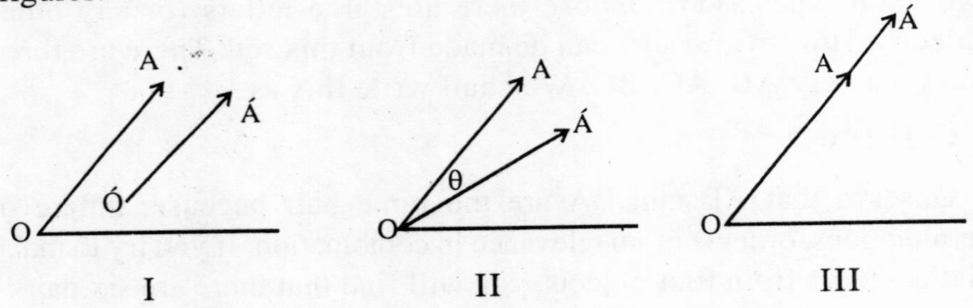

Fig 7.9 Geometrical Transformations

Fig. 7.9 I shows translation in which the entire segment OA is 'shifted' to O'A' so that OA & O'A' are parallel and have the same the length. II shows the rotation of OA through angle θ without there being any change in the length. Fig III is a case of magnification in which OA expands to OA'. Of course there can be contraction also under magnification. We have already seen what mirror reflection is.

When a figure undergoes any of these transformations its internal structure does not change. It can of course, undergo successive transformations.

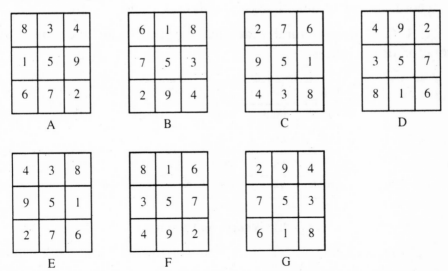

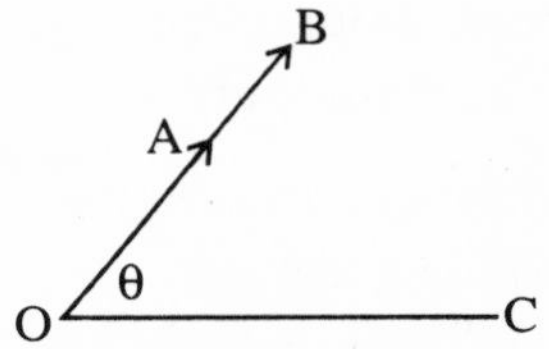

Fig 7.10 Successive Transformations

In fig. 7.10, OA undergoes two successive transformations.

$$OA \xrightarrow{m} OB \xrightarrow{r} OC$$

where m and r stand for magnification and rotation.

It should be obvious to you that translation and rotation do not change the internal structure of the figure. Magnification appears tricky. You might feel that the structure is not identical but only similar, because there are more points in OB and OC than in OA. This is actually not so. It can be proved that OA, OB and OC, have the same number of points and we can establish 1-1 correspondence between the respective points. We need not discuss the proof because it would lead us to the domain of "infinity" which is a treacherous terrain.

Transformations and permutations abound in yantras. The former tell us that several yantras may appear different but have the same structure. The latter show that a structure can give rise to a number of related structures in a methodical way. A few examples will illustrate this point.

8	3	4
1	5	9
6	7	2

A

6	1	8
7	5	3
2	9	4

B

2	7	6
9	5	1
4	3	8

C

4	9	2
3	5	7
8	1	6

D

4	3	8
9	5	1
2	7	6

E

8	1	6
3	5	7
4	9	2

F

2	9	4
7	5	3
6	1	8

G

Fig 7.11 Yantras and Transformation

The yantras shown above when used with appropriate mantras are believed to be useful for various purposes as mentioned below.

A - For easy delivery in pregnancy
B - For terrorizing enemies
C - The celestial cow with her calf descends to the earth.
D - For becoming invisible
E - One can see any object one wishes to
F - For acquiring clothes and houses.
G - For curing diseases, influencing people etc.

'Arabic' numerals are used for the convenience of readers.
We can easily perceive the following relations

$A \xrightarrow{r} B \xrightarrow{r} C \xrightarrow{r} D \xrightarrow{r} A$ (rotation through 90^0)
$A \rightarrow E$ (interchange of 1st and 3rd column)
$B \rightarrow F$ (interchange of 1st and 3rd column)
$D \rightarrow G$ (interchange of 1st and 3rd column)
The last two incidentally, are reflections into the central columns.
The following diagram will summarize these interrelations.

$A \xrightarrow{r} B \xrightarrow{r} C \xrightarrow{r} D$
$\downarrow \; \downarrow \qquad\quad \downarrow$
E F G
where $\downarrow$ refers to interchange of columns 1 and 3

A, B, C, D are structurally identical since each can be obtained by rotation of the others.

na	Śi	ya	maḥ	vā
ya	maḥ	vā	na	Śi
vā	na	Śi	ya	maḥ
Śi	ya	maḥ	vā	na
maḥ	vā	na	Śi	ya

*

Fig 7.12 Yantra and Rotation

The advanced students of tantra who worship Śri Vidyā use a yantra which contains 25 squares. In the squares are inscribed the elements from the mantra "*om namaḥ śivāya*" (Oṃ, salutations to Śiva). It is believed that every letter of the Devanāgarī script is a mantra and hence all inscriptions should be in this script for the yantra to be effective. However, since our purpose is structral analysis, we have used transliterations in fig. 7.12. There are 24 tridends symmetrically arranged along the boundary of the yantra, not shown in the figure.

To understand the rotational transformations, start with column 3(*) and read from the bottom to the top (na maḥ Śi vā ya). Rotate the third column in the plane perpendicular to the plane of the paper, so that to you the column appears to move upwards. All other columns will appear one by one before you as follows:

Columns 3 → 5 → 2 → 4 → 1

This is an example of 'pattern completion' discussed in Chapter 8.

8

RITUALS IN GENERAL

8.1. The Nature of Rituals

Ritual is a stereotyped or stylized behaviour which to a large extent is determined by social milieu. Rituals may be simple or complex, short or long, flexible or rigid, and play an important role in all aspects of human life.

A few rituals are listed below merely to indicate the vast area they cover.

Social life—manners, etiquettes, customs and mores relating to greeting, eating, bathing, courtship, dressing and excreting.

Religion—rites of passage, burial and cremation rites, modes of worship, conduct of religious institutions, code of conduct for priests and religious officials.

Politics and law—election procedure, government formation, parliamentary procedure, enactment of laws, international law, international protocol.

Defence—parade, war games, rules of behaviour relationg to rank.

Science and technology—lectures, exhibitions, seminars, societies.

Education—rules relating to educational institutions, code of conduct among teachers and students.

Recreation—music, dancing, sports, gymnastics.

An example of an exceedingly simple ritual is greetings. If you are attending a privately organized entertainment programme, the sponsors' representative may greet you at the entrance with "good morning" and you may never exchange a single word with her subsequently. Religious rituals on the other hand, may be very complex consisting of diverse acts and incantations which may last for many days.

In informal rituals there is considerable flexibility. If two friends bump into each other after a long time, and each of them has about five minutes to spare, we may guess what they will speak about : health, their families, common friends and business. But we cannot predict their exact conversation because within these probable areas there is an ample choice of linguistic expressions.

Formal rituals, on the other hand, are quite rigid. Religious rites provide many examples of inflexibility. In Hindu rituals, for example, the mantras have to be chanted in the exact prescribed manner with the right pronunciation and intonation. If there is a mistake, the mantras may have to be repeated. Some prolonged rites terminate with expiatory rituals which serve the purpose of tendering apology to gods for the mistakes which may have been inadvertently committed in the main body of rites.

Rigid rituals usually accompany solemn occasions. For example, when after the elections, a council of ministers is sworn in by the President of India or when the American President is installed, the prescribed procedure is followed without deviation.

However, rigid rituals need neither be long nor complex. A holy man may bless you with a mere touch on the head. A simple ritual need not be short. You may repeat a simple mantra for several hours.

Why do we follow ritualistic or stylized behavior? Rituals make social interactions easy. We know exactly how to behave in a given situation. Rituals thus may be looked upon as a cohesive social force. At the individual level, however, different explanations may be offered. The existentialist might contend that the certainty and determinacy inherent in a ritual reduces the existential anxiety. The argument certainly has some substance, and is reinforced by the observation of some emotionally disturbed people who engage in repetitive behaviour without any apparent stimulus. In religion rituals are sometimes interpreted as magic.

Social milieu decides the nature and duration of informal as well as formal rituals. If you are an Indian belonging to a certain community, you may not enquire after your friend's wife. If you are an Indian student you will address your teacher as 'Sir' and not as 'Mr. *A*'. if you happen to be in a country where a despot reigns, the rules may make it necessary for you to bend down when you approach the dictator, unless you prefer to be beheaded

All rituals have do's and don'ts. The latter are particularly important in religious rituals and are called taboos. They indicate prohibitions and restrictions related to the sacred. In Polynesia when a ritual specialist (tohunga) performed his rituals, he could not feed himself; young virgins had to perform the task for him. Makados were Japan's spiritual emperors. They were considered so holy that they could not touch the ground with their feet. The Makado was carried from one place to another on men's shoulders.

Mantras are sometimes chanted in relay by a number of priests. It is necessary to ensure that there are no gaps when one priest takes over from another. The priests are so horrified at the propect of an inadvertent breach of this rule that a priest starts chanting his portion before his predecessor has ended. This overlapping ensures that there is a continuous flow of mantras.

Frazer calls taboos negative magic whose function is to avoid an undesirable event. Taboos appear to be as important as rituals themselves in many cases.[1]

The different types of rules are sometimes distinguished in connection with rituals, regulative rules and constitutive rules. Regulative rules govern a pre-existing activity. Law courts administer justice but there are procedural rules which regulate their conduct. Constitutive rules are those which constitute and also regulate an activity. The activity itself is logically dependent on these rules.

Thus the rules of a game such as tennis are constitutive, but handshakes and applause are not. According to Staal Vedic rituals are constitutive not regulative, that is, they logically depend on the ritual rules. This is based on his thesis that ritual and mantras are rules without meaning a topic which is discussed later.

8.2. Transactional Analysis

Transactional Analysis (TA) offers many insights into the genesis of social rituals. According to TA every infant needs to be stimulated. This stimulus hunger is satisfied by patting, hugging and coddling of the child by parents and relatives. The stimulus hunger transforms into what is called recognition – hunger when the child grows. When you do an act which implies the cognition of someone else's presence, you are not only expressing the recognition of his presence, you are also giving a 'stroke' to him. TA treats a stroke as the fundamental unit of social action. An exchange of strokes is called transaction, which is the unit of social intercourse. Strokes tend to satiate the recognition hunger to the extent that depends on the nature of the strokes. Transactional analysts rightly believe that a mild punitive stroke (say, a repreimand) is far better than no stroke or total ignorance.

Next in the hierarchy of hunger comes the structure-hunger – the problem of how to structure our time when we are awake. According to Eric Berne all social living in the cooperative aspects addresses this problem.[2] While unsatiated stimulus hunger and recognition hunger can lead to sensory and emotional starvation, structure hunger can lead to boredom. If all these hungers are allowed to grow without strokes, they should ultimately result in the biological deterioration.

For TA a ritual is essentially a social transaction. When two people engage in a ritual like greetings they intuitively know how to give the right quantum of strokes to each other. Rituals originate in our upbringing and are shaped by social conditions in which parents play the most important role. In our adult life these 'parents' inside our mind in the form of conscience determine our rituals to a great extent. When we participate in a ritual we invite soothing strokes and our guilt and anxiety (concomitants of conscience) are reduced. Rituals also structure our time and make our life enjoyable. TA also maintains that many rigid rituals which have been passed down for generations have lost their contextual relevance, but are still performed as a matter of faith.

Transational analysis lays greater stress on structure than on the contents of a ritual. Nevertheless these structures are not really abstract in the sense the word was used in Chapter 7. Transactional structures center around three ego states: Adult (reality), Child (parts of the childhood in the mind) and Parent (conscience or the parents inside the mind.) For them structural analysis is not independent of semantic interpretation. Further, for them ritual is only one of the options for structuring time, the others are pastimes, games, intimacy and activity. Every stylized behaviour in their jargon is not a ritual. Moreover, a game usually involves an ulterior transaction. When two persons play a game they try to manipulate each other.

8.3 Animal Rituals

Ritualistic behaviour among mammals has been recorded by a number of investigators. Young chimpanzees learn by trial and error percussive drumming though they never reach the complexity of human percussive expression. They also indulge in swaying and jigging movements which may be called the precursors of human dancing. Chimpanzees like young children engage in rhythmic gymnastics.

Scientists have concluded that despite the rigidity involved in it, a ritual is the result of exploratory urge of mammals. Two opposite tendencies, neophilia (love of the new) and neophobia (fear of the new)play a role in determining a ritual. Neophilia creates new rituals or complexities within a ritual while neophobia freezes the pattern, making ritual rigid. Because the primates' ability to learn is limited, their rituals do not flower into human percussion, dancing, gymnastics, or games. Humans on the other hand are successful in stylizing various types of rituals. However, since rituals appear in all mammals, biology rather than culture appears to be the main determinant of ritual.

In connection with what we may call play rituals, Desmond Morris lists six 'play rules'[3] (1) the unfamiliar is investigated until it becomes familiar, (2) Rhythmic repetition is engaged in relation to what is familiar, (3) Various permutations and combinations are tried to vary the repetition, (4) The most satisfying variation is given preferences over the less satisfying pattern, (5) All these variations are combined and recombined and (6) The ritual activity is an end itself.

We will find the relevance of (5) when we discuss the structure of human ritual. Rule (6) will also be recalled when we discuss the role of 'meaning' in mantras and religious ritual.

Higher animals also display rituals other than 'plays'. Most of them engage in ritualized combat which consists of threatening gestures and counter gestures till one of the adversaries accepts defeat without engaging in actual fighting. The animal often faces a situation which is ambiguous – there is a conflict between his instinctual responses of attack and flight. These entail a number of physiological processes which oppose each other. It is believed that in the course of evolution, these responses have been ritualized into threat or crouching postures. The ambiguous signals are reflected in such rituals as rhythmic shaking.

Thus we can see complex threat rituals and combat dances in which animal contestants circle around each other, "they may bow, nod, shake, shiver, swing rhythmically from side to side or make repeated stylized runs"[4] Our own ritualistic behavior resembles that of primates cleanching of fists, rhythmic gestures of blows, begging gestures to seek mercy, all have their counterparts in the behavior of primates.

While these rituals are goal oriented there are some others which are displaced, activities. When the hostility between two rivals reaches a point when they are about to engage in a combat, there may be a sudden change in their behavior and they may switch over to rituals like yawning, stretching or even going to sleep. Humans engage in similar displacement rituals. If we are under stress we may play with our tie, drum the table, whistle or sip a drink. These activities or rituals are engaged to relieve stress. When we whistle, we may not be even conscious of the tune, and when we sip a drink, its taste may not register in our mind.

The studies of animal behavior seem to indicate that there are – at least on surface three types of rituals, (1) those which are an end in themselves e.g. 'playing', (2) those which are goal directed. e.g. throttling gestures and (3) those which are displacement activities undertaken uncouciously to relieve tension.

8.4 Ritual Structures

A ritual consists of a series of ritual elements arranged temporally i.e. the elements appear in succession in time. A ritual can be conveniently denoted by

ABC ...

Where A, B, ... are its elements. This does not mean that spatial relations are not present. A game like football can be fully described only in terms of a spatio-temporal structure. Similarly in case of religious ritual spatial elements may be important. When a number of priests participate in a ritual they may be seated in a certain manner, each facing a certain direction. Idols, utensils, fruits etc. used in a ritual may be arranged according to standard rules. However, in rituals time element is more important than space elements. What's more, a complex ritual can usually be broken into a number of simple temporal sequences.

A number of structural forms can be noticed in rituals. In this chapter we shall identify structures found in general. They will be called 'general ritual structures' or GRS; Special structural characteristics of particular areas (religion, music, poetry etc.) will be discussed later.

1. *Iteration (Repetition)* – In iteration an element is repeated successively. The general structure appears as

   ABB ... BC

Sometimes the repeated block may appear in the beginning or at the end.

A japa or repeated chanting of a mantra is an instance of iteration. In cricket when a batsman takes more runs than one, he is repeating the to and fro movement. When you applaud continuously at the end of a concert your acts amount to iteration, and so do those of the conductor who bows repeatedly. When soldiers march, their hands and feet perform iteration.

2. *Palindrome (also called mirror, retrograde.)*

   Suppose you walk from a pole *X* to pole *Y* and return to *X*. your activity can be described as

   AA^{-1}

   where A denotes your going from *X* to *Y* and A^{-1} your returning to *X*. A^{-1} may be called the 'inverse' or the mirror image of A. Consider a more complicated case consisting of the following series of acts

   Open the book – read – close the book, which can be written as

   ABA^{-1}

Where A^{-1} (close the book) is the inverse of A (open the book). Such structures as AA^{-1} or ABA^{-1} will be called palindrome or mirror. Palindrome is a word which reads the same backwards as well as forwards.

You will observe that there is some difference between AA^{-1} and ABA^{-1}. In the second, B is an extra element which is not inversible (reading cannot be inverted). We ignore such niceties because in practice perfect mirror images are seldom found, and call both patterns the palindromes.

Notice that the inverse of the inverse of an element is that element itself.

i.e. $(A^{-1})^{-1} = A$

For example, the inversion of 'open' is 'close' and the inversion of 'close' is 'open' which takes you back to the starting point.

A little deliberation will convince you that

$(AB)^{-1} = B^{-1}A^{-1}$

and $(ABC)^{-1} = C^{-1}B^{-1}A^{-1}$ etc.

Consider the mantra,

om namaḥ śivāya \ śivāya namaḥ om = A B C / C B A, say

which is a palindrome. Strictly speaking however, the individual words are not inverted. In most inversions we find some basic blocks whose relative order is inverted but the words themselves do not undergo internal inversion. For example, om does not become 'mo'. Such deviations can be ignored and the structure may be called palindrome.

If we assume that the basic blocks are non-inversible, the general structure of A palindrome would appear as

a) A_1, A_2......... A_{n-1} A_{n-1} ... ...A_2 A_1
b) A_1 A_2......... A_{n-1} A_n A_{n-1} ... ... A_2A_1

When an A can be inverted it can be replaced by A^{-1} on the right hand side.

Napoleon the Great, when he was captive in the prison of Elba after his defeat is said to have written the following palindrome on the prison walls.

Able was I ere I saw Elba

In cricket when a batsman takes two runs in a ball, the structure can be represented as

$A\ A^{-1}\ A\ A^{-1}$

The block AA^{-1} is iterated, and is itself a palindrome. The following example also shows a combination of iteration and inversion.

Go to college – study math – study physics – Return home, which can be represented by

$A\ B\ B\ A^{-1}$

where B denotes 'studies' without distinguishing the subjects

3. *Refrain* – In verse a refrain is a line or a part of a line or a group of lines which is repeated, usually at the end of stanza. For our purpose it will mean a ritual act that periodically appears at the end of a sequence, but which may sometimes appears in the beginning or in the middle.The structure containing a refrain can be shown as:

   a) A B ... ... R.........MN ... ... R.........ST... ...R
   b) RAB... ... ...RMN ... ... RST... ... ...
   c) ARBC ... ... MRNP....... ... ... SRTQ ... ... etc.

where R is the refrain and other letters are variable elements. Refrains abound in almost every type of ritual. A few illustrations are given below:

i) The school bell rings when lessons begin, a new period starts and when the last lesson ends.
ii) A boss is briefing his assistant on a new assignment. The refrains of 'yes sir' are uttered periodically by the assistant.
iii) At the end of every confirmed sale, the auctioneer strikes the table with a hammer.
iv) In verse a refrain may be introduced for euphony and may have no meaning. In Shakespeare's, *It was a lover and his lass* the refrain " with a hey, and a ho, and a hey nonino " is a purely technical device.

4. *Multiplets* – A muliplets is a group which recurs, but not with regularity to be classified as refrain. Triplets are especially common in Indian religious texts, verse and ritual "*om namaḥ Śivāya*", "*om tat sat*", "*bhūr bhuvaḥ svar*", (earth, sky, heaven) are some of the well-known triplet.
A symbol of trinity, threesomes were common in church music. In Hinduism it appears as trimūrti, the triad of three gods *Brahmā* (creation), *Viṣṇu* (preservation), *Śiva* (destruction). *Dattātreya* a Brahmin saint is supposed be the incarnation of all these three gods and worshipped. The triplet 'Brahmā, Viṣṇu, Maheśa (Mahesa for Śiva) is also common.
According to Staal triplets enjoy a special position among multiplets because three is the most common number of subdivisions of larger units.

5. *Embedding* – Consider the daily routine of a businessman
Go to oftice –work – lunch – work – return home
which can be written as $ABCBA^{-1}$
where A^{-1} (return) is the inverse or image of A (go).
Suppose his intenerary is slightly modified on Mondays when he reads a book before and after lunch. We have seen that reading a book itself is a ritual.
Open the book –read-close the book or $D = E\,F\,E^{-1}$, say.
Ritual D is independent in the sense it can be undertaken at home, in office or when you are at your friend's house. The

modified itinerary would appear as

$A\ B\ D\ C\ B\ D\ A^{-1}$

This is a case of 'embedding'. D is embedded in a larger pattern. Embedding usually gives rise to a complex hierarchy of structures. For example, snacks may be embedded in a meeting of executives, which in turn is embedded in their office work. An example of progressive embedding would be :

$$A \longrightarrow A_1 B A_2 \longrightarrow A_1\ B_1\ C\ B_2\ A_2$$

B is embedded in A splitting it into two similar portions A_1, A_2; C is embedded in B splitting it into subdivisions B_1, B_2 of B.

6. *Relay* – An activity may be completed by a chain of people who take over the tasks from their predecessor and hand it over to their successor. The 'relay race' found in sports is an obvious example. In India people go on 'relay fast' as a mark of protest against a government's action or an oppressive law. Every person fasts for a certain number of hours or days by turn. This is an innovative method of registering a protest which gives a wide publicity to a grievance without endangering the individual protester's health.
   Relays are also used in factories and offices which employ a number of shifts. A person who has been on duty for a certain number of hours is relieved by his successor and the work goes on continuously.

7. *Cycle* – A cycle begins and ends with the same element and has the structure.

   ABC ... A

   Though not common, a cycle is found in music and religious rituals. A mantra sometimes begins with 'om' and ends with 'om'. An activity closely similar to a cycle is a 'cyclic activity' in an ordinary sense. Your daily routine if stereotyped is cyclic. On a race track when a runner has completed a circuit, he has described a 'cycle'. Such rituals are covered by the definition above. In fact all the latter rituals can be exhibited as iteration.

   AA...

8. *Chorus* (concord, unison)

In chorus there is a simultaneous performance of similar activities by a number of people. A few illustrations follow :

a) The entire audience may join the singer in singing the refrain of a song.
b) In a bhajana (devotional song), certain portions of the song are sung by the entire audience.
c) After a political leader completes his speech the audience may raise the slogans like 'Long live *X*", "We will do or die", "Down with *Y*"
d) In villages you can see women singing and pounding the grain in unison.
e) It is interesting to see how a gang of laborers shifts a huge weight from one place to another. The gang leader utters a refrain which may or may not have any meaning. This is a signal for his team-mates, who in chorus utter some meaningless word and at the same time give a jerk to the weight in unison. In this example chorus is only a secondary activity which facilitates the main goal.

9. *Structure completion (Pattern Completion)* – Suppose you are reading an interesting novel. It is 5 p.m., your usual time to go for a walk and you find that you have only one or two pages to complete the book. In all probability you will complete the novel postponing your walk by a few minutes. You are watching a cricket match on TV and your favorite batsman has made 97 runs. You find that it is time to leave for your office. You are likely to wait for a few minutes hoping that the magic figure of 100 is reached, though your going late to office might invite a mild reprimand from your boss.

You invite a friend to dinner who is visiting you after a long time. You offer her a number of courses followed by dessert. Although it was an informal dinner, you realize that it was becoming structurally formal – only the last step mentioned in your book of etiquettes was missing – coffee. You decide to serve coffee though your friend is not very keen on it. You have the satisfaction of completing a formal ritual.

These are the examples of what I call 'pattern copletion' or 'structure completion' which involves the motive to leave a thing unfinished. It may involve conformity with formal etiquettes and manners, completion of symmetry or order, cyclic movements permutations and combinations, magic numbers, and even superstitions and taboos. I shall provide one more example. Suppose you find three letters A, B, C arranged as ABC, BCA. You feel that only one arrangement CAB is left out from the cyclical rotation A, B, C. You add the third arrangement. Similarly, if the arrangements ABCD, BCDA,CDAB are given to you, which involve successive cyclical rotation, DABC will complete the pattern.

10. *Overlapping* – If a task consists of a number of activities, it may be possible to replace a relay be overlapping activities. One of the obvious reasons for overlapping is economy of time. There may be other reasons in religious rites which are discussed later.

A ritual is sometimes slightly modified. For example in your daily routine of going to office and returning home you may take a train instead of driving to office. If a father has the habit of delivering a sermon to his son every evening, occasionally the sermon may accompanied by a slap if the son has misbehaved on that day.

In fact a ritual may be modified by (1) omission of a few elements, (2) addition of a few elements, or (3) modification of a few elements. We shall denote a modification of a ritual or ritual element by a prime or dash. Thus 'Á' is a modified from 'A'. It will be assumed that such modifications are slight and do not warrant re-classification of the structure. For example : Chant a mantra for 101 times-meditate –chant the same mantra for 101 times is a palindrome ABA

If the second A is modified to chant the mantra for 100 times, the ritual can be written as

ABÁ

and will still be treated as a palindrome.

8.5 Ritual and Abnormal Behaviour

It is interesting to compare ritualistic behaviour with some types of repetitive behaviour which is recongnised as pathological.

In Tourette's syndrome, a person develops multiple tics, repetitive urges like throat clearing, yelps or barks. This involuntary repetitive behaviour is believed to be a neurogical disorder.

Closely resembling this is the obsessive compulsive disorder (OCD) which is usually treated as psychological or emotional disturbance. Obsessions are intrusive thoughts which a person cannot drive away. Compulsions are the stereotyped acts which the people with OCD are compelled to perform. These may include repetative rituals like writing the same sentence again and again, uttering an obscene word repeatedly, checking and re-checking to ensure that gas is turned off and performing a religious act repeatedly for no ostensible reason. The person usually feels that if she does not indulge in the compulsions, some catastrophic event may follow. Unfortunately the compulsive acts give only a temporary relief from tension.

Interestingly almost every structural pattern mentioned in connection with rituals is found in the behavior of the person afflicted with OCD. The person may be compelled to perform a series of acts which include refrain, iteration (repetative acts), inversion (counting in a normal way and backwards), symmetry (arranging objects in symmetrical patterns), pattern completion (arranging objects in different orders using permutations and combinations)

The compulsive usually has a doubt whether she has performed a ritual properly and tends to repeat the ritual several times. In this respect she resemble a priest who always dreads that the ritual may not have been performed according to the prescribed rules, and he may add an expiatory ritual as a precautionary measure.

The compulsive ritual has some outstanding features. The compulsive is more rigid than the most rigid priest who insists on performing a ritual exactly in the prescribed manner.

Compulsive rituals appear to be almost totally structure-oriented. The ritualists themselves do not know the meaning, nor do they have any goal except performing the ritual under compulsion. We may use the word *morphocentric* (Gk. morpho, form) to denote a ritual which is structurally oriented and whose manifest content has little meaning. Compulsive rituals may change their forms. For instance, the compulsive may indulge in counting for some time, then switch over to compulsive washing followed by compulsive writing. While the forms may change, the ritual will have most of GRS, that a solo ritualist can perform. Sometimes these ritualists may also request their close relatives to participate in these rituals, which may lead to greater complexities.

While abnormal anxiety is believed to be the root of OCD, psychoanalysts go further and assume that rituals have hidden meaning, and interpret such compulsive behaviour in the same manner as they interpret dreams. The analyst may spend years and decades in decoding the compulsive rituals of a patient, but the only important inference that can be drawn from such interpretation is a general conclusion that the ritualist suffers from excessive anxiety and the rituals involve an interplay of the id (instinctive impulse, mostly sexual), the ego (self) and the superego (conscience).

Another fascinating feature of the compulsive ritual is recursion. Recursive rules in grammar and śrauta ritual can theoretically create infinite possibilities out of the finite data. The compulsive ritualist, too, is a potential creator of infinity, but can use many more tools. The following example will elucidate the point.

I.1. *A* is a compulsive ritualist. On a certain day he has an urge to touch an idol (X_1). When he touches X_1, he feels that he has soiled X_1, and starts cleaning it. He then realizes that X_2, the pedestal on which X_1 is mounted is also polluted through contagion and needs cleaning, a ritual which occupies him next. X_2 is near other objects X_3, X_4, X_5 which also must have been polluted because of their proximity. These objects also need cleaning. The polluted objects and the rituals appear as branches, potentially infinite in number, as shown in fig. 8.1

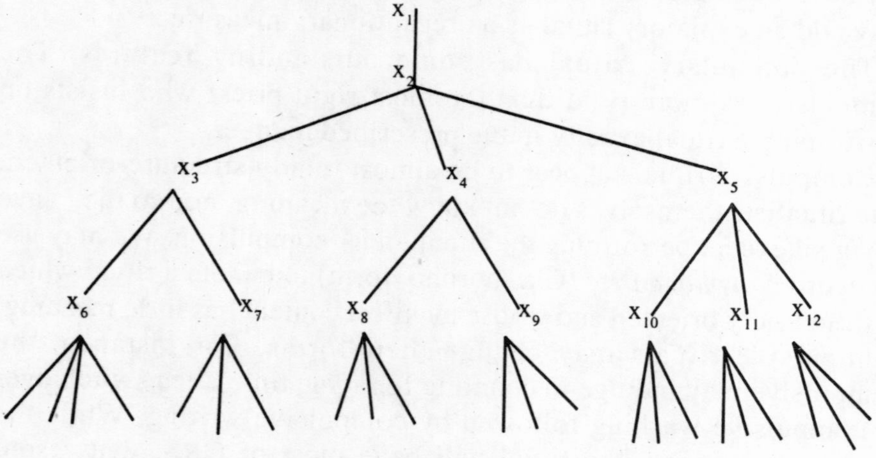

Fig. 8.1 Compulsive Ritual

I.2. *A* is compelled to count numbers from 1 to 100. However, there are a number of taboos in his repertory. While counting these number, if a prohibited object, sound or thought (taboo) appears, he has to count odd number 1, 3, ...after the normal counting is over. During this expiatory counting, if another toboo appears he may have to do the 'expiation of the expiation', say counting squares of 1, 2, 3,... i.e. 1, 4, 9, ... The ritual can be almost endless and may involve permutations and combinations and pattern completion. It should be obvious, to you that the performance of 'rituals within rituals' amounts to self-embedding.

Psychologist and psychoanalysts usually interpret the compulsive acts as exaggerated defences against the anxiety a person harbours.

Recent advances in neuroscience show a remarkable connection between Tourette's syndrome and OCD. In the core of the brain is situated the neo-striatum, consisting of two parts, the caudate nucleus and putamen. The former is the 'automatic transmission station' for the front part of the brain which controls thought. The latter is a similar control station for that part of the brain which controls physical movements. Malfunctioning of the caudate nucleus results in obsessions and compulsions while that of the putamen leads to the Tourette's syndrome. Psychiatrist Jeffrey M. Schwartz aptly likens this situation with the car whose gearshift is stuck[5]. Two other areas in the brain, The orbital cortex or 'the error detecting system' and the cingulate gyrus of the limbic system in the brain also appear to play a role in OCD. These two parts interacting with the caudate nucleus give the afflicted person a sense of exaggerated dread and anxiety which he tries to reduce by performing compulsive rituals.

Ritualistic 'fixation' also occurs in case of some aboriginal tribes that have failed to 'grow'. Such neophobic societies live isolated with their own rigid rituals and taboos. Many people, who are fed up with the modern 'fast' life yearn to 'go back to the nature' and idolize such apparently simple societies as a symbol of pristine living. However, they seldom realize that more often than not they are the specimens of 'frozen' societies which have stopped evolving.

8.6 Existentialism

We briefly considered in passing the rationale for ritual. While explanations have been suggested by psychologists, psychoanalysts, biologists, sociologists and anthropologists, the contribution of existentialists appears to be surprisingly novel.

Existentialism was perhaps depicted in chapter 6 in a bad light because those existentialists who entered hermeneutics could interpret a text in almost infinite number of ways making a mockery of the very word meaning. One also finds it difficult to evaluate them because of their penchant for making paradoxical and puzzling statements such as Heidegger's " das Nichts nichtet " (nothing nothings)

However, in case of rituals existentialism can offer a plausible explanation. Its merit is that it is applicable to both normal as well as abnormal behaviour, animals as well as humans (though many existentialists may not be aware of this). It does not have to posit a special meaning, a goal or does not have to deal with symbols, the unconscious and context-related interpretation. Anxiety is built into the very existence of man, which he tries to allay through ritual.

According to Soren Kierkgaard (1813-1855) our personal experience comes through "a direct feeling rather than through the abstract activity of intellect". He also regards personal experience in absolute contradistinction with non-personal existence. Each individual is faced with a situation either of 'being' or 'not being himself'.

Heidegger maintains that we have a dread or anxiety which is rooted in our existence. Paul Tillich describes three types of anxiety which can be attributed to human existence. Since this anxiety is present in all normal humans, Tillich's thoughts can give us some insight into one of the causes of rituals. He calls the first type 'ontic' anxiety (In Greak 'on'means being). According to him fate and death constantly threaten our existence. The dread of death is the most basic one. Anxiety of fate is a derivative dread and arises from " contingency" or uncertainty inherent in the situation we meet at every step. Our anxiety abouf fate is based on our awareness of this 'contingency'.

The second type of anxiety is the anxiety of emptiness and meaninglessness. Man tries to self-affirm spiritually every moment. What this means is that he is engaged in a creative activity – the way of living spontaneously. Such spontaneous interaction with the surrounding is 'creative' since it alters the environment. This spiritual self-affirmation is threatened by non - being. The absolute threat of non-being leads to emptiness whereas a relative threat in a specific sense gives rise to meaninglessness.Meaninglessness has the relationship to emptiness as the threat of fate has to the anxiety about death.

The third type of anxiety is that non-being threatens our moral self-affirmation. Man is responsible for his own actions. But man is also a moral judge of his actions. When the judge within him assesses his moral rectitude of the actor within him, there is a conflict which produces anxiety of guilt in specific situations. In the absolute sense it is the anxiety of condemnation and rejection.

These three types of anxiety are not independent ; usually all of these co-exist though one of them could be dominant.

Rituals vary in their degree of rigidity and form a continuum. At one end are the rituals like informal greetings which are extremely flexible. While at the other end of the spectrum are such rigid rituals as religious rites accompanied by taboos. These rituals may be regarded as our shields against anxiety - the greater the anxiety, the greater is the rigidity and perhaps complexity of the rituals. All these types of anxieties are in fact reflected in our ritual. What's more when anxiety exceeds a certain limit it can lead to psychological disorders in which, as we have already seen, develops a ritualistic behavior strikingly similar to some of the complex, and rigid formal rituals.

Part III

RITUALS AND SCIENCE

9

LANGUAGE

9.1 Semiotics

A sign is a mark, an object, an event or an action, which denotes another object, event, or action. For example, the configuration CAT consists of three marks on this page, but they stand for a particular species of quadrupeds according to the accepted convention.

A sign system may be used to convey information. The branch of knowledge concerned with sign systems is called semiotic or semiotics. Sign systems are used in language, mathematics and logic. The Morse code and the Braille are examples of sign systems.

There are three sub-systems of a sign system: (1) syntactics which deals with the internal structure of the signs irrespective of the functions they perform, (2) semantics which is concerned with the relationship of signs with meaning, and (3) pragmatics, which studies the relationship of the system with the user.

In chapter 7 we studied structures. Some of these structures are non-symbolic, while some structures are signs for something else. A complex can be used as a sign of another complex when the two complexes are structurally similar, i.e when the elements of one can be correlated with those of another.

9.2 The Features of Language

Language is a sign system but the perception that it is used only for communication is not correct. It serves many purposes, and can be used (1) to indicate a fact – an object, an idea or a situation, (2) to express the state of the speaker, and (3) to change the state of the hearer. If you inadvertently touch a hot object you may, under pain utter "oh" or "ayyo" depending upon your social background. Here (2) is operative. If you are in an art gallery and come across a beautiful painting you may exclaim, "An excellent painting!". Here (1) and (2) are present if there are no hearers. If your order your husband to shut up, you are using (2) and (3).

Communication, of course, is the most important function of language. People have always wondered whether animals can talk. In mythology and children's literature, they do – in fact even inanimate objects like chairs may communicate. However, scientists agree that animals do communicate, but they also assert that this communication is so primitive that it cannot be called language.

The best way to compare their communication with human language is to consider the key properties of a language and find out if some of them are shared by animal communication. Before we consider these properties a few concepts in linguistics (the science of language) need to be mentioned.

A phoneme is a unit of sound, which cannot be analyzed further. The phonemes of a language stand in contrast with each other. For example, in words pat, bat, rat, sat, the initial consonants give rise to the phonemes denoted by / p /, / b /, / r /, / s /.

However, the phonemic analysis is much more complex, but we need not go into its details. For instance, / p / itself is not a constant sound and slight variations are found, but these nuances are generally ignored. Phonology or phonemics deals with a system of sound used in a language. The most important function of phonemes in a language is to keep two utterances apart.

A morpheme is the smallest meaningful element of language. The grammatical system consists of the set of morphemes and the arrangements in which they appear. A morpheme is not only a word but includes prefixes, suffixes and host of 'non-words ' For example in the sentence "He is my brother's son" and "This farm belongs to my brothers", 's' in both sentences are morphemes, but they are different morphemes.

The most important characteristics of language are duality, productivity, arbitrariness, interchangeability, specialization, displacement and cultural transmission.

Duality: When you utter a sentence you are using two sub-systems, though unconsciously, the phonological and grammatical systems in which there is a correspondence between a morpheme and a phoneme or a group of phonemes. To understand how the principle of duality plays an important role in language, let us consider a simple case.

Suppose your language has only one word (phoneme) and you are permitted to use exactly three words. How many sentences can you form? If you denote the identically pronounced words by A, the only sentence you can form is AAA. You can assign a meaning to this sentence, but your one-sentence language can hardly be of any use to you. Suppose now, you have two different words A and B, the sentences you can form are: AAA, AAB, ABA, ABB, BAA, BBA, BAB, and BBB. Their number is 8 (2x2x2). This is, of course the maximum number of meaningful sentences possible assuming that a meaning is assigned to each sequence. In practice, a language has thousands of phonemes, and sentence need not be confined to three words. Millions of meaningful sentences can be created out of such phonemes with a grammatical system.

Productivity: Humans can not only reproduce the sentences they have already heard, they can also create new sentences. Theoretically productivity implies that there is no limit to the number of sentences one can construct. In constructing new sentences to meet novel situations, we use what linguists call the principle of analogy.

Cultural Transmission: Unlike other creatures, we not only learn, but also teach. We can pass habits and customs including language, form one generation to another. A new generation does not have to start from scratch. What this means is that as time passes, human knowledge tends to multiply rapidly.In this respect man differs from other social animals: he is said to belong to the socio-cultural system while the latter belong to the bio-social system.

Arbitrariness: To understand this characteristic, consider a map of a territory. There is a geometrical resemblance between the symbol (map) and its meaning (land). This element of resemblance is called iconicity. The design of a language, on the other hand, is arbitrarily based on a semantic convention. There are only a few exceptions. For example in onomatopoeia a word is formed in imitation of the sound associated with its source – cat's mewing or the ding-dong of the bell. Iconic representation has some advantages, but these are far outweighed by its limitations. Unlike the iconic mode, language can describe abstract ideas and emotions.

Interchangeability: Interchangeability exits if the organism capable of transmitting a massage is also able to receive it. Human speech and most of the communication gadgets have these characteristics. In courtship signalling of most animals, males and females cannot change their roles.

Specialization: Suppose a house in your neighbourhood is vacant. You see two truckloads of household articles being unloaded and taken into the house. Later you find that a new family has moved in.

Your friend has not seen these events but has been told by someone that a new family has just occupied the house. In the knowledge which you gained there was a close connection between the antecedent and the consequence, a sort of functional relationship existed between them. Your friend on the other hand received the knowledge verbally without going through the chain of events. The communication he received was 'specialized '.

Displacement: A communication is said to be displaced when the main characteristics of the antecedent and consequence can be removed from time and place of transmission. For example, a message meant for a certain person may have been transmitted hours or days before the person received it, and who may be thousands of miles away from the person who transmitted the message. In the era of modern gadgets of communication and storage, 'communication' from *A* to *B* is not a single event, it is chain of events which may create a gulf of many years and thousands of miles between *A* and *B*.

A few inustration will elucidate the difference between the animal and human communication systems.

I.1. When a bee worker finds a source of nectar, it returns to the hive and performs a dance, which conveys information about the source of nectar, to other workers. The dance has two parameters, one showing the direction and other indicating the distance of the source, from the hive. This system has productivity because the bee can pinpoint a new source, displacement because the dance takes place away from the source. There is no cultured transmission; the behavior is instinctual. There is no arbitrariness and only one type of information is transmitted. Duality if present is negligible. There is, however interchangeability and specialization.

I.2. Gibbons are one of our closest relatives. They have a language–like communication system consisting of a few distinct calls which can take care of limited number of situations. Some of their calls relate to avoidance behavior and friendly approach.

However there is no duality, productivity or displacement. There is only slight arbitrariness and cultural transmission if any is negligible. Interchangeability and specialization are present. But their ability to utter different phonemes is biologically limited and their intelligence level far too low to make use of the scanty resources for a developed communication system.

In relation to the animal's ability to communicate recent researches by anthropologists such as Lyn Miles have led to interesting results. It has been found that primates like orangutang can be taught sign language if raised in human environment. An intelligent primate can display the grammatical comprehension of a 2-year-old human child, and have a vocabulary up to 3000 words.[1] However, these are the examples of the 'languages' taught to primates by humans and not their native language. It shows the primate's ability to use its intelligence rather than evolve a language. It is doubtful, that once taught, they can culturally transmit it to the next generation without the help of humans.

9.3 Syntax and Semantics

Syntax in its broadest sense is the order in which different parts or elements of a complex are related to each other. The complex fitted with these relations is called a system. The word structure was used in Chapter 7 to indicate a system as well its syntax.

When the system happens to be a symbolic or a sign system it also 'means' something. Semantics is the study and analysis of meaning. In particular, it is concerned with the relations between expressions or elements of the system with their meaning. It was pointed out in Chapter 6. I.1 that the given data can be semantically interpreted in several ways.

The following illustration will show that an expression can have several syntactic views and many semantic interpretations.

Consider the expression
C D A B A D C.

Its syntax can be described in various ways.

1. The expression consists of seven elements.
2. It is the mirror image of itself.
3. It is part of the structure N M C D A B A D C Q.

4. All its elements consist of continuous lines.

It can also be semantically interpreted in different ways depending upon the 'meaning' of A, B, C, D.

1. It is a sequence of activities eat, read, work, sleep, work, read, and eat.
2. It is a number 1230321.
3. It is a ritual consisting of the following steps: prostration, recitation of a mantra oblation, meditation, oblation, recitation of a mantra, prostration.
4. 5+7 = 7+5.

An unfortunate tendency prevails in the fields of religion, art and psychology to "semanticize" almost every structure - shapes, articles, acts and utterances. Many people seem to believe that every structure should have a hidden meaning i.e. it should be a sign-system. This was discussed in Chapter 6.

There is a relation between the syntax and semantics of a language, which is of course, purely conventional. To understand this aspect, consider three words 'Lincoln', 'Booth' and 'Killed' which can be arranged in six ways.

(a) Lincoln Booth killed.
(b) Lincoln killed Booth.
(c) Booth Lincoln killed.
(d) Booth killed Lincoln.
(e) Killed Lincoln Booth.
(f) Killed Booth Lincoln.

Structures a, c, e, f are meaningless. While b and d possess meaning only d is true. However, it would be wrong to think every grammatically correct sentence has meaning. For example, the sentence

Happiness stands on two legs

is grammatically correct, but is meaningless unless it is "interpreted" metaphorically or poetically. These examples illustrate the distinction between the different types of a sentence: true, meaningful and grammatically correct.

9.4. Phylogenetic Changes

As time passes the design of a language changes. The change is so gradual that usually we do not perceive the process of change. Such a historical change is called phylogenetic change.

Two examples one from old English (OE) and one from middle English are given below.

1. Grendel gongan,godes yrre baer (A line from epic Beowulf).
2. That thee is sent reeyve in buxomnesse.(From Chaucer 14th Century CE).

The first is totally unintelligible to most of us. It means "Grendel going god's bore" in modern English. The second makes a vague sense but some words need to be explained. For example "that" means "that which" and "buxomnesse" means cheerfulness.

Phylogenetic changes are of various types. For example, OE did not have the phoneme 'sh' such as in 'shy' in modern English and 'r' was a trill. As an example of grammatical change we may cite the inflection of nouns for case which prevailed in OE, which no more exists in modern English. There are also semantic changes. For example in OE "Klyppen" meant "to hug or accept". The words now appears as 'clip', to fasten.

While these changes can be brought about by different mechanisms, for us the most important mechanism is the interaction of two languages. When two language groups come into contact with each other each language influences the other. There is mutual borrowing of various kinds.

The borrowing is usually motivated by two factors; prestige and need. After the Norman Conquest, upperclass Englishmen borrowed words and expressions from French, the language of their conquerors.

When the British colonized India, they came across several objects for which there were no English words. Instead of coining new words, They adapted the Indian words to their phonology. Pundit, brahmin, mantra, yoga chukkar (in polo) and sandhi(in linguistics) are some of the words India has given to English. Words adopted from other language are called loanwords.

There is another kind of borrowing which is important for us, loan translation. The phrase 'marriage of convenience' has been created by translation of French 'mariage de convenance'. Idioms like 'his days are numbered' have been loan-translated into Indian languages from English.

The final shape of a borrowed word depends upon a number of

factors the most important being prestige, need, and the design of the borrowing language. The process by which the loanword undergoes a change, if any, is called adaptation.

When prestige and practicability compete with each other, the borrowing language may face a dilemma. For example, English has borrowed a number of words from French for prestige. There are nasal sounds in French, but nasalization does not exist in English. Those proficient in French may pronounce 'entree' exactly as the French do, but what about the common people? In such cases more pronunciations than one prevail concurrently for some time till one of them may supplant the others. In case of the loanwords borrowed from French by English nasal sounds seem to have been replaced by the nearest non-nasal sounds available in English.

The word restaurant, a loanword from French provides an interesting example of the role of prestige among Indians. The speakers of English usually pronounce it without nasalization. In Hindi it is written in a nasalized form closely resembling the French pronunciation. However, most educated Indians prefer to pronounces it as the British do as a matter of prestige.

What happens when an entire work of science or language is exported? The importing language usually translates it in the following manner.

1. Words are translated when their equivalents exist in the borrowing language; else a few words may be borrowed as loanwords.
   The loanwords may undergo adaptation or may be written in italics in the original form. If extensively used they will ultimately be naturalized after a long time and enjoy the status of any other native words in that language.
2. Usually phrases are translated when possible. Very rarely idiomatic expressions may be translated ('action at a distance' from Latin 'actio in distans'), but most are retained in the original form of foreign phrases ('esprit de corpse').
3. Sentences are usually translated.

It is important to remember that whole sentences are translated and not transliterated. This has an important bearing in deciding the status of mantras vis-á-vis language, and will be discussed later.

9.5 Verse

Of all the structures sharing common characteristics with rituals, verse is unique because it has three distinct syntax:

1. As a linguistic expression it is subject to the syntax of the language in which it is written.
2. Unlike prose, it has a ritual-like verbal structure.
3. It has a metrical structure resembling that of rituals. This may be called its musical syntax.

These structures compete with one another and the net is result is the dilution of the linguistic syntax. Thus in poetry we find the rules of syntax are often relaxed and we come across constructions which are not found in prose. But this deviation may sometimes affect semantics and the poem may become unintelligible or admit of several interpretations.

Rhythm is a pattern of sound determined by the relations of long/ short or stressed/unstressed syllables. In verse this pattern is regular, recurrent and euphonic. A unit of such a pattern is called a meter. In English the meter is usually of the stress-and-syllable type.

Consider the following line from Thomas Gray's *Elegy written in a country Churchyard.*

Thĕ cúr' fĕw tólls' thĕ knéll' ŏf pár' tĭng dáy'

If the unstressed syllable ˘ and the stressed syllable ′ are denote by A and B respectively the pattern may be written as

1. AB \ AB \ AB \ AB \ AB
   The block AB which is repeated constitutes the 'foot' of a meter called iambic and is the most popular meter in English. Since there are five feet in a line, it is an example of iambic pentameter.
   Other standard meters are.
2. Anapestic AAB \ AAB \ AAB \ AAB (tetrameter).
3. Trochaic BA \ BA\ BA \ BA \ (tetrameter).
4. Detylic BAA \ BAA (dimeter).
5. Spondaic BB \ BB \ AB \ AB \AB (pentameter).
6. Pyrrhic BA\ AA \ AB \ AA \ABA (pentameter).

A few remarks are in order. First, in practice all feet are not identical and the meter is identified by the predominant foot. In (5) and (6) above, the meter is identified by 'BB' and 'AA' respectively. Many trochaic lines lack the last 'A', for example, in Blake's *The Tiger*

Tíger' Tíger' búrn ĭng' bríght'

Secondly, the pattern is repeated (with some variations) in other lines, a fact that has to be borne in mind while identifying structures.

Iteration: This characteristic is really striking. For example, in the illustration of the iambic meter, the entire block AB is repeated four times. You must also remember the entire pattern of the line, say, L may be repeated with same modifications.

There can also be verbal iteration such as in

The woods decay, the woods decay and fall (Tennyson).

Refrain: Refrain is called 'burden' in poetry. In the pyrrhic meter illustrated above 'AA' can be treated as a refrain, which will also occur in other lines.

There are many kinds of verbal refrain found in verse. The refrain 'with a hey and a ho, and a hey nonino' from Shakespeare has already been mentioned.

The first stanza of the French poem *Malbrough s'en va-t-en guerre* is

1. Malbroughs'en va-t-en guerre.
2. Mironton, ton, ton, mirontaine.
3. Malbroughs'en va-t-en guerre.
4. Ne sais quand reviendra, Ne sais quand reviendra, Ne sais quand reviendra.

The second line is repeated in all other stanzas (not shown above), and is a refrain. There is also an 'internal ' refrain –the first and the third lines are the same. In fact this characteristic is common to all stanzas. For instance the first and the third lines of the second stanza are "I1 reviendra-z-a' paques".

Palindrome: Though this structure is not as frequent as iteration or refrain, a few examples can be cited. Consider the three lines of John Keats' *Endymion*

Ă thíng' ŏf béau'tў' ís' ă jóy' fŏr évĕr:'
Ĭts lóve' lĭnéss' iň créašĕs; // ít 'wĭll névĕr'
Páss ĭn 'tŏ nóth' ĭngnĕss' // bŭt stíll' wĭll kéep'

(lines // indicate pauses, called caesura.)

The opening foot of the third line (BA) is the inversion of the second (AB) as well as first which gives conversion of the iamb into trochee.

Verbal palindrome appears in the following French poem *Sur le pont d'Avignon*

Sur le pont d'Avignon L'on y danse
L'on y danse, sur le pont d'Avignon.

Rhyme: Rhyme resembles refrain- In the first two lines of *Endymion* above 'ever' and 'never' rhyme with each other. However, the rhyme may appear in different forms. In Wordsworth's poem "I wandered lonely as a cloud", the first six lines appear as follows:

I wandered lonely as a cloud
That floats on high oer vales and hills
When all at once I saw a crowd
A host of golden daffodils;
Beside the lake, beneath the trees
Fluttering and dancing in breeze

There is rhyming between the first and the third line, the second and the fourth and fifth and the sixth. The above rhymes are called end-rhymes for obvious reason. The rhyme may be 'internal 'such as in

The ice was here, the ice was there
The ice was all around:
It cracked and growled, and roared and howled
Like noises in a swound !

(Coleridge)

Rhyme may be treated as a sub-class of refrain.

Alliteration: Alliteration is the repetition of a consonant in conspicuous position. This can be observed in William Langland's *Piers Plowman*. The opening line is

In somer seson, when soft was the sonne

Or in Chesterton's

A reeling road, a rolling road, that rambles round the shire.

Alliteration may be treated as a sub-class of 'internal' refrain or repetition depending upon its pattern.

9.6 Sanskrit verse

Like Latin and Greek verse, the meters of Indian poetry are 'quantitative' i.e. they are based on the order of the short (⏑) and long (-) syllables. A syllable is treated as long if it contains a long vowel (ā, ī, ū, ṝ, e, o, ai, au) or a short vowel followed by two consonants.[2] A long syllable takes twice as much time as a short syllable.

The most common Vedic stanza was *Tristubh* consisting of four lines (pāda) each of eleven syllables. The last four syllables have the cadence -⏑-⏓. Each of the lines can be metrically expressed as XC or XC where X is a variable of seven syllables. The last four syllables give rise to the metrical refrain of C.

The courtly poets preferred long and rigid meters. Over 100 meters of this type are described in textbooks.

In Sanskrit prosody eight types of feet consisting of three syllables each have been devised. Denoting short and long syllables by A and B, these can be written as:

bha (BAA), ja (ABA), sa (AAB), ya (ABB), ra (BAB), ta (BBA), ma (BBB), na (AAA).

Notice that this classification is a pattern completion giving all possible (2x2x2) arrangements.

A meter is called *sama* when all the quarters are similar. It is *ardhasama* if alternate quarters are similar, and *viṣama* if no two quarters are similar.

A few examples of the *sama* and *ardhasama* meters may be provided.

Sama

1. *Indravajra*	4 × 11	BBA	BBA	ABA	BB	
2. *Līlākhela*	4 × 15	BBB	BBB	BBB	BBB	BBB
3. *Bhujaṅgaprayāta*	4 × 12	ABB	ABB	ABB	ABB	

Ardhasama

4. *Upacitra*	odd	AAB	AAB	AAB	AB
	even	BAA	BAA	BAA	BB

All sama meters provide instances of metrical iteration, and ardhasama display the refrain of the whole line. Both the types shows the iteration and refrain of blocks. The most interesting case is (2) in which the long syllable is iterated throughout the poem.

Verse composed in whatever language has the characteristics mentioned earlier, with some degree of variation. There is therefore, no need to illustrate verbal iteration or refrain though one singular example of refrain may be cited. In *Avadhūta Gītā* the last lines of each of the twenty-two successive stanzas (Chapter IV 3-24) is "*svarūpa - nirvāṇam anamayo ham*" (I am free from disease - my form has been extinguished.)

10

MUSIC

10.1 Indian Music

Before we compare the structures of music with those of ritual, a few words must be said about Indian Music.

The history of Indian music is usually divided into four periods : Vedic, ancient, middle and modern.

Vedic period (upto 1000 BCE.). During this era, music was used mainly for chanting Vedic Sāmans. Initially only three notes called udātta, anudātta and svarita were used. This scale was later expanded to contain seven notes. According to a śloka from the Vedic text *Pāṇinīya Śikṣā* these seven notes emerged as follows:[1]

Udātta	—	niṣāda (ni), gandhāra (ga)
Anudātta	—	ṛṣabha (re), dhaivata (dha)
Svarita	—	ṣaḍja (sā), madhyama (ma), pañcama (pa)

The Vedic music is also known as 'mārgī' saṅgīta (music). Its knowledge was confined to priests and rsis. However, gradually it came to be used for entertainment, and the music used by the entertainers was known as Gandharva music.

Ancient Period (1000 BCE - 800 CE): The music which prevailed during this period is called 'jātigāyana' which has been described in the famous text *Bharata Nāṭyaśāstra*, which is also a treatise on drama and dance. The jātigāyana is believed to be the precursor of the music based on rāgas which were possibly born at the end of this period. The rāgas were first mentioned in *Bṛhaddeśi*, a text written by Mataṅga Muni.

Middle Period (800-1800 CE): The jātigāyana was supplanted by the rāgasaṅgīta (the music based on rāgas). The Indian music in the North was also influenced by Persian and Arabic music through Muslims.

Modern Period (1800 CE): Indian music has made great strides during this period. There have been many innovative experiments to create new rāgas. The Western music also has had some influence especially in popular music. New instruments such as harmonium, violin and piano have been introduced from the West, and the first two have become part of the paraphernalia of the 'classical' music.

The modern Indian music has two main branches, Karnataki which is confined to South India, and Hindusṭani, mainly played in the North, though its practitioners are also found in South. Hindusṭani music has been influenced by Persian music to some extent, while the Karnataki music can be treated as a descendent of the ancient Indian music.

The seven notes mentioned above constitute a *saptaka* or a group of seven notes. The notes sā, re, ga, ma, pa, dha, ni roughly correspond to C,D,E,F,G, A, B of the Western major scale. It is interesting to observe the difference between the Indian and Western nomenclature. The saptaka indicates seven notes (unlike the Western 'octave' – eight), because the next harmonic of sā is not treated as part of the saptaka. Technically the saptaka is divided into 22 microtones (nādasthāna) but in practice only twelve tones are of importance.

1. sā (achala)
2. *re* (komaḷa)
3. re (śuddha)
4. *ga* (komala)
5. ga (śuddha)
6. ma (śuddha)
7. ma' (tīvra)
8. pa (achala)
9. *dha* (koṃala)
10. dha (śuddha)
11. *ni* (komala)
12. ni (śuddha)

Two notes 'sā' and 'pa' are 'achala' or stationary having no variants. Komala ('soft') indicates the flat variant and tīvra is the sharp varient of the basic note called suddha (pure). Only 'ma' has a tīvra.

The three saptakas used in Indian music are called mandra (lowest), *madhya* (middle) and *tāra* (highest). The mandra note is denoted by a dot below the note, e.g. pa. The tāra note is denoted by a dot above the the note e.g. p'a'. The notes without dots belong to the madhya such as 'pa'

To avoid confusion the usual phonetic diacritical marks will be omitted from the musical notations. Thus the madhya 'sā' will be indicated by 'sa'.

Indian music derives its strength from melody. Harmony is rarely used because the concept of chords is alien to it. Recently, however, under the impact of the Western music, some musicians have tried to introduce harmony as a new dimension, especially in popular music.

Indian classical music is based on rāgas. A rāga may be defined as the melodious group of notes subject to some rules. Some of the important rules are:

1. 'Sa' cannot be omitted from a rāga.
2. 'Ma' and 'pa' cannot be simultaneously omitted from a rāga.
3. A rāga should have at least five different notes.
4. Every rāga has an āroha (a specific sequence of ascending notes) and an avaroha (a specific sequence of descending notes)
5. There are certain rules which prohibit the inclusion of a note or certain combinations of notes.

A few technical words may now be mentioned Mukhyāṅga ('main body') or pakaḍa is the group of notes which recurs in the rāga. Each rāga has a distinct mukhyāṅga. For example, in the rāga sāraṅga it is ni sa re ma re pa ma re sa.

A vādī svara is that note which occurs most frequently in a rāga. Saṃvādī svara is the note whose frequency is next to the vādī. For example, in rāga Lalita ma is vādī and sa is saṃvādī. Svara-saṃvāda is a euphonic combination of two notes. For example, 'ṣaḍja pañcama bhāva' is the combination sa-pa or re-dha, ga-ni or ma-sä (The dot represents the higher harmonic) in which the second (pa) note is fifth in the scale from the first (sa). 'Ṣaḍja madhyama bhāva' is a similar combination of a note and another which is sixth from it in the scale.

Ālāpa is a technique in which the notes are sung with a vowel 'a' giving the appearance of a continuous flow of notes.

In tāna, the notes are sung rapidly with the vowel 'a'. The tāna may be called the rapid ālāpa.

Kampana (vibration) is the technique of extending a note for some duration (at the same frequency) without repeating the consonant. For example,

Maaa...

Sthāyi varṇa is the method according to which a note is repeated. For example,

sasa, gaga, nini etc.

Rāga-rāgiṇī. Rāgas are often identified with specific gods and rāgiṇīs are female rāgas or the wives of the gods. For example, the rāga Bhairava (Śiva) has five or six rāgiṇīs. The group of notes from sa to ma is called the pūrvāṅga and that from pa to sa is called the uttarāṅga. In the Western music they are called the lower and upper tetrachords.

Before we proceed, two differences relating to nomenclature must be mentioned. A note in the British parlance is a sound of a definite pitch which Americans call tone. Second, a saptaka can be built on any base note which then becomes the sa of that scale. In the terminology of Western music, if a scale is built on D as the base, it would be called D major, i.e. D does not become C.

10.2 Musical Structure

Iteration: As in verse, iteration is very common in Indian as well as Western music. In Indian classical music it appears in the form of kampana and sthāyi varṇa as mentioned earlier. Another type of iteration occurs in jamajamā, a style in which the same note appears in *druta* (fast) tempo such as dha dha dha dha dha or gamaga gamaga.

In popular songs, folk songs and nursery rhymes iterations are abundant.

I.1. In nursery rhymes like'Baa baa black sheep' or 'Jingle bell' a simple structure like the following appears.
AB-AB or AB-AB́ showing the iteration of AB.
In simple *bhajanas* (devotional songs) and 'āratis' sung at the time of a pūjā the pattern
AB-AB is very common.

I.2. The most popular songs in India are from movies – a movie without songs is likely to be a flop. Mukesh's 'Avara Hum' would appear as

AABA ... C D E F A A B A ...
The repetition of A is striking.
Talat's "Itanana mujhase tu" which is based on a Mozart's symphony appears as
ABAB ... CCD ... AB...
Showing the repetition C and AB.

I.3. There is no dearth of iteration in the Western pop.
Abba's 'Fernando' looks like
ABABCDECD...
showing the iteration of AB and CD.

Refrain: While refrain usually occurs in verse at the end, in music it also occurs in the beginning and in the middle. In fact, there are more refrains than one.

In I.1 above, both A and B are refrains.

I.2 above A, B are refrains.

In I.3 A, B and C are refrains.

The vādī and saṃvādī svaras are types of refrain though perhaps trivial since they consist of single notes. But in mukhyāṅga the entire group appears as a refrain. For instance, in rāga Yamana the refrain is ni, rega, regamapa, madha, pamagare, niresa. The mukhyāṅga is also called pakaḍa.

In church music Amen and Alleluia are refrains which resemble bījamantras.

It is really not necessary to make a detailed analysis for detecting iteration and refrain. If you are familiar with the Western pop music you will find them in Elvis Presley's "Tutti fruiti", Beatle's "Hippy hippy shake" or Frank Sinatra's "South of the border". If you know Indian 'film' songs, such as Talat's 'Ai mere dil kahin aur chal' or Rafi's 'Meri kahani' you will have not doubt about their abundance. In fact, you will find it difficult to choose a song without either iteration or refrain.

Palindrome: The mirror image is also called a rerograde. Staal cites Debussy's *Prelude No.10* as a composition in which palindrome occurs. Canonical and fugal compositions too contain mirror images.[2]

Before the rāgas came into existence (c. 6th century) Indian music was based on grāmas or a group of tonal sequences. A mūrchanā consisted of seven ascending (āroha) and seven descending (avaroha) sequences. For example, *U*ttaramandra consisted of sa re ga ma pa dha ni – ni dha pa ma ga re sa and Rajani.

Ṇi sa re ga ma pa dha – dha pa ma ga re sa ṇi.

There were 21 such mūrchanās, all palindromes.

In the rāga system though not all āroha – avaroha form palindromes, a few do. For example, in rāgas 1) Durga and (2) Śivarañjanī the palindromes are (1) sa re ma pa dha sā – sā dha pa ma re sa and (2) sa re *ga* pa dha sa – sa dha pa *ga* re sa.

In what is called śuddha tāna, the singer uses a group of notes which is a palindrome e.g. ma pa dha ni sa, ni dha pa ma.

Cycle: A cycle may appear in the form

ABC ... ... A

Or a modified form ABC ... ... A′

In I.2 "Avara hum" is a cycle and so is Lata Mangeshkar's "Meri bina tuma bina roye" which would appear as

ABA ... C D A B Á Á

It also appears in Indian percussion which is discussed later.

Staal gives a few examples of cycles in Western music.[3] I have discussed a few cycles under minuet, rondo and sonata.

Chorus: In Chapter 8, I used the word chorus in a broader sense, not restricted to vocal synchronization. When a number of musicians play the same tune, there is chorus. This is found in Indian as well as Western music. Devotional songs called bhajana and 'samūha gāna' or 'group singing' are examples where chorus appears.

Relay: Though not as common as iteration or refrain, relay does occur in music. When one instrument 'takes over' from another. In Indian popular music duets are very common and a couplet started by, say, a male voice may be completed by the female voice, though a few lines especially refrains may be sung in chorus.

A variation of relay occurs in Indian classical music when there is a friendly competion between two or more instruments. For example, a musician may play a piece on sitar, which will be 'copied' by a purcussionist.

Overlapping: This feature can occur only when two are more musicians are participating in a piece. It is common when a large orchestra is used both in Indian and Western music, classical as well as popular.

Multiplets: Triplets occur in sonata and symphony[4]. It was pointed out in Chapter 8 that '*Bhūr bhuvaḥ svaḥ*' is a triplet in Indian rituals. When set to music it becomes a musical triplet.

Minuet, Rondo and Sonata: The classical minuet appears as

A B A

which is a palindrome.

In rondo the main theme played at the outset returns at intervals and also closes the piece. It is an extension of the ternary form A B A into, say,

A B A C A D A

The form exemplifies a cycle, a part of which is the palindrome ABA.

Sonata is an instrumental piece which is in three or four movements the first movement is in Sonata Form followed by minuet (optional) or scherzo and finale. The Sonata Form consists of exposition, development and recapitulation and may be written as

A B Á

showing the mirror-like structure.

When 'D' in the rondo mentioned above is replaced by B, we get

A B A C A B A

Which is a palindrome and is sometimes called sonata-rondo.

Harmony: Harmony uses chords or simultaneous sounding of two or more notes. However, chords are not a mere aggregate, their progression forms a musical syntax. While harmony is called a mere clothing of melody, many critics point out that without the harmonic component Beethoven's music would cease to be the product of a genius.

Hormony, however, is alien to Indian music, though some composers under the influence of Western music have experimented with it.

Symphony: Symphony is an 'orchestral sonata' consisting of four movements – the first is a substantial movement, the second is a slow movement followed by a minuet or scherzo and the finale. A modern orchestra playing symphony can have about seventy instruments. The second movement has the same structure as the third viz. ABA. The first and the fourth are in the Sonata Form. ABÁ.

While Á is a function of A, we cannot create ABÁ from ABA by the 'context - sensitive rule'

BA → BÁ

since A in the middle movements is not to be charged. The rule adopted is called 'transformation rule' and can be expressed as: [5]

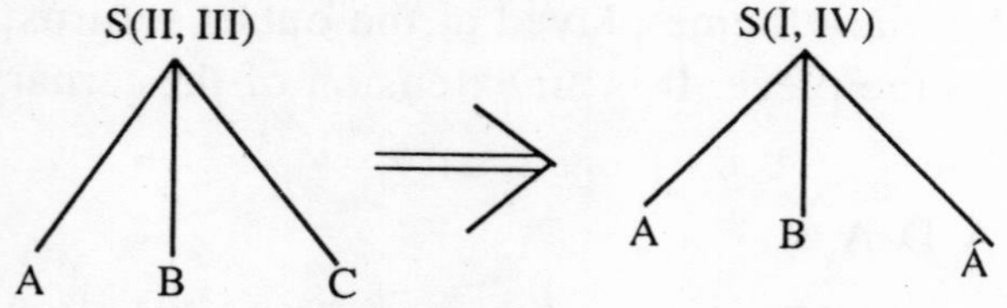

Embedding: An interesting case of self-embedding may now be described. As mentioned earlier the minuet has the structure

A B A

which can be formed from the recursive rule A → ABA. Applying this rule once more, ABA → ABABABA. It will be seen that the sonata-rondo ABACABA is only a modification of this.

We have already mentioned that the minuet appears as ABA. Each of these elements sometimes has the same structure.[6] This can be treated as the embedding of the minuets (or palindromes) into a minuet.

Pattern Completion: The Indian penchant for classification and manipulation of figures is reflected in a variety of pattern completion.

It was mentioned earlier that each rāga has an āroha (A) and an avaroha (B). Based on the combination A and B types (jātī) of ragas are determined. Both A and B can have three values since they can consist of 5, 6 or 7 notes. This leads to 3x3 = 9 AB combinations or jātīs. For instance (5, 5) is called oḍhava-oḍhava (5, 6) is called oḍhava-ṣāḍava, (5, 7) is oḍhava-sampūrṇa, (6, 5) is Ṣāḍ,ava-oḍhava and so on creating a complete pattern.

Pattern completion is also found in what is called 'thāṭa'. A thāṭa is a sequence of seven notes form which rāgas are created. In the seventeenth century Vyankaṭmakhī, a Karnataka musician created 32 and 72 thāṭas from which 480 ragas were extracted. To understand this mechanism consider the sequence of a saptaka.

Notes -	Sa	re	ga	ma	pa	dha	ni
Numberof varients -	1	2	2	2	1	2	2

The numerals indicate the varients śuddha, komala or tīvra as the case may be. For example sȧ being achala has only one type, re has two variants śuddha and komala. How many different permutations or sequences can have if the relative positions of sa, re,... are not changed? The answer is 1×2×2×2×1×2×2=32, which is the number of thāṭas.

Vyankaṭamakhī also created second order 72 thatas using a different approach. He divided the eight notes

Sa re ga ma pa dha ni saฺ

Into two euphonic blocks of four notes each.

	A	B
1.	Sa *re* re ma	pa *dha* dha sa
2.	Sa *re ga* ma	pa *dha ni* sa
3.	Sa *re* ga ma	pa *dha* ni sa
4.	Sa re *ga* ma	pa dha *ni* sa
5.	Sa re ga ma	pa dh ni ṣā
6.	Sa *ga* ga ma	pa *ni* ni sa

To each of A you can attach 6 lines of B giving 6x6 = 36 combinations. For example one such combination is A1-B1, i.e. sa *re* re ma pa *dha* dha sa.

In these combinations ma is śuddha. Let it be replaced by its tīvra variant ma′ in each combination. We shall have 36 more varieties, giving in all 72 thatas.

It may be contended that a thāṭa is a hypothetical entity like a geometrical point or some roots in Sanskrit whose existential status is debatable. However, there are many rāgas called āśraya rāgas or janaka rāgas which have a correspondence with the thāṭas. For example the rāga toḍī has āroha-avaroha as

Sa *re ga*, má pa *dha*, ni sȧ
Sa ni *dha* pa, ma’ *ga*, *re* sa.

which is the replica of the corresponding thāṭa and its mirror image.

In Hindustani music, however, there are ten thāṭas from which different rāgas are composed.

10.3 Percussion and Rhythm

Indian music has a well-developed art and science of percussion. A beat is called mātrā, and the interval between two beats is known as laya analogous to tempo. There are three speeds in Hindustani music slow (vilambita), medium (madhya) and fast (druta).

A pattern of the rhythm is called tāla which may be treated as a 'meter'. A tāla is divided into khaṇdas or sections. When the tempo of percussion agrees with that of rāga gāyana, the tāla is 'barabara'. If the number of beats in a given interval is doubled it becomes 'dugunā', if trebled it is tigunā. Cauganā is the tāla that is four times faster than the original barābara. There are rules regarding the combination of the rāgas and the tālas of the accompanying percussion instrument.

Tabla is the most popular versatile percussion instrument used in Hindustani music. Mṛdaṅgam and ghaṭam are used in the Karnataka music.

A tabla consists of two drums called ḍaggā and tabla ṭo be struck with the left and right hand. A distinct feature of the tabla is that all its beats are not identical. Varṇa or bola is the basic sound that can be struck from the tabla. There are four bolas that can be obtained from the ḍaggā (e.g. gi, dhi) and nine from the tabla (e.g. ta, na). Over twenty complex sounds can be created with the combination these basic sounds e.g. tak, tirakita etc.

Following are a few tālas

Eka tāla 2/2/2/2/2/2

which means there are six khaṇḍas, and two beats in each khaṇḍa.

Tri tāla	4/4/4/4
Keravā	2/2
Rūpaka	3/2/2
Zapatāla	2/3/2/3

Let us show two beats by A, 3 by B and 4 by C. Then tālas have the structure.

1. A A A A A A
2. C C C C
3. A A
4. B A A
5. A B A B

A is iterated in 1, 3 and 4. C is iterated in 2 and there is a refrain of A and B in 5.

It was mentioned earlier that more than twenty complex sounds can be generated from the tabala. This allows us to associate another type of structure with beats which may be called 'verbal' or 'acoustic'. Let us consider a few 'pieces' called ṭhekā, peśakāra etc., without defining these technical terms.

I. Tīn tāla (peśakāra)[7]
Dhikd dhindha dha dhikd dhindha dha dhikd dhindha
Tikd tinta ta tikd dhindha dha dhikd dhindha
The structure can be written as
ABCABCAB
A'B'C'A'BCAB
The following patterns can be observed:

1. The second line is the iteration of the first.
2. ABC is iterated in each line.
3. There is a refrain of AB (or A'B') in each line.
4. The whole piece is a near – palindrome.

II. Ek Tāla (peśakāra)[8]
Tirkakita dhit dhagadha tirakita dhit dhagadha tirakita tit takata tirakita dhit dhagadha
which can be written as

ABC ABC AB'C'ABC

which gives iteration of ABC, refrains of A, B and C

III. Tīn Tāla (ṭhekā)[9]
Dha dhadha dhim dha dhimdhim dhakr dhim dhim dha
Dha tata tim ta timtim dhakr dhimdhim dha
Symbolically it appears as

A AA B A BB C BB A
A A'A' B' A' B'B' C BB A

This has a number of iterations and refrains. What's more, it is also a cycle.

11

THE STRUCTURE OF RELIGIOUS RITUAL

11.1 Rituals, Mantras and GRS

The structure of religious ritual can be studied in three aspects, the structure of ritual acts, the structure of mantras and correlation of these two structures. Both mantras and ritual acts have most of the structural patterns displayed by rituals in general (GRS) discussed in Chapter 8, and a few illustrations have already been considered.

Staal has concentrated on Vedic ritual and especially the śrauta type. However, it was mentioned in Introduction that one of our goals was to investigate if non-Vedic rituals, too, share the characteristics of Vedic ritual. Accordingly, we shall consider the religious ceremonies which are practiced today and have different sources, Vedic, Purāṇic and tantric.

A few comments are in order before we proceed. First, rituals vary from place to place to some extent though they have similar structure. Most of my sources are from the Indian state of Maharashtra. Second, some of the words I have used in connection with ritual may not be purely Sanskrit; they are adaptations which are firmly established among the general populace.

It may be contended that since mantras are in verse which has already been discussed, there is no need to discuss mantras again. However, they need to be considered separately in order to find out if they have special features not possessed by ordinary verse.

1. Iteration

I.1. It was mentioned in Chapter 2 that every male who has undergone the initiation (upanayana) ceremony has to perform sandhyā twice a day. The ritual consists of about fourteen steps.

Iteration appears in the following subordinate rituals.

a) In arghyadāna three successive oblations of water are offered to the sun.

b) At the end, the Gāyatrī mantra is chanted 10, 20 or 108 times.

I.2. Every 'japa' of a mantra involves repetition of the mantra several times. According to the mantra śāstra, depending upon the nature of the mantra and the purpose for which it is used, the japa may consist of tens, thousands and even millions of repetitions.

2. Refrain

I.3. Acamanam in its simplest form consists of the following sequence of acts. (1) The right palm is held in the gokarṇa mudrā which gives it the shape of the cow's ear. (2) A small measure of water is placed on the palm. (3) The water is sipped off the middle portion of the palm called *brahmatīrtha*. (4) The process is repeated thrice (5) A spoonful of water is then taken over the *brahmatīrtha* and discharged into a receptacle.

According to *Manu Smṛti*, the ācamana is to be performed (a) after waking up (b) after drinking water (c) after meal (d) after sneezing (e) when one is hungry (f) after telling a lie. (g) after completing lessons and so on. It is believed that periodical intake of water in small quantities improves digestion and excessive intake at any time is harmful. The refrain on any day appears as

AR BR CR DR ER... where R is the ācamana

There is also an internal refrain in step (4)

The ācamana also forms the first step of the sandhyā mentioned in I.1 but is more complicated and its structure is

AR BR CR DR ER... where AR, BR ... are mantras in which A, B... are 24 names of Viṣṇu and R is the refrain "namaḥ". The three sips of the ācamana synchronize with AR, BR and CR and the praying posture follows CR.

3. Palindrome: Mirror images though not as frequent as iterations and refrains, do occur occasionally. The following mantra appears in the Yajurveda and Sāmaveda.

Agnir jyotir jyotir agnir
Indro jyotir jyotir Indraḥ

Sūryo jyotir jyotih Sūryaḥ
(SV 1831)
(YV 3-9)

Each line is a palindrome

I.4. Staal has studied in detail śrauta rituals called Agniṣṭoma or "praise of Agni" and Agnicayana. The first lasts five days and second twelve days. These are Soma rituals and very complex. In Agnicayna when each layer of the atlar is constructed, it is preceded and followed by two ceremonies called pravargya and upasad. The usual pattern is one of the following:

ABCAB (1)
OR ABCBA (2)

where A, B, C stand for pravargya, upasad, and the construction of layer. Both can be treated as palindromes if in (1) AB is taken as a non-inversible unit and in (2) A and B are treated as two distinct non-inversible units.

There is also a further dimension to this structure. The priest (Adhvaryu) recites specific mantras before C and after C creating a 1-1 correspondence between the mantras and the ritual acts. For example (1) can be written as

AB C AB
↕ ↕
M N

where M and N are the mantras.

I.5. Heesterman describes the odana ritual which consists of preparing rice stew that is subsequently eaten by priests.[2] The ritual occurs before and after the horse sacrifice and the structure would appear as a palindrome:

ABA

4. Multiplets: Triplets and quartets are quite common. Longer recitations from the Rig Veda attract the rule : first and last to be recited thrice. The structure appears as

AAAB ... CDDD

In sandhyā mentioned in I.1 modified triplets appear as follows

Āchamana – sipping of water three times
Arghyadāna – oblation of water three times
In many recitations '*bhūḥ bhuvaḥ svaḥ*' appears as a triplet.
Another triplet which often appears is '*idam na mama*' or 'not for me' which is a renunciation formula (see Chapter 12)

5. Relay: In many rituals, the recitation is 'handed over' by one priest to another or by a priest to the *yajamāna*, the person of whose behalf the ritual is performed.

6. Cycle: Staal mentions a quasi–cycle appearing in Agnicayana. There are seven oblations of cooked rice.

AB-S/BC-S/CD-S/DE-S/EF-S/GA-S/
where A, B,... G are mantras S the oblations with "svāhā"

I.6. One of the ways in which a Hindu devotee pays obeisance to god is walking round the idol in clockwise direction. Each circuit she describes is called pradakśiṇā. A variant of this is circling around oneself for a number of times and then prostrating before the idol. These circular movements constitute cycles.

Mt Kailaśa is believed to be the abode of god Śiva. There is a lake called Mānas which is revered by Hindus. Those pilgrims who visit these places consider themselves lucky if they can make a circumambulation (parikramā) around the lake. The greater the number of circuits a devotee makes in his life the greater his merit, and the greater is the respect he commands.

In many rituals a lighted lamp or camphor is circularly moved clockwise in a vertical plane before the idol for a prescribed number of times.

All these rituals involve cycles.

7. Overlapping: One often finds overlapping of the units of ritual. While relay can be attributed to the division of labor, overlapping seems to stem from the desire to maintain a continuous flow of the religious process. Possibly, it was believed that any gaps may indicate carelessness on the part of the participants and would invite gods' wrath, or possibly, the vacuum arouses existential anxiety mentioned in chapter 8 which the rite was supposed shield. In any case, such interpretations are not important for structural analysis.

8. Chorus: It has already been mentioned that a devotional song (bhajana) is often sung by all the devotees.

9. Pattern completion

I.7. Before a rosary (mālā) is used, it is consecrated or subjected to a saṃskāra called mālā saṃskāra. The mālā is placed on a fig leaf. Keeping the right hand on the mālā the following sequence of bīja mantras is recited.

om hrīṃ aṃ āṃ ... kaṃ...laṃ... kṣaṃ

Barring a few bījas, the sequence is nothing but nasalization of the alphabet, which was mentioned earlier in Chapter 2.

I.8. The structure of the kuṇḍalinī cakras was discussed in Chapter 3. The association of the bījamantras obtained from nasalization of the alphabet with the petals of the cakras display a 'pattern completion' of which there are two aspects. First, each cakra is 'pattern-complete' inasmuch as the letters are 'nasalized'. Second, there is a 1-1 correspondence between the alphabet and cakra systems as can be seen in table 11.1

Table 11.1

Cakra	Sequence of letters on petals
ājñā	Ha through kṣa
Viśuddha	A through aḥ
Anāhata	Ka through ṭha
Maṇipūra	Ḍa through pha
Svādhiṣṭhāna	Ba through la
Mūlādhāra	Va through sa

Observe that in the above table the sequence 'ājñā through mūlādhāra' is obtained by rotating cyclically the sequence 'viśuddha through ājñā', and the latter sequence has a 1-1 correspondence with the letters of the alphabet in order.

I.9. In a major pūjā ceremony which will be described in the next chapter, there is sometimes a subsidiary pūjā in which about 21 devatās are worshipped. Let X_1, X_2,...X_{20} and X_{21} be the set of devatās' names containing 21 elements, (A_1,A_2) the set of elements, 'praying' (A_1) and 'inviting' (A_2). Each devata is thus first prayed and then invited. This gives us 42 combinations (21x2) of the type 'XA' completing the combination pattern.

10. Embedding and recursion: Embedding abounds in ritual. For example the ācamana is embedded in a number of other rituals such as sandhyā and worship rituals. Recursion and self embedding appear to be the special characteristic of śrauta rituals. Staal has shown that the following pattern occurs in Agnicayana.

$A_1A_2A_3A_4A_5 \ldots A_5A_3A_4A_2A_1$

which is a near - palindrome. Moreover, this can be obtained from the recursion formula

$A \rightarrow BAB$

mentioned in Chapter 7. Theoretically such recursive formulas can lead to rituals of infinite length and are called sattra rituals. In respect of recursion śrauta rituals have a close resemblance with language in which similar recursive rules appear.

However, recursion does appear even in non-śrauta ritual through not as frequently. One often finds a pūjā within a pūjā in worship ritual. Recursion also appears in yantras and will be discussed at the end of this chapter.

11. Affixation : A peculiar pattern prevails in religions rituals, which may be called affixation. Certain ritual elements are prefixed, suffixed or infixed ostensibly to enhance the ritual power. The most frequently used affix is om, the sacred bījā. Many other bīja mantras also serve the purpose. The triplet 'bhūh bhuvaḥ svaḥ' and its components are also used usually as infixes.

Affixes are used to 'activate' a mantra. If m is a mantra, one of the methods or saṃskāras performed on it is to use the prefix 'haṃsa' and the suffix 'soham' so that the new mantra appears as
Haṃsa m soham

This new mantra is then recited several times. Affixes appear to have the status of catalysts or magical devices.

Affixation prevails in other rituals too, but with a lesser degree. An introduction by an eminenant person affixed to a book, an introductory lecture preceding the main lecture to be given by a celebrity, praying to god before a major secular ceremony begins, the appearance of a film star at the launching of a new product are all instances of affixation.

11.2 Yantras and Ritual

We have already described several characteristics of yantras. Many of these characteristics have a close resemblance with those of ritual acts and mantras. This should not surprises us, for time plays the same role in ritual as space plays in yantras. While rhythm is the basis of ritual, symmetry is the cornerstone of yantras. This should make us wonder if yantras are not disguised ritual. The following table shows the equivalence of yantric and ritual structures.

Ritual	*Yantra*
1. Iteration	Juxtaposition
2. Refrain	Recurrence of pattern
3. Palindrome	Mirror symmetry or rotation through 180^0
4. Multiplets	Multiplets
5. Cycle	A closed figure
6. Embedding, self-embedding,	Embedding, enclosure
7. Recursion A→AB	Recursion A→AB
8. Pattern completion	Pattern completion including saptial symmetry.
9. Relay	Any continuous line or shape
10. Overlapping	Overlapping
11. Chorus	

Table 11.2 Equivalence of Yantric and Ritual Structures

It is not difficult to translate the ritual idiom into the idiom of yantras. Iteration means successive repetition in time. In case of yantras this would mean repetition of the same figure in space. Palindrome creates problems because we can not have the exact spatial equivalent in terms of mirror symmetry. The closest equivalent is the rotational symmetry through 180^0 (see Chapter 7). We must realize that time has only one dimension unlike space, which prevents us to extend comparison between ritual and yantras beyond a certain point.

Overlapping is the intersection of two figures. Relay implies continuity in time, which in space would mean continuity in the line or pattern.

These features can be explained with reference to the Śrī Yantra (Chapter 3)

Iteration – outer circles in succession, petals, borders.

Refrain – triangles

Palindrome – There are two axes of symmetry, the vertical and horizontal lines passing through the center. The whole yantra can be treated as a palindrome in two directions.

Cycle – Every closed circuit such as circle, border or triangle is a cycle, so are the petals arranged circularly.

Pattern completion is inherent in the geometrical symmetry of various types.

Embedding – many yantras are embedded in the śrī Yantra. (A) Hanumāna yantra (inverted triangle), (B) Dhana-yaśa-prāpti yantra (see Chapter 3)

If you watch the yantra carefully you will find that A itself is embedded into another A or B giving a hierarchy of embedding.

Recursion : A→AB. Let A be the point at the center and B the innermost circle. The sequence A→AB→ABB→ABBB give point→ point and one circle→point and two concentric circles→point and three concentric circles.

Relay – All continuous figures

Multiplets – Multiplets such as '*om namaḥ śivāya*' are found in some yantra.

There is no correlate of chorus in yantras.

11.3 Awakening of Mantras

It was mentioned in Chapter 2 that even mantras have to undergo certain saṃskāras so that they are fit to be used. The following are the rituals performed for activating the Vedic mantras.

(a particular symbol has the same meaning in all steps)

1. *Jananam* The mantra is written on a birch leaf with the letters from a to ha in a certain geometrical figure. The goddess is then invoked and worshipped.
2. *Dīpanam* consists of repeating the following chain a number of times :(hih)(hih) ...
   where h = *haṃsa*, i = *iṣṭamantra*, h= *soham*
   giving the iteration of the palindrome (h i h)
3. *Bodhanam* consists of the japa
   (hih)(hih) ... several thousand times
   which may be treated as the iteration of a palindrome (h i h)
4. *Tāḍanam* consists of repeating the palindrome
   (pip)(pip) ... several times
   p= phaṭ. This is the iteration of the palindrome (pip)

4A. *Abhiśekam* – the following mantra is written on a brich leaf which is then subjected to bathing (abhiśeka)
jha – i – jha
j=eṃ, h= haṃsa, a= om
The mantra is a palindrome
5. *Vimalīkaraṇam* consists of reciting the following 1000 times
(a t q – i – qta) (atq-i-qta) ...
t = *trauṃ*, q = *vaṣaṭ*. Observe that each bracket is a palindrome which is iterated.
6. *Jīvanam* consists of repeating the following one thousand times.
7. (sqiqs)(sqiqs) ... where s = *svadhā*. The brackets are palindromes
8. *Tarpaṇam* : In this ritual the mantra *i* to be awakend is written on a birch leaf and oblations of milk, yoghurt and water are made one thousand times, which gives the iteration of a ritual act.
9. *Gopanam* – The following sequence is recited one thousand times
(rir) (rir)...
(rir) is a palindrome which is iterated, r = hrīṃ
10. *Āpyayānam* consists of the japa of the following derived mantra, one thousand times.
hsau – i-sauh
which is a near - palindrome of the type ABÁ
The bracketed expressions above are mirror images which in turn are repeated several times.
The saṃskāras of mantras also afford an illustration of recursion since they use 'mantras for a mantra'

Theoretically the mantras used to activate a mantra in turn should be awakened and the process would continue *ad infinitum*. These rites also provide the illustrations of 'prefixing' and 'suffixing' of a mantra or a ritual act.

11.4 Gāyatrī Mantra

(A particular symbol stands for the same word in this section)
The Gāyatrī mantra is one of the most sacred mantras. It provides an excellent example of break-and-make. Its constituent parts are used as elements to compose new mantras. Consider the basic Gāyatrī.

tat saviturvareṇyam bhargo devasya dhīmahi
dhiyo yo naḥ pracodayāt (Rv 3-62-10)

If the first and the second line are denoted by k and l we can writ the Gāyatrī as

G=kl ...(1)

When om is prefixed to (1), we have what is called 'ekāpada'. Th ekapāda japa appears as

akl, akl,...

where a = om

When om is prefixed and suffixed to 'kl', its repetition is calle *sampuṭa japa* of the Gāyatrī which is the iteration of the cycle akla

akla, akla,...

j = *bhūḥ bhuvaḥ svaḥ*, is a triplet which frequently appears embedded in several mantras. Bhuḥ, bhūaḥ, etc. are called *vyāhṛtis*. The Gāyatrī tripāda is

om bhūrbhuvaḥsvaḥ om tatsaviturvareṇyam bhargo devasya dhīmahi om dhiyoyanaḥ pracodayāt.

Thus the tripāda japa is

ajakal

Or $a(j_1j_2j_3)a(k_1k_2k_3k_4)al$

where the suffixed letters correspond to the words in j and k or j_1 = *bhūḥ* j_2 = *bhuvaḥ* j_3= *svaḥ* k_1 = *tatsaviturvareṇyam* k_2 = *bhargo* k_3 = *devasya* k_4 = *dhīmahi*

In the *pañcapāda* five oms are affixed / embedded.

$aj_1aj_2aj_3akal$

The *ṣaṭpāda* japa consists of the iteration of

$aj_1aj_2aj_3ak_1ak_2k_3k_4al$

in which om occurs six times and the elements the Gāyatrī are split.

The *śatākṣarī* Gāyatrī consists of 100 letters in which the original Gāyatrī is embedded.

ajklx where x consists of other letters.

In the *Nārada Purāṇa* an accretion to the Gāyatrī appears as follows:

$aj_1aj_2aj_3$a(*mahaḥ*)a(*janaḥ*)a(*tapaḥ*)a(*satyam*)akl

j_1(*bhūḥ*), j_2(*bhuvaḥ*), j_3(*svaḥ*), *mahaḥ, janaḥ, tapaḥ* and *satyam* are called seven *vyāhṛtis*

A most interesting case is that of the Brahmāstra mantra which is obtained by writing the Gāyatrī from the right to the left.

Yātdacopra naḥ yo yodhī himadhi sya vade bhargomaṇyarevaturavisatta

which is the inverse of the Gāyatrī

There are also many cycles formed out of the Gāyatrī such as

ajkla

You can observe the bits of Gāyatrī embedded in the following Sāvitrī mantra

tatsaviturvarṇīmahe । *vayam devasya bhojanam* ।
śreṣṭham sarvadhātamam । *turam bhogasya dhīmahi* ।
(Rv 5-82-1)

The Sāvitrī mantra of the Gupta sect consists of three subordinate mantras.

Viśvāmitra - aj_1zak_1
Gāyatrīchanda - $aj_2zk_2k_3k_4$
Savitā devatā - aj_3zla
where z = *Savitrīm praviśāmi*

Observe that the elements of the Gāyatrī are distributed in these three mantras, and also the last mantra is a cycle.

It should be borne in mind that the various 'derived' mantras mentioned above are recited several times giving iteration, and are used for specific purposes.

Gāyatrīkavaca, a composition is often chanted before the japa of the Gāyatrī. Each stanza from 17 to 24 of this composition contains a letter from 'kl' (*Gāyatrī*) affording an instance of embedding as well as pattern completion.

The above *Gāyatrī* is called '*Savitṛ Gāyatrī*' Many Gāyatrī mantras relating to other deities have been composed in which the elements of the Gāyatrī are incorporated. For example

Śrī Rāma Gāyatrī – *om daśarathāya vidmahe* । *sītārāmāya dhīmahi* । *tanno rāmaḥ pracodayāt.*

Gāyatrī elements are also embedded in the 'karanyạsa' and

'hṛdayādi nyāsa' in which the elements of the Gāyatrī are "deposited" on the various parts of the palms in karanyāsa and the torso in the 'hṛdayādi nyāsa', with mantras incorporating the Gāyatrī elements.[4]

The Gāyatrī and om were discussed at length because they provide almost all structural patterns, iteration, refrain, embedding, prefixing, suffixing and infixing. You should especially observe the process of break-and-make which involves permutation and combination. The Gāyatrī elements when attached to other mantras often appear as aliens showing that the syntactic approach sometimes yields a rich material where the semantic approach may appear futile.

11.5 Pūjā

Pūjanam or pūjā (puja) means worship or veneration. It may be very simple consisting of a few steps, or may have a complex structure extending over several hours or even days.

A number of subordinate rituals called upacāras accompany a pūjā. Tantra texts prescribe 3,5,7,... 64 or even more upacāras appropriate for the relevant ceremony. For the daily pūjā a five-step ritual (pañcopacāra) or a sixteen-step upacāra (ṣoḍaśopacāra) are used depending upon the time the worshipper can spare. The mantras used are either Vedic or Purāṇic.

The ṣoḍaśopacāra is briefly described below. This ritual is important because it appears in several major religious ceremonies. But the fact that is of greater importance is that it happens to have as many steps as the number of stanzas in the famous Puruṣasūkta of the Rig Veda. This is not fortuitous – each stanza is recited with each step of the pūjā. What's more, the associated verse has absolutely no relevance to the pūjā ritual. As an alternative to the Vedic recitation, mantras from Purāṇa are used. These mantras appear relevant in the sense they describe the meaning of the ritual. This dichotomy leads to a puzzle which is difficult to solve.

On the one hand, the use of the Vedic mantras gives credence to Staal's contention that the Vedic ritual is meaningless. On the other hand the Purāṇic verses appear to rebut this thesis. This point will be discussed later.

Before the pūjā starts, the devotee performs a ritual called saṅkalpa. It is a kind of vow to complete the rites relevant to the ceremony to be performed. It incorporates such details as time, place and prayer to the god. In major pūjās considered in the next chapter, it appears after 'pūrva pañcāṅga' (see chapter 12). In the daily pūjā containing 5 or

16 steps, it usually precedes the first step (āvāhana). The contents of the saṅkalpa vary from pūjā to pūjā. In the simple saṅkalpa the devotee takes a portion of water on his right palm and asserts that the pūjā is performed for gaining gods' favour. The water is then discharged into a receptacle.

1. *Āvāhana* or invocation
   The deity is invoked and requested to accept the pūjā.
   The Vedic mantra is
   The man has a thousand eyes and thousand feet. He has pervaded the earth on all sides and has extended beyond it to the extent of ten fingers.
   The Purāṇic mantra is
   O God of gods, Brilliance incarnate, protector of the world, the best of gods, come Accept my pūjā. Salutations to gods
   The worshipper says om and offers rice grains (akṣatā) and flowers.
2. *Āsana* or ṣeat
   The god is offered a seat
   Recitation of (apparently irrelevant) Vedic verse or meaningful Purāṇic verse as in (1)
3. *Pādya*
   The deity is offered water for washing his/her feet.
   Recitation of a Vedic/Purāṇic verse.
4. *Arghya*
   The god is offered water for washing his hands
   Recitation of a Vedic/Purāṇic mantras
5. *Ācamana*
   The god is offered water for rinsing his mouth
   Recitation of a Vedic/Purāṇic mantra.
6. *Snāna* or bath
   The god's idol is bathed in water or in a mixture of milk, yoghurt, ghee, honey and sugar (pañcāmṛta)
   Recitation of a Vedic/Purāṇic mantra
7. *Vastra* or apparel
   Two apparels are offered to the deity
   Recitation of a Vedic/Purāṇic mantra.
8. *Upavastra* (quasi – apparel)
   The god is offered *yajñopavīta* (see Chapter 1)
   Recitation of a Vedic/Purāṇic mantra.

9. *Candana or gandha samarpaṇa*
The god is offered sandal-wood
Recitation of a Vedic/Purāṇic mantra
10. *Puṣpa samarpaṇa*
The god is offered flowers
Recitation of a Vedic/Purāṇic mantra.
11. *Dhūpa*
The deity is offered burnt perfume
Recitation of a Vedic/Purāṇic mantra.
12. *Dīpa samarpaṇa*
This consists of offering 'light' to the god. Oil lamps are moved in a circle in the vertical plane. Usually in clockwise direction. There are specific rules regarding the number of ārati. (circular motions) to be offered. In certain cases the ārati is moved to and fro. The arati is thus either a cycle or a palindrome.
Recitation of a Vedic/Purāṇic verse.
13. *Naivedya*
Naivedya symbolizes the food offered to the god. Recitation of a Vedic/Purāṇic verse. In a minor pūjā milk with sugar or sugar porridge etc. are offered. In a major pūjā the offering is called mahā naivedya ('great' naivedya) when rich sweet dishes are offered.
While offering the food the worshipper behaves as if he is feeding the god. The following mantra is recalled in silence
om prāṇāya svāhā, om apānāya svāhā, om vyānāya svāhā, om udānāya svāhā, om brahmaṇe svāhā.
Observe the double refrain in the above (a and b)

$ax_1b, ax_2b, \ldots ax_6b$

These mantras correspond to six mudrās or gestures. The worshipper can make these mudrās if he knows them while he is 'feeding' the god. This is followed by a few minor etiquettes such as offering water to the god for washing hands etc.
14. *Namaskāra or obeisance*
The devotee prostrates before the idol once, thrice or five times giving an iteration
Recitation of a Vedic/Purāṇic mantra

15. *Pradakṣiṇā*
    Recitation of a Vedic/Purāṇic mantra
    The worshippers makes pradakṣiṇās as explained in I6 in this chapter.
16. *Mantrapuṣpa* or "flowers of mantra"
    Recitation of a Vedic/Purāṇic mantra.

A number of mantras and national anthem may be sung praising the gods and seeking their blessings. This step may also involve āratī, prayers offering of flowers and final prostration. A variant of Gāyatrī mantra incorporating the concerned deities may also be recited.

Sometimes a kṣamā prārthanā is also sung.[9] This is a prayer seeking god's forgiveness for any inadvertent omissions in the ritual.

The pūjā is terminated by chanting an appropriate mantra.

The ṣoḍaśa is sometimes interspersed with several salutations which have the sequence

xbxbxb...

where x is the name of the god and b = namaḥ (I pray). This is especially so when the worshipper does not use the Vedic / Purāṇic mantras.

We recall that the sixteen Vedic mantras used in the ṣoḍaśa above are from the Puruṣasūkta or the 'Hymn of Man' (Rv 10.90). We have not given the mantras in detail, but they do not accord with the ritual acts as you can see in step 1.

The pūjā ritual also has a few variants. For example while making an offering the devotee may utter x_1a, x_2a,... where x_1, x_2.. are the things offered and a= samarpayāmi (I offer), which creates refrains of 'a'. Many minor steps have been ignored in the above description.

The concise five-step pūjā runs from step 9 to step 13.

12

MAJOR RELIGIOUS RITUALS

12.1 Worship Rituals and their Structure

We are now ready to describe some major ritual ceremonies. As mentioned in Chapter 2, there are different types of religious rituals. We shall consider worship ritual in detail. Another important type viz. rites of passage will be mentioned only briefly.

The worship ritual is called pūjā. In any major pūjā there is a main deity who is primarily worshipped though other gods and goddesses may be included. A major pūjā is a complex ceremony and consists of several subsidiary rituals. However, some rituals or a group of rituals (sometimes with a slight modification) appear in most of these pujas. They will be called *ritual constants*. There are also rituals which are of the same type but whose contents differ from one pūjā to another. These will be called *ritual variables*.

It must be mentioned that rituals may vary from place to place and from one 'school' to another. Again, priests may use Vedic or Purāṇic mantras. There is reason to believe that despite these variations, the ritual structures are similar. My analysis is based on those sources which are listed in the Bibliography. Some of them are ritual manuals used extensively in the Indian state of Maharastra. These sources contain Vedic, Purāṇic and tantric mantras and some even suggest concise mantras adapted to the present-day life style. However, the structures usually show similar characteristics whatever the sources of mantras.

The component rituals, **A, W, B,** etc of a major pūjā are briefly described below. Table 12.1 is a summary of the internal structure of these rituals.

A . This is a 'constant' consisting of five rituals, sometimes called *Pūrva Pañcāṅga* (First Quintent)

1. A mark is made on the forehead of the devotee who pays obeisance to gods, guru etc.
2. *Ācamana*, which has already been mentioned, is interspersed with mantras that consist of 24 refrains,
   $x_1e, x_2e, \ldots \ldots \ldots \ldots$
   where $x_1, x_2 \ldots \ldots$ are 24 names of Viṣṇu and e = namaḥ.
3. The devotee wears a holy ring (pavitra) made of kuśa grass. A few mantras are recited.
4. *Prāṇāyāma* which consists of inhaling through the left nostril (*pūraka*), retaining the breath (*kumbhaka*) and exhaling through the right nostril (*recaka*) accompanied by (silent) mantras. The breathing pattern amounts to a palindrome.
5. A ritual pertaining to time, place etc. A few mantras are recited.

W. *Saṅkalpa* (vow) which is a ritual variable (see Chapter 11)

B. 1. *Gaṇeśa pūjā* – It was mentioned that Gaṇapati is an important god who is invoked at the beginning of important ceremonies. This 'pūjā' is a pūjā within the main pūjā. It recapitulates many elements of the main ceremony affording an excellent example of self-embedding. The pūjā consists of the following elements.

a. Nāmamantra consisting of several sequences
   $X Y_1 Y, X Y_2 Y, \ldots \ldots \ldots \ldots$
   where X = Śrī Mahāgaṇapate namaḥ, $Y_1, Y_2 \ldots$ are the names of the of offerings and Y = samarpayāmi.
b. Naivedya which contains six refrains (See *naivedya* under **X**)

2. This ritual relates to the seat (*āsana*). The devotee prays to the earth amidst a few mantras.
3. The pūjā of the copper vessel (*kalaśa*)
4. The pūjā of the conch (*śaṅkha*)
5. The pūjā of the bell (*ghaṇṭā*)
6. The pūjā of the light (*dīpa*)
7. A purification ceremony

The seven steps in **B** are sometimes called *Madhya Saptāṅga* (Middle Septet)

C. The pūjā of Varuṇa who is symbolized by a vessel (*kalaśa*).

The pūjā includes an installation ritual, *nāmamantra* and *naivedya*. It is again a *pūjā* within a *pūjā* providing an example of self-embedding. However, it is not performed in all major pūjās. The triplet '*om bhūrbhuvaḥ svaḥ*' appears several times.

D. This ritual which, is included in some major pūjās, is again a subsidiary pūjā in which 21 gods are invoked and worshipped.[1] The invocation has several refrains and triplets :

om bhūrbuvaḥ svaḥ X_1 *namaḥ* X_1 *āvāhayāmi*
om bhūrbhuvaḥ svaḥ X_2 *namḥ * X_2 *āvāhayāmi*

---------------- -------- -------- where X_1, X_2...etc are the names of the deities.

The invocation is followed by a prayer and offering of the type

XY_1Y, XY_2Y, ...

where X are prayers to the gods invoked, Y_1, Y_2 ... ... are the substances offered, and Y is the verb 'offer' sometimes with modifications. This is followed by the naivedya. The multiplet '*om bhūrbhuvaḥ svaḥ*' appears several times.

X. This is the main pūjā for which the vow was made. It consists of the following elements.

1. The main deity is bathed during which the Vedic mantras specific for the deity should be recited. In practice, however, a concise mantra is recited which can be treated as a ritual constant (**N**)
2. In some pujas there are embedded minor pūjās of the 'body', flowers, leaves, names and cover (āvaraṇa) of which there may be as many as five and vary from deity to deity. They will be denoted by $\mathbf{J_1}$, $\mathbf{J_2}$, $\mathbf{J_3}$, $\mathbf{J_4}$.
3. In some pūjās there is the reading of stories relating to the god (*kathāvācana*). In that case such reading is preceded by recitation of a few mantras constituting 'initial' obeisance. This reading will be denoted by **K**.
4. The pūjā of Sarasvatī, the goddess of learning, is a constant ritual denoted by **L**. Apart from other structures, the multiplet *"prāṇāya svāhā, apānāya svāhā, vyānāya svāhā, udānāya svāhā, samānāya svāhā, brahmaṇe svāhā" appears thrice in the pūjā*
5. The pūjā of brahmins, denoted by **M**.

6. This is the core of the pūjā and includes the 'great āratī' (mahā āratī), and 'great naivedya' (mahā naivedya). Apart from the basic elements of a pūjā, it includes several refrains of 'Samarpayāmi'. The naivedya is 'shown' to the god. In the ritual the refrain svāhā appears in *prāṇāya svāhā\ apānāya svāhā \ vyānāya svāhā \ udānāya svāhā \ samānāya svāhā \ Brahmaṇe svāhā* \\ There is also the repetition of the entire verse. Moreover six gestures (*mudrās*) corresponding to each element above (*prāṇa mudrā, apāna, mudrā,* etc.) are made with the hand. This gives us a 1-1 correspondence and pattern completion. While performing the *mahā ārati* a hymn for Gaṇeśa is sung first, followed by the āratī for the main deity. This is followed by other āratī song for other deities.

F. This again is a ritual constant consisting of five steps, also called *Uttara Pañcāṅga* (Second Quintent)

1. The āratī of camphor (*karpūra*), *pradakṣiṇā* and obeisance; the first two are cycles.
2. Offering of the holy grains, flowers and the 'flowers of mantras'.
3. The prayer to the god or the goddess as the case may be. (with gender modification).
4. Sipping of holy water (tīrtha)
5. Partaking of the prāsāda - the food which was earlier offered to the god, 'Prāsāda' also means favour or gift from the deity.

G. A second ācamana, a variant of the first performed in **A** now follows.

H. Before the Prāsāda meal (bhojana) a few mantras are recited, which involves honoring a married woman, an initiated bachelor, a spinster etc. with a few minor ritual acts.
The pūjā ends with salutations to gods.

I. A minor pūjā called 'uttara pūjā' ('uttara' mean late) is performed usually on the next day. In the pūjās of some deities this is not performed.

Table 12.1

Symbol	*Ritual*	*Ritual Status*	*Internal Structure*
A	First Quintet	Essential constant	I T, R F, P L, E M
B	Middle Septet	Essential Constant	I T, R F, E M, C L, M L
C	Varuṇa Pūjā	Constant	I T, R F, C L, M L
D	Pūjā of other deities	Constant	R F, C L, M L, P C
F	Second Quintet	Essential Constant	C H, I T, R F, C L
G	Second Ācamana	Essential Constant	I T, R F
H	Holy Meal	Constant	C H, R F
I	Uttara Pūjā	Constant	C L
J	Minor Pūjās	Constant $\subset$**X**	R F
K	'Story' Reading	Variable $\subset$ **X**	I T, R F
L	Sarasvatī Pūjā	Constant $\subset$**X**	I T, R F, M L, C L
M	Brahmin Pūjā	Constant $\subset$**X**	R F, R L
N	Holy Bath	Constant $\subset$**X**	I T, R F
W	Vow	Variable	I T, RT
X	Pūjā of Main Deity	Variable	I T, R F, R L, E M, CH, CL, P C

1. 'Constant' is a ritual whose structure usually does not depend on the nature of **X**, the main pūjā.
2. 'Essential Constant' is a constant which is usually found in most of the major worship ceremonies.
3. 'Variable'is a ritual whose structure depends on the nature of the main deity or **X**.
4. $\subset$ means 'embedded in'.
5. G R S – I T (iteration), R F (refrain), P L (palindrome), P C (pattern completion), C H (chorus), C L (cycle), E M (embedding), R L (relay), M P (multiplets).

12.2 Major Pūjās

We recall that **A, B, C, D, E, F, G, H, I, J, K, L, M, N** are ritual constants and **W** and **X** are ritual variables as mentioned in the last section. We add another convention. If **S** is the symbol for the main ceremony, **W (S)** and **X (S)** will indicate the ritual **W** and **X** in relation to **S**. Those of you who are familiar with higher mathematics or symbolic logic will realize that this is a mode of indicating a functional relationship. While **F (S)** is the more common mode of writing a function, **W (S), X (S)** ... ... are more useful in that they identify the functions **W, X** ... ...

The general formula for a major worship (Pūjā) ceremony can be denoted by **P** :

P = A W B C D X F G H I ... ... (1)

Ritual constants **J, K**, ... etc. may be embedded in the variable **X** and have to be specified when a particular pūjā is considered. It may also be noted that some of the rituals like **C** and **D** may be dropped in certain ceremonies. The most outstanding feature of the ceremony is the existence of ritual constants like **A,B, F** ... ... which are obligatory. A consequence of this aspect is structural predictability. A new puja can be designed using this formula and we shall cite a ceremony which could not have existed in the distant past.

We have already considered the intra-elemental structures and one inter-elemental structure namely the pūjā within a pūjā which is an example of self-embedding. There is another cycle pattern which begins with ācamana ($\mathbf{A_2}$) and ends with the second ācamana in **G**. The latter is called *karmānte dvirācamana* or the second ācamana at 'the end of the task' indicating the technical end of the ceremony.

1. Satyanārāyaṇa (S)

   This is a popular ritual regularly performed by many devotees. Nārāyaṇa is one of the names of Viṣṇu. The structure of the ceremony is

   P (S) = A W (S) B C D X (S) F G H I

   N, J = $\mathbf{J_1\ J_2J_3J_4}$**, K, L, M** are embedded in **X** in the same order.

   Each **J** has refrains 'namaḥ' and 'samarpayāmi'

   The most interesting is $\mathbf{J_4}$ 'nāmapūjā' in which 'namaḥ' appears 1000 times :T_1 namaḥ, T_2 namaḥ ... ... where T_1, T_2, ...are one thousand names of god Viṣṇu. The sequence is sometimes reduced 108 or 24 names.

2. Gaṇeśa Caturthī (G)

   This pūjā celebrates the birth day of Gaṇeśa. As a community ritual it has become immensely popular during the last century. In addition to the communal celebrations, many families have their own idols.

   The structure is

   P (G) = A W (G) B Q X (G) F G H I ... ... (3)

   C, D are missing while **Q** (*Prāṇapratiṣṭhā*) which means activating the idol (*Prāṇa* - life force, *pratiṣṭhā* – installation) is an additional ritual. This ritual consists of reciting mantras of tantric origin. *om aṃ hrīṃ kroṃ \ āṃ yaṃ raṃ laṁ vaṃ śam ṣaṃ sam haṃ laṃ ksaṃ aḥ* \ appears three times giving iteration and pattern completion. '*Haṃsa soham*' is a palindrome which, too, appears.

N, $\mathbf{J_3}$ (patra pūjā) are embedded in **X**. As usual there are the *mahā āratī* and other steps mentioned in (6) in **X**.

3. Lakṣmī pūjā (R)
Lakṣmī is the goddess of wealth and Viṣṇu's wife. Its pūjā is very important especially to the business community. Its structure is

P (R) = A W (R) B C X (R) F' G

N is embedded in **X**. **F'** is a slightly modified form of **F** and contains an additional salutation to the goddess between the second and third step of **F**.

4. Swami Samartha Puja (Z)
Swami samartha a 17th century saint and the guru of the Maratha King Śivājī is sometimes regarded as an incarnation of Dattatreya. His devotees make a vow (*Vrata*) to perform this pūjā. In the pūjā a portrait of the swami may be used instead of an idol.

The pūjā has the same structure as that postulated in the general formula which shows that worship ritual has a well-established design.

The structure of the pūjā is

P (Z) = A W (Z) B C D X (Z) F G H I

N, $\mathbf{J_1}$ $\mathbf{J_2}$ $\mathbf{J_4}$, **K,L, M** are embedded in **X** in the usual order. $\mathbf{J_4}$ contains more than 100 refrains of " *namaḥ* ". **X** also has a kathā ('story') which is quite long and describes the life of the saint.

It would be interesting to juxtapose the structure of the four pūjās, which we have just discussed, for comparison.

P (S) = A W (S) B C D X (S) F G H I

P(G) = A W (G) B Q X (G) F G H I

P(R) = A W (R) B C D X (R) F G

P(Z) = A W (Z) B C D X (Z) F G H I

These structure should be examined in the light of what we studied in Chapter 6. The double-arrows show a 1-1 correspondence between the variable elements.

(1) There is a very high degree of structural similarity. (2) The preponderance of the ritual constants is striking. What's more some constants **A, B, F** etc. appear to be ubiquitous. (3) All the ritual constants and variables have internal structures replete with the patterns like iteration, refrain embedding etc. (4) They are qualitatively similar.

Structures which are identical are called isomorphic and those which are similar are called homeomorphic. The worship rituals thus display a very high degree homeomorphism and are also qualitatively similar.

One of the most striking features of the worship ritual is the pūjā within a puja which is a kind of self-embedding though it is true that not all pujas have the same degree of complexity (Fig. 12.1)

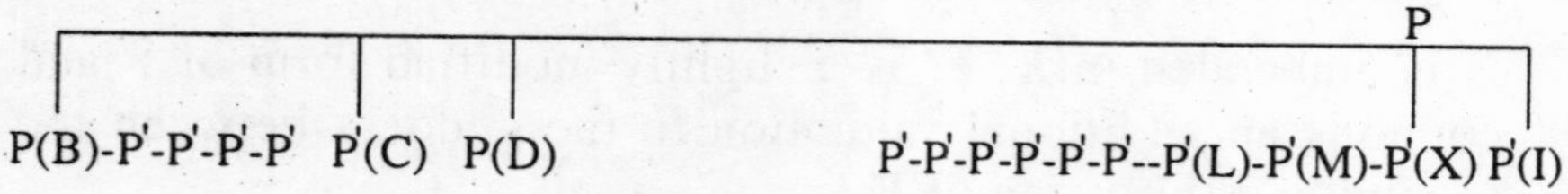

Fig. 12.1 The Puja hierarchy

P may be called minor pūjās since they are not structurally complex (though some of them may be long). **C, D** are major pūjās showing all the intricacies of the worship ritual.

The most interesting puja is the pūjā of Gaṇeśa in which his own puja **(B)** is embedded.

The structure of the worship ritual depicted above shows different 'orders' of pūjā.

1. At the apex is the entire ceremony which is called the pūjā **P** named after the main deity **X.**
2. The next lower order contain **B, C, D** and **X** which formally have at least the five-step (pancopacara) worship.
3. **P** belong to still the lower order which are simple like **L, M** and **I** or are nominal like the puja of the light or bell.

12.3 The Rites of Passage

It was mentioned in Chapter 2 that scriptures mention some 48 saṃskāras of which about sixteen are still followed by the orthodox Hindus. All the rites of passage display the ritual characteristics mentioned earlier. However, they do not show 'a standard' design as the worship rituals show possibly because though they are all the rites of passage they have distinct individuality inasmuch as they are performed at different stages of life. Birth, initiation and marriage though all are Saṃskāras, their goals are different. Nevertheless, there are ritual components which are common to them. There are even rituals which are found both in the rites of passage and worship rituals.

It would take hundreds of pages to describe the various Saṃskāras, but we may briefly consider those rituals which are embedded in most Saṃskāras. These are (1) Yajña-homa in which Agni is worshipped. (2) Gaṇapati pūjā (3) Puṇyāhavācana in which the confirmation of the auspicious time for the ceremony is obtained from the priest and others (4) Mātṛkā pūjana in which several goddesses are worshipped. (5) Nāndi Śrāddha. Śrāddha, as we saw, in Chapter 2 is a funeral ceremony. The Nāndi is, however, a peculiar śrāddha which is performed at the time of most saṃskāras to avert any hurdle. (6) Ācārya *varaṇa*, in which the right ācārya or the priest is 'accepted'.

Many of these rituals embed elements which we have already considered. Some of them are modified forms. We shall not elaborate the structure.

1. *Yajña* – homa. Some of its elements are :

   a. Ritual regarding place time etc. (See **A** (5)) above.
   b. Saṅkalpa (See **W** above)
   c. Invocation of Agni (See 1 under pūjā Chapter 11)
   d. Installation of Agni (Similar to Āsana in pūjā Chapter 11)
   e. Praying to Agni with a number of Vedic mantras.
   f. Oblations to Agni and other mantras.

   One of the sequences is replete with the refrains :
   Om bhuḥ A X_1 B
   Om bhuvaḥ A X_2 B
   Om svaḥ A X_3 B
   Bhubhuvah svaḥ A B
   where, A = svāḥā, X_1, X_2 ... ... are the names of the gods
   B = This oblation is for him (X) not for me (*idam na mama*)

2. *Gaṇapati Pūjanam* (Modification of **B** (1) in 12.1)
3. *Puṇyāha Vācana*

   a. Ritual regarding time and place as in **A** (5) in 12.1
   b. Vow like **W**
   c. *Varuṇa pūjā* (Similar to **C** in 12.1)

4. Mātṛkā pūjana
   About 23 goddesses and four deities including Gaṇeśa are invoked and worshipped according to ṣoḍaśopacāra (Chapter 11)
5. Nāndi śrāddha – contains a saṅkalpa
6. Ācāryavaraṇa – contains a saṅkalpa

13

MANTRAS AND LANGUAGE

13.1 Pre-linguistic Sounds

We may now address an interesting question : are mantras language? Many mantras contain bījas and stobhas which appear unintelligible. It is also found that many bījas resemble the utterances of babies. It may therefore be guessed that bījas and stobhas are either meaningless or originated as mood signals, though it cannot be deined that many bījas were later added as a matter of "pattern completion."

Animals, too, utter such sounds. Scientists once believed that these sounds, especially those uttered by higher animals constituted some kind of language system. It is now realized that even if these sounds perform the function of 'communicating' they are so crude that they can hardly be called language.

If animals function at the pre-linguistic level, it would be interesting to compare their utterances with sounds made by humans which are not part of their language. This means we have to find out if there are some definite patterns in mewing, neighing, bleating, cackling, grunting, twittering and chirping.

Even the layperson can easily identify two structures, iteration and refrain. In fact it is the repetitive feature which has given rise to onamatopoeiac words like caw, mew and roar. If we listen carefully we can also hear chorus and relay in a crude form.

13.2 Bird Songs

But it is the birds that offer a variety of acoustic structures, and much research has already been done in this area. The words bird 'song' may appear a caricature – it may not sound music to all of us, but in syntax it seems to resemble music rather than language.

We often hear the following sound patterns in the bird songs, though we may not be able to identify the birds who utter them.

1. A A A ...
2. AB AB AB ...
3. ABC ABC, ...
4. ABA ABA, ABAABA ...

where A, B, C are notes. All display iterations and refrains while the fourth also shows palindromes (which are also cycles)

However, bird songs are more complex than the above, and in order to appreciate its structure it is necessary to break them into basic units comparable to those of mantras. A few songs analysed by François – Bernard Mâche are given below.[1] The letters do not indicate notes but a group of notes which can be considered as a recurring unit.

1. A B C B C B D E /
   B' C B C B C B F É
   A B C B C D /
   B' C B C B C B F É
   (Black Flycatcher *Ficedula hypleuca*)
2. A B A B C Á BB́ A" B́B
   (*Sylvia communies*)
3. ABBC / AAAAB / ABCB / AAABCB / A
   (A part of the song of *Acrocephalus dumetorum*)

These structures confirm what we ordinary people would expect from our own experiences related to simple notes.

Like other scientists ornithologists have tried to search for meaning in bird songs. While in some cases they have been able to explain a correlation between the song pattern and its ultility or function (feeding, courtship etc.), they realize that most songs have no function or goal. Birds sing because they feel like singing in much the same way we sing or play.

It is quite clear that bird songs and mantras resemble each other and bird songs fall in the same category of the rituals in general as described in Chapter 8.

13.3 Are Mantras Language?

We can now have a closer look at mantras and language and compare them in respect of two aspects, syntax and semantics.

We shall discuss semantics first because many mantras are so intelligible, they can be recognized as language. On the other hand there are mantras which are totally unintelligible to us. Let us consider the following examples.

I.1. Saṅkalpa
asya kumārasya upanayana kartu tatprācyaṅgabhūta vāpanādi kariṣye.
(For the upnayana of this boy I undertake to complete all rituals (shaving the scalp etc.)

I.2. *om āṃ hrīm koṃ / aṃ yaṃ raṃ laṃ vaṃ śaṃ ṣaṃ saṃ haṃ laṃ kṣaṃ aḥ / kroṃ hrīṃ aṃ haṃsaḥ soḥaṃ / devasya jīva iha sthitaḥ // Om āṃ ...*
(From śrī Ananta Vratam)

I.3. *Om doṃvasāsejarropa om tyadacopra naḥ yo yo dhi himadhīsyavadergobha yam nirervatu vitsata, om lajvapra lajvapra yardama yardama nria om rhaṃ rhāṃ rhaṃ auṃ oṃ, kyoṃ kaṃ srīṃ om // iti*

(Brahmadaṇḍdāastra mantra)

I.1 shows a vow (*saṅkalpa*) to be taken by the father of the boy who is to be initiated into the *upanayana*, one of the sixteen *saṃskāras* (See Chapter 2). The text is quite intelligible.

I.2 These are the lines from Ananta (Gaṇeśa) pūjā. The verse relates to *prāṇa pratiṣṭhā* or infusing life force in the idol, which was mentioned earlier. Most of the words are unintelligible except the last few which indicate that god's life force (jīva) is being 'installed'.

I.3 Like I.2 these lines contain a number of bījas, but some words are certainly not the usual bīja mantras, nor do they convey any meaning. But if we inspect them carefully, they are found to be the inverses of meaningful mantras. For example, you will find the Gāyatrī mantra embedded in the inverted form (*tayadacopra naḥ...*)

We thus see two types of meaningless texts (1) those which contain bījas (2) those which are manipulations of the meaningful words. The second case is in fact a type of ritual syntax – permutations under 'pattern completion' which we have already considered. The inverted words are clearly treated as a separate genre.

In connection with śrauta rites Staal furnishes graded

illustrations, the first being completely intelligible while the last containing a sequence of 'stobhas' such as *hā bū hā bū hā... ...*[2] In case of gṛhya rites that are practiced today, most mantras make sense while those which appear unintelligible are due to bījas (I.2 and I.3) which probably have tantric origin. However, when the Vedic mantras are used in the gṛhya rites, many times they appear to be vague or even out context. In Chapter 11 we mentioned that the sixteen verses of the Hymn of Man from the Rig Veda used in 'pūjā' appeared totally irrelevant. We give below the second and the third step of the ṣoḍaśopacāra alongwith the Vedic and Purāṇic mantras juxtaposed.

I.4. *Second step*: Seat (āsana) God is offered seat. (a) "The universe is nothing but this Man who is the ruler of immortality. It is because He willed so that He appeared through food needed for all creatures." (RV 10-90-2) (b) "O God of gods. This diamond-studded steat of gold is offered to you in order to please you. Please accept it." (Purāṇic)

Third step: Offering water to God for washing his feet. (c) "His glory is indescribable. Man is greater than all the entire visible universe. All creatures are quarter of him, three quarters are what is immortal in heaven". (RV 10-90-3). (d) "O God of gods. Our well-being is the result of your blessings. O the ruler of people, I offer you with divotion pādya (water) for washing your feet." (Purāṇic)

In both the steps the Vedic mantras appear out of context while, the Purāṇic mantras describe the rites.

We may say that this is the third type of meaningless variety in which the mantra per se has meaning but does not fit into the context.

Based on the terminology of ornithologists Staal explains the distinction between the śrauta rites and gṛhya rites. German bird watchers use the word *Abetungsmoglichkeit* (possibility to deduce) to indicate that a certain behaviour can be "explained". Staal points out that this word is appropriate in case of the gṛhya rites but it cannot be applied to śrauta rites. We have already pointed out that some mantras having tantric elements are meaningless and some (Vedic) may be out of step with the ritual acts relating to gṛhya ceremonies.

However, when we say that a bīja mantra has no meaning, we face a dilemma. It was mentioned in Chapter 3 that each bīja has a specific use. In fact according to a well-known śloka,

"Vaṣaṭ for influencing (people), *phaṭ* for dislodging, *huṃ* for jealousy, *kheṃ* for causing injury, *svāhā* for winning favour, *namaḥ* for gaining a high post, and *vauṣaṭ* for wealth."

Hence if we inspect a mantra, it is not difficult for us to 'sense' the meaning. Do we then have a right to say that the words like 'phaṭ' or 'huṃ' are meaningless? In the widest sense in which the word 'meaning' is used (Chapter 6) probably the answer is that they do convey some meaning to us. However, in a restricted sense the bīja do not have meaning because (1) Like other words they are not usually listed in ordinary dictionaries (2) They do not decline as other words do in Sanskrit. Their status is more like magical utterances which have specific purpose.

It was shown in Chapter 10 that mantras have structural features of general rituals (GRS) such as iteration, refrain etc. These patterns are not found in language except in verse which was discussed in Chapter 9.

For example, such linguistic constructions would appear ridiculous.

1. I I I I I am going to office (iteration)
2. *A* is working, *B* is working, *C* is working, *D* is working, *E* is working (refrain)
3. I am going am I (palindrome)
4. He went to school, he (cycle)

A strutterer may use 1, a clown may use 1, 2, and 3, a poet perhaps 3 and 4 and we may all use 4 rarely for emphasis.

14. Suppose *A, B, C* constitute a team entrusted with a certain project. Their supervisor *S* enters the office and faces one of the following scenarios.

    a. *A, B, C* tell *S* in unison, " We have completed 20% of the project. We need additional funds immediately" (chorus)
    b. *A* " We have completed 20% of
       B " the project. We need additional
       C " funds immediately" (relay)
       S is bound to feel either that he is ridiculed or that his juniors need psychiatric treatment.

It looks strange, but it is true, that while our social behaviour usually follows ritualistic pattern, our language has a different syntax.

It is interesting to compare mantras with language in other respects. When a literary work produced in one country reaches another country, it is usually translated so that it is intelligible to those who do not understand the language in which it was originally written. Thus the Bible, *Das Kapital* and Stephen Hawkings *The Brief History of Time* have been translated into a number of languages.

When mantras are exported, they are not translated, but transliterated, though they may undergo phonological adaptation in the new environment. If a work also includes non-mantric text, it is found that the text is translated while the accompanying mantras are transliterated. The 'non-translatability' of mantras is not confined to the bīja or stobhas, it is also applicable to mantras having apparent meaning. For example, '*Namo Buddhāya*' and '*Śivāya namaḥ*' are not translated as "Hail to Buddha" or "Hail to Śiva", but its original form is retained.[3]

For example, the Sanskrit mantra *om vajra karma kam* (Om thunderbolt rite) becomes in Japenese

On bazaar Kyarna Ken

there being 1-1 correspondence between the original words and those adapted to the Japanese environment.

Some other adaptations are; Sanskrit 'mantra' to Tamil 'mantira', Sanskrit 'homa' to Japanese 'goma', Sanskrit 'bhuḥ' to Japanese 'kham'.

There are other differences between language and mantras. We have already mentioned three types of mantras, japa, which is muttered upāṃśu which are murmurs and the meditative mantras (manasā) which are recalled in silence. Staal rightly refers to this gradation of intensity as a distinct characteristic of mantras not shared by ordinary language.

It is not difficult to guess how the mono-syllabac bīja emerged. They represent the remnants of sounds produced by our ancestors before language came into existence. Some evidence can be found in the utterances of babies. R. Jakobson has pointed out that the easiest or natural mode of sound production consists in opening and closing the mouth. The emergence of sounds like om, him, hom can be easily ascribed to the baby's earliest experiments with acoustics. More complicated syllables like *lam, ram, clim, vam* etc. possibly indicate the next stage of development in the hierarchy of utterances.

Staal rightly guesses that mantras appeared before language. It was mentioned in Chapter 8 that rituals exist even among animals. The earlier monosyllabic sounds are quite handy to be used in ritual either alone or in conjunction with rites (ritual acts)

It would be worthwhile to briefly describe how the human child acquires language. The newborn has certain genetically transmitted capacities. His earliest 'active' contact with the world is through such responses as crying and wriggling in responses to the stimuli like hunger and pain. His primitive communication system is based on non-verbal conditioned reflex. For example, a touch on the shoulder may mean that he is going to be lifted by mother (or mother substitute). The fact that nonverbal conditioned reflex constitutes 'meaning' was discussed in Chapter 6.

The first signals the infant can send has biological or physical connections with antecedents or consequences. His communication system is also iconic to some extent, there being some resemblance between the signal and its meaning. For instance the touch on the shoulder is a condensed form of the anticipated manipulation by mother. In fact, there arises a mutually 'accepted' communication system between the baby and the mother which consists of the baby's understanding of the mother's signals and the mother's interpretation of the infant's signals.

It is only when the child begins to 'imitate' adults that he picks up words through association though in a babyish way. Adults react to his incorrect pronunciation sympathetically and try to mimic him, from which arises the baby talk.

It is believed that the child does not learn words in the same sense as the adult regards them – components of language which can be fitted into various constructions. In the child's repertory – called closed repertory – there are verbal signals which have 1-1 correspondence with meaning. He learns through the whole signals and not through its constituents. He does not know the complicated manner in which a word may be inflected or used in a sentence which is not part of his repertory. He may not even be familiar with the different intonations of 'papa' which are used on different occasions by grown-up children. It is only later that he begins to 'analogize' and can construct his own sentences. His repertory then becomes the 'open repertory'. This stage gives him a big leap forward in the acquisition of knowledge.

It is interesting to find that the names of the objects the baby first comes into contact are also the words that can be pronounced most easily, usually monosyllabic or bisyllabic.

In the following list 'I' means "in some Indic languages" 'E' means "in many European languages", 'D' stands for "Dravidian languages."

Abu, aba, abba, abbe (father – Semtic, I)
ammā (mother – I,D); akkā (sister – I,D)
ānnu (father – I); aṇṇā (elder brother – I,D)
bābā (father –I, Persian); baby (infant – E)
mā (mother I,E)
mummy, mom, mama (mother – E), māmā, mamu (maternal uncle – I)
māmī (maternal uncle's wife – I); pa, papa (father – E)
phūphī (aunty – I) and phūphā (her husband – I)
munnā and munnī (male and female child – I)
kākā, cācā (uncle – I); kākī, cācī (aunty – I)
bhubhu (dog); miau (cat)
tāi (elder sister – I); tātā (sleep I)
tāi (mother – D); tātā (bye – E)
dādā (elder brother, grandfather – I); nānā (grandfather – I)
dādī (grand mother – I); nānī (grandmother – I)

However, what is still more interesting is that the infant utters some of these syllables before he is taught what they (e.g. mama or mom) mean.

Many psychologists have been influenced by Haeckel's biogenic law according to which ontogeny (The development of the individual organism) recapitulates phylogeny (the development of the species). If we accept this law we can assert that mantras antedate language on two grounds.

1. The babbling and monologues of babies reveal that these utterances have resemblance with mantras and their ritualistic features. Babies often utter and iterate the sounds resembling the bijas and stobhas such as *uṃ, hṃ, ūṃ*..., bā bā bā..., go go go... etc.
2. In Chapter 8 we made reference to the abnormal ritualistic behaviour. According to the Freudian theory the abnormal behaviour among the emotionally disturbed reflects the fixation

> at an earlier stage of the patient's development. When the biogenic law is applied to this, the abnormal ritual behaviour which includes repeated mantra-like utterances as well as tics should be ascribed to the pre-linguistic stage in the human evolution.

Before we conclude the Chapter the process of break-and-make must be explained in detail. It was mentioned in Chapter 1 that the Vedic society was non-literate and the Vedas were transmitted by oral tradition from one generation to another. Scholars have no doubt that the Vedic saṃhitās have been transmitted intact for two reasons. First, utmost care was taken in preserving the form (structure with pronunciation) and secondly, mnemonic methods were employed to ascertain that the original verses were not distorted.

However, the mantras used in the ritual context seem to have had a different fate. They could be broken into smaller pieces; these elements from different sources could be rearranged to form new mantras. Some of the smaller bits could be used as 'fillers'. What's more, mantras originally meant for some purpose could be attached to other rites, appearing as foreign elements. Recall that the Hymn of Man was broken into pieces and attached to different steps of the ṣoḍaśopacāra puja. The peculiar ritual syntax allowing iteration, refrain, inversion (some points of the Gāyatrī have been inverted.) implies that over several hundred years there was considerable distortion in the mantras used in ritual as well as the mantra – ritual act linkages.

Language, though it undergoes changes over time, is subject to different rules. The process of break-and-make does certainly not operate.

It is interesting to compare the Vedic mantras used in ritual with Purāṇic mantras and the mantras constructed in recent years : the latter are more intelligible and seldom out of context. If distortion is treated as a function of time, the rite – mantra complex which appear intelligible today may appear strange after another thousand years.

While the fact that mantras antedate language is indubitable, Staal goes even further and asserts that language developed from mantras.[4] He divides the mantras into three types. Type I represents the earliest stage of human development when the bīja and stobhas came into existence. The second type involved some syntactic constraints on type I mantras. The final stage shows mantras of Type 2 which appear more meaningful such as 'Vācam yaccha' (control your speech)

I think the best way to depict the language-mantra connection is by a Venn diagram such as is shown below:[5]

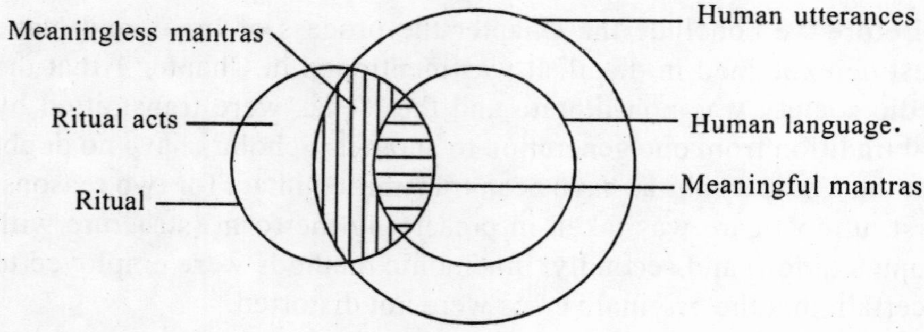

Fig. 13.2 Language, Mantras and Ritual

On the right are two circles (drawn concentric for convenience). The larger circle covers the space allotted to human utterness. The inner circle contains human language which is obviously a sub-class of utterances. The left-hand circle shows religious ritual. The intersection of the utterance-circle and the ritual-circle gives rise to mantras. These fall into two categories:

1. Meaningful mantras shaded by horizontal lines (intersection of language and ritual)
2. Meaningless mantras shaded by vertical lines (intersection of non-linguistic utterances and ritual)

The unshaded portion of the ritual shows the ritual acts.

The diagram incorporates the present state of knowledge, but keeps the question whether language developed from mantras, open.

14

THE INTERPRETATION OF RITUALS

14.1 Meaning and Meaninglessness

Religious rituals have been interpreted in several ways. Before we try to discuss these interpretations we should recall that in Chapter 6 we pointed out that there are different meanings of the word 'meaning' itself. This fact will have to be borne in mind as a qualifier of every interpretation we are offered.

Ritual may have one of the following ostensible goals.

1. It may have a lofty goal of maintaining the equilibrium of the universe.
2. Ritual may be used to fulfil one's wishes such as acquisition of wealth and power or destruction of enemies.
3. Ritual may be used as a means of liberating oneself from the cycle of birth and death.
4. Ritual may be performed as a matter of duty or tradition. The goal may be implicit : avoidance of gods' wrath. Very rarely, no goal may be specified or inferred.

It must be mentioned that these goals are not mutually exclusive. Secondly, where more goals than one are contemplated there may be a logical conflict which is usually resolved by some ingenious argument.

When a goal is stated to exist, it may be achieved in one of the following methods.

1. a) Sacrifice and offerings are made to gods or other supernatural forces who will ensure that the goal is attained. When the sacrifice is made to *Agni* (fire), he plays a dual role : he is a god as well as the intermediary who delivers the sacrifices to other gods.

b) The participant may believe in magic and use mantras and other acts to achieve the goal.

When there is no specific goal, the purpose of performing ritual is usually to avoid any evil that may befall in the future.

The ritual may sometimes be self-explanatory. For example, the worshipper offers sweets to gods and asks for a specific favour. However, when the ritual is not intelligible it is often interpreted in several ways. Traditionally, it is the Brāhmaṇas which have interpreted ritual. These interpretations suffer from the same drawbacks which every hermeneutic technique does. This question was discussed at length in Chapter 6.

According to Indologist Louis Renou these explanations contain fabricated accounts of the origin of various details in liturgical ceremonial. Staal maintains that these explanations are ad hoc and adds that in *Śatapatha Brāhmaṇa*, which has influenced the Western scholars immensely, "almost everyone can find something to suit his taste or support her theory."[1]

In connection with the yajṇa-homa (Chapter 2) it was mentioned that after making oblations the *yajamāna* adds, "For Agni, not for me". This refrain appears in a number of rituals including *Agniṣṭoma* and leads to apparent contradictions. This renunciation is called tyāga which is one of the constituents of the ritual according to the śrauta Sūtras, the other being substance (*dravya*) used in oblation and deity (*devatā*). The following contradictions may be observed with reference to *Agniṣṭoma*.

1. Agniṣṭoma is performed for acquiring a place in heaven. But after making oblations the yajamāna renounces the fruits of action.
2. *Agniṣṭoma* is an obligatory (*nitya*) rite; but since its goal is heaven it is at the same time optional.
3. According to the *Mīmāṃsā Sūtra*, rites lead the yajamāna to heaven while according to *Ṛjuvimalā*, a commentary, this rule is not applicable in case of obligatory ritual.
4. After the ritual is over the *yajamāna* does not go to heaven, but continues to perform the *Agnihotra* till he lives.

These contradictions lead Staal to conclude that the rituals are to be performed for their own sake.[2]

We have discussed the Mīmāṃsā philosophy in detail (Chapter 2) in which it was pointed out that it offers a rationale for ritual. However, it was also observed that its interpretative methods had the same defects which were mentioned in Chapter 6. The contradictions noted above should not surprise us since conflict is the common denominator of hermeneutics.

Western scholars have explained ritual in one of the following ways:

1. Ritual reflects a myth and symbolizes its enactment.
2. Ritual reflects social milieu.
3. Ritual is used to transmit cultural and social values especially in preliterate societies.

Staal has made forceful counter-arguments to rebut these explanations.[3] Why should a myth be re-enacted? Or why should social values be transmitted to the next generations in such a roundabout manner when the same purpose can be achieved by telling the young ones in plain language? In any case since a number conflicting interpretations are always possible, we cannot fathom the true meaning of ritual.

But Staal goes further and makes a bold hypothesis : ritual has no meaning goal or aim. It constitutes its own aim or goal. [4] The following arguments can be put forward to support the theory that rituals are meaningless. Of course, the hypothesis is confined to śrauta rituals.

1. Ritual differs from ordinary activity. In the former what matters is 'orthopraxy' (right action). In the latter it is the goal that is important. If the goal can be achieved through different routes we are generally free to choose the route that suits us. Ritual on the other hand has to be followed according to the rules exactly in the prescribed manner.
2. There is considerable similarity between games and ritual. In the former the constitutive rules are the meaning as well goal – the game is played for its own sake. In fact while in a game you might lose, you are always the winner when you perform ritual. *A fortiori*, ritual must be meaningless.
3. The Vedic mantras were transmitted without any change. Though some mantras appear like language, they do not undergo the changes which a language is subject to over a period of time. (Chapter 9)

4. Some mantras especially the bijas and stobhas make no sense. Some mantras like *Puruṣa Sūkta* though having meaning appear out of context when used with ritual acts such as *Ṣoḍaśopacāra*.
5. Animals, too, perform rituals. They dance and indulge in 'acrobatics' and also have aspersion rites. We saw in Chapter 8 that this prompted Morris to infer that animal ritual-at least the type called 'play ritual' - was an end itself. It can be argued that since animals are not able to cogitate, plan or ratiocinate we should conclude that their rituals are meaningless. Hence human rituals, too, must be meaningless.
6. Interpretations of a ritual are innumerable and conflict with each other and in fact "anything goes". These are usually after - thoughts or rationalizations created to suit the interpreter's convenience.
7. The very premise that a ritual or for that matter any phenomenon should have a meaning is itself untenable. For example, we do not point at an elephant and ask the zookeeper, "What is the meaning of this?"
8. The same rites are used in different ceremonies which necessitates ascription of different meanings to the same rite depending on the context. These ambiguities were pointed by such scholars as Hubert, Mauss and Durkheim.
9. The priests who perform these rituals are not able to provide a satisfactory explanation except that they do it as a matter of tradition. Sometimes the priests may not understand what the mantras mean; they have only learnt to recite them by heart in the prescribed manner.
10. If ritual had any symbolic meaning, this would have been conveyed in simple language rather than making the message deliberately obscure.

While many of these arguments are convincing some of them can be challenged. The counter-arguments would appear as follows :

I. While some mantras are unintelligible, there are many mantras which make sense and appear contextually sound. In fact in the six graded illustrations furnished by Staal only the last mantra is totally meaningless.[5] Of the remaining, one or two may be said to be context-relevant. The phenomenon of mantras being out of context is singular in case of the *ṣoḍaśopacāra pūjā* where the Vedic mantras make no contextual sense but the alternative Purāṇic mantras are in tune with ritual acts. It is possible that the contextual distortion results from the process of break-and-make described earlier. The older mantras appear more as magical formulas unlike the recent ones, and may be used like 'om' whenever one feels like using magic. We may contend that originally the ritual was 'self-sufficient' in all respects but in due course many new mantras, acts or gods were added which made the ritual distorted and thus now appear meaningless. Hence, what originally was a meaningful ritual became, after several generations a traditional compulsion.

II. While many animal rituals appear to be devoid of any ostensible goal, it was pointed out in Chapter 8, that the ritual behaviour may at once express anger and the desire to avoid combat. It was also observed that ritual may be a mechanism to reduce (temporarily) anxiety. Hence, in a wider sense these rituals cannot be said to be meaningless. There are a few instances of animal rituals which definitely have meaning. In Chapter 9, it was mentioned that the honey bee indicates through the dance the location of the beehive. Though this ritual is instinctive it certainly has meaning and a goal.

Secondly, even if animal rituals are assumed to be meaningless, can we conclude that human rituals, too, are devoid of any meaning? There are many examples which indicate the contrary. The worship rituals designed recently have a clear goal and meaning. Performing arts afford another example. Dance and drama are rituals though not religious rituals. The actors in the drama behave in a way they do not do in real life. They may declaim, sing in chorus and soliloquize loudly for several minutes. The play thus has the indubitable characteristics of the rigid ritual, but at the same time it conveys a meaning. This does not, of course, prove that Vedic ritual should have meaning. But it should make us wonder why the ritual-like structures should radically differ from each other.

III. As against argument 6, one may contend that merely because there are many interpretations of a phenomenon, we cannot conclude that the phenomenon has no explanation or meaning.

IV. It is true that an elephant has no meaning. But an elephant is an object, not a process. If the same elephant moves his trunk repeatedly in a certain way we may ask the zookeeper "what does it mean" and he may, from his past experience, be able to enlighten us.

V. The fact that the same rites appear in different ceremonies may be ascribed to the process of beak-and-make. For example the mantras considered magical may be inserted in any ceremony. If one rightly treats such mantras as foreign bodies and reads the ceremony without them, then there would not be any confusion. But some scholars feel that every utterance or act should have a meaning and try to ascribe one to this *odd man out* in such a way that the whole ceremony is interpreted with these mantras artificially. This leads to the ascription of different meanings to the same mantras or acts in different contexts.

VI. It is true that the priest may neither understand the meaning nor the context of some mantras. This certainly shows that tradition emphasizes the correct formal (in form) transmission of the mantras and acts from one generation to the next. However, it does not prove that the ritual was not consciously designed in a meaningful way in the remote past.

VII. It may be contended (to counter argument 10) that symbolism is sometimes more useful than plain language. For example, ritual may involve avoidence of taboos which cannot be openly mentioned. Or ritual which is repetitive may be easy to remember. It is also a fact that what can be conveyed plainly is also sung or dramatized.

Those who believe in the unconscious (like Sigmund Freud) or the collective unconscious (like Carl Jung) may argue that some rituals are the expressions of unconscious goals of which the performers may not be aware.

To conclude, most rituals appear to possess 'meaning' in the wider sense which includes 'symbolism, instinctual reaction, association, function, goal, teleology, cause etc. as described in Chapter 6. However, when meaning implies merely symbolism, some rituals do appear either meaningless or admit of countless meanings such as in some of the religious rituals and compulsive rituals.

Any theory which purports to explain religious ritual must take into account the following findings:

1. While the śrauta and gṛhya rituals may have distinct

characteristics, they have a common ground. In fact, all religious rituals, Vedic, Purāṇic or tantric have common structural features.

2. Religious ritual is only one type of stylized behaviour which is called ritual in general and which is found in other fields such as games, politics, education etc. as was described in Chapter 8. The theory must reflect the connection between ritual in religion and ritual in generic sense.
3. Rituals in general have characteristics such as iteration, refrain, palindrome etc. Some characteristics like iteration and refrain are found in all types of rituals whereas some like chorus may be found only specific types. For instance, chorus is found in religious ritual and music.
4. Rituals appears as pathological behaviour such as in OCD and Tourette's syndrome (Chapter 8).
5. Animals, too, perform rituals.
6. Some rituals and mantras have meaning while others appear meaningless or contextually irrelevant.

   1-2 imply that the theory should enable us to treat the gṛhya/śrauta rituals as the subsets of religious rituals, and the religious rituals as a subclass of rituals in general. The corresponding Venn diagram would appear as in fig.14.1

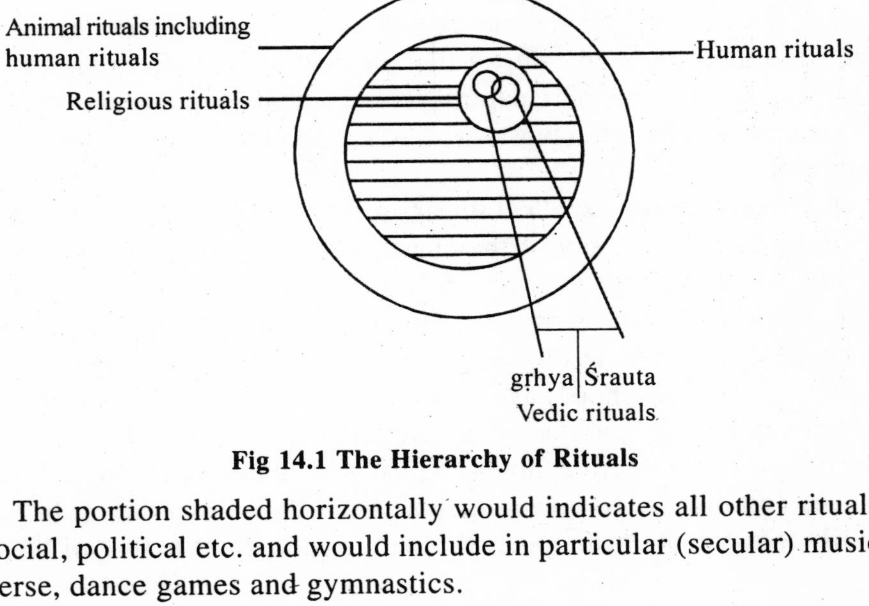

Fig 14.1 The Hierarchy of Rituals

The portion shaded horizontally would indicates all other rituals, social, political etc. and would include in particular (secular) music, verse, dance games and gymnastics.

The compulsive ritual was treated at some length in Chapter 8. A comparison between the śrauta ritual and compulsive ritual shows striking similarities between the two. Both rituals are highly morphocentric (Chapter 8). Both have manifest contents which may be devoid of any meaning apart from the syntactical rules. It is true that compulsive rituals have been 'interpreted', but the vagueness inherent in any hermeneutic technique usually admits innumerable interpretations. Hence, if meaning is used in the sense of 'symbolic meaning', we may consider these rituals semantically irrelevant or as pure structures.

Another common feature of these rituals is their potential to 'create infinity', which has already been mentioned.

14.2 Rituals and Culture

The fact that other animals perform rituals strongly suggests that ritual is rooted in biology. However, humans have culture which no other animals possess. We know that the expression of our instincts such as sex and hunger is controlled by culture. It would be proper to think of the interaction between biology and culture. Such institutions as marriage, homes, schools, government and nations are all the products of this interaction.

Supposing ritual to have biological origin it would be quite appropriate to assume that it is subject to the influence of culture in case of humans. Ritual undoubtedly precedes language but once man acquired language his cultural development accelerated at an unprecedented pace. It is natural to think that language may have influenced ritual in the same way as it has influenced other biological expressions.

Dance provides an excellent illustration. Dance, like music, is rooted in rhythm and has many of the characteristics of rituals in general. Animals have their own ways of swaying rhythmically which may be called a precursor of human dancing. In case of humans, dance has ceased to be a mere biological expression, it has been tailored by culture. Choreographers have consciously designed ballets to tell a story or to convey moods. Many classical dances in India perform the function of enacting mythological and historical scenes. Such dances certainly have meaning apart from the rules relating to the bodily movements, which constitute the syntax or structure of these dances. This meaning is not the result of any subsequent interpretations, but exists before the dance was performed because the dance is 'designed'.

A similar process appears in case of religious ritual. New rituals have been created and mantras have been composed consciously. In Chapter 12 we elaborated the worship ceremonies in which the mantras have Vedic, Purāṇic or tantric sources. Of course, some mantras especially the bīja appear meaningless and some Vedic verses appear out of context. But in most cases the meaning appeared fairly clear. The distortion, it was pointed out, can be ascribed to two sources (1) meaninglessness of the bīja and stobhas (2) the process of break-and-make. It must be remembered that while culture does control ritual to some extent, the biological aspect which gives it its structure is always present, nor is the process of break-and-make dead. It is reasonable to predict that in the future the element of meaninglessness and distortion will decline as the proportion of the 'designed' rituals increases, but the incongruent features can never be totally expelled.

In *Ritual and Mantras,* Staal often mentions the 'potter's principle' in grammar ascribed to Panini's commentator Patañjali. When you need pots, you go to a potter; but when you need words, you don't go to a grammarian; you go to the people who speak the language. [6] The principle emphasizes that the grammar was not prescriptive but was based on usage. The same principle seems to be valid in case of ritual. When applied to the present-day rituals in India, it implies that we have to find out what the religious people are doing today rather than what they should be doing according to the original scriptures. This means that we have also to consider the mantras composed recently including those in regional languages, and the rituals designed by the modern worshippers. The impression we get is that most of the rituals used in the present form make sense.

If this is so where does Staal's hypothesis that rituals (at least Vedic or śrauta type) are meaningless stand? We may say that rituals demonstrate primacy of syntax over semantics. We may go even further and assert that the syntax or structure is the essential aspect of rituals, while meaning is an inessential dimension, i.e., a ritual can exist without meaning. One may postitulate that man as well as many animals have an urge to perform ritual. Of course ritual can be clothed with meaning for some advantage but that is a cultural accretion or rather an appendage. Meaning thus can be looked upon as incidental or a mere 'excuse' (nimitta). Staal's hypothesis that rituals are devoid of meaning should be interpreted in this light.

Rituals in general which include all sorts of formalized behaviour has rhythm as the basis and include music, verse, dance and gymnastics. We may hypothesize that ritual is an instinctual expression. Such theory can take care of Staal's assertion of 'meaninglessness' without in any way denying the cultural effect on the ritual expression. Such a postulate should, however, satisfy all the six conditions mentioned earlier in this Chapter.

14.3 Rituals and Instinct

In ethology or the comparative study of animal behaviour in natural setting instinctictive behaviour is the innate or unlearned behaviour which is found in all 'equivalent' members of a given species ('equivalent' roughly means of the same category such as male, female, infant, adult etc.). Instinct is believed to be genetically determined.

Instinctive patterns can be easily observed in case of insects, birds and some animals in their 'natural state'. We find that birds build nests without being taught. Many instincts in lower animals are specialized. We have already seen how the honey bee's dance can indicate the source of honey. The butterfly at a certain age of her life lays eggs on leaves only of a particular plant which are homes for the caterpillars.

In order to study the unlearned behaviour scientists concentrate on these members of the species who have been isolated from birth. A study of bird songs is particularly important for us. M. MePessel's study of the isolated Roller canaries kept in sound proof cages from the time they were hatched, shows that at the appropriate age they sing the elementary songs characteristic of the species.[7] However, even in case of birds and animals it has been found that experience and teaching can improve their behaviour.

Many instincts have been mentioned in the past; sex, self-preservation, maternal care, and even the instinct for acquisition which shows the urge to hoard things which has little value. Then there are social instincts such as gregariousness which make us seek company of fellow beings, or herd instinct which prompts us to follow the majority blindly.

An instinct, unfortunately, is complex unlike a simple unlearned reflex. What's more, humans have weaker instincts of all kinds than other animals, possibly because they no longer live in natural conditions. Some instincts seem to be overlapping, and the existence of some appears doubtful, Harry Harlow's study of monkeys over 30 years shows that 'maternal instinct' may be a myth.[8] In case of humans since baby-bashing is not uncommon a similar conjecture can be made. A large part of maternal or paternal, instinct may be due to social values inculcated into parents, i.e. on account of learning. In any case, instinctive patterns seem to appear in verying degrees among the members of the same species.

While there may be a conflict of instincts it is found that they can be blended harmoniously. Social customs, norms and laws play a vital role in this area and usually in case of a conflict between the 'individual' instincts and social instincts, the preservation of species is given precedence over the interest of the individual.

Because instincts are difficult to handle, psychologists use other terms to describe human instinctual behaviour. They speak of needs and drives. Some drives arise to meet specific needs; sleep, hunger, thirst etc. Some needs are less specific which can be gratified through different ways and which may be controlled in the sense their gratificatious may be delayed or even denied. These include sex, maternal drive (which many psychologists regard as innate) and the need for love and affection.

Guilford also mentions some general needs such as the urge to escape from fear, the urge to struggle which includes the urge to fight, exploratory urge (which was mentioned in Chapter 8), the desire for humor, beauty and play.[9] Some psychologists like Freud have also postulated the existence of destructive instincts like 'death instinct' – a person's unconscious wish to die. Of all those needs and drives, the need to play seems to be closely connected with ritual instinct.

It is now necessary to examine whether the assumption that ritual is instinctual is consistent with six prerequisites mentioned earlier.

Since instinctual expression is modified by socio-cultural forces, the differences between the śrauta and gṛhya as well as those between religious and non-religious rituals can be accounted for. As explained earlier, meaning (in the symbolic sense) is an inessential aspect of ritual. If meaning is absent, what you find is a purely instinctual expression. If it is present, it is a product of culture which can coexist and interact with instinct. Meaning then determines, to a great extent, the type of ritual; religious, śrauta, social, political and so forth.

Pathological ritual needs a little amplification. It was mentioned in Chapter 8 that most psychologists agree that rituals tend to allay anxiety and leads to a sense of well-being (at least temporarily). But it was pointed out that isolated animals who had no opportunity to socialize also indulge in ritual behaviour. That both anxiety as well as boredom should trigger ritual mechanism might appear paradoxical. But instincts sometimes have different manifestations – Morris describes no less then ten functions of sex.[10]

It may therefore be guessed that the satisfaction of ritual urge is a homoeostatic mechanism which keeps organism in balance. In case of OCD (obsessive – compulsive disorder) the urge is excessive and its satisfaction yields only temporary relief. In Freudian psychoanalysis the OCD symptoms are defence mechanisms and the id, the repository of instincts is involved in the inner conflict. Although sexual instinct assumes primacy in the Freudian views, there is something like 'displacement activity', which zoologists have observed in animals, that may be playing a role in OCD or any other emotional disturbances for that matter. Zoologists contend that when there is an inner conflict (say between the urge to flee and the urge to attack) animals display a displacement activity. For example a bird when tense on account of conflict may start building a nest. What's more, such displacement activities are usually of the nature of ritual. It may argued that the person suffering from OCD whose sexual instinct is thwarted uses a more convenient or acceptable expression; ritualization. It appears that in humans as well as other animals ritual comes as a handy (and perhaps a poor) substitute for other drives which cannot be easily fulfilled.

Neuroscientists have provided a physical explanation of OCD. Serotonin is one of the neuro-transmitters (chemicals which transmit messages between two nerve cells). In morbid conditions, this chemical is deactivated by certain molecules called 'reuptake pumps', as soon as it is released. This results in a chemical imbalance which may be rectified by administering such drugs as fluoxetine (Prozac) which inhibit the reuptake pumps.

It should be left to neuroscientists and geneticists to find out how ritual instinct is codified and how it appears uncontrolled in OCD.

Tourette's syndrome though involving ritualistic patterns like OCD is usually treated as a neurological disorder. It was pointed out in Chapter 8 that in both cases the striatum of the brain is affected.

It is believed that Tourette's syndrome and OCD are genetically related.[11]

There is therefore a reasonable ground to believe that ritualistic behaviour is instinctual and genetically determined. It may be possible for the researchers, in the future, to identify its genetic configuration.

15

SCIENCE, NON-SCIENCE AND PSEUDO-SCIENCE

15.1 Falsificationism

It is now necessary to enquire whether science exists in mantras and rituals. We are not concerned here with the science which ancient Indians produced and whose fruits we are enjoying today : the decimal system, algebraic equations, astronomy, medicine (ayurveda) and linguistics. We are particularly interested in such claims which the historians of science have not been able to substantiate, and especially those which relate to miracles and supernatural powers which, many believe, can be acquired through ritual.

But before we proceed, we must acquaint ourselves with Popper's falsificationism theory. This is especially important because a scientific theory is subject to revision in the light of new evidence. Popper's theory affords a powerful tool to decide whether a theory lies in the province of science or not. A knowledge which is not within the ambit of science will be called non-science.

An interesting theory called the principle of falsificationism was advanced by Karl Popper (1902-1994), Austrian philosopher, logician and sociologist. According to him scientific generalization cannot be conclusively verified, but it can be falsified by a counter-instance.

To understand this recall the two statements A and B of Chapter 5

Hypothesis $\Rightarrow$ Observed predictions A
Observations agree with predictions $\Rightarrow$ Hypothesis B

It was pointed out there that from B, the scientist cannot deduce A, but under certain circumstances when B is confirmed through repeated experimentations, she assumes that A is probably true. Let us write A symbolically as

$$H \Rightarrow O \qquad C$$

This is logically equivalent to

$$\text{Not } O \Rightarrow \text{not } H \qquad D$$

For example A is a man ⇒ A is mortal is the same as A is not mortal ⇒ A is not a man.

Recall also I1 D Chapter 4.

It is necessary to remember that the inference D is not probabilistic but logical or certain. D implies that if we have a single counterinstance (i.e. not O), the hypothesis H stands refuted (i.e. not H). This means that H needs to be revised as already explained.

The falsification principle provides us a powerful tool to decide whether a statement is scientific or non-scientific. If a statement can in principle be falsified, it is a scientific statement, if it is not falsifiable, it is not a scientific statement. Similarly, a theory can be called scientific only if it makes predictions that are testable. According to Popper, psychoanalysis and Marxism are not scientific theories, because they are not falsifiable.

A few illustrations will elucidate the point.

I.1. A man claims that he can walk on the surface of water.
This is a scientific statement in the sense that it is falsifiable. Interestingly, such a claim was made by L. S. Rao, a Haṭha yogī, in 1966. The yogī agreed to demonstrate his feat in Bombay (now Mumbai). The event was given wide publicity. Though he miserably failed, it is worth mentioning that about 500 spectators had come to witness the feat and each had paid a huge sum to buy a 'donor card'.[1]

I.2. Although there are a few doctrinal differences, both Hindus and Jains believe in the law of karma according to which the sum of our actions is carried forward from one life to the next. It is the accumulated karma which determines our fate in a particular life. According to Jainism, liberation from the cycle of birth and death can be achieved through two stages. We can stop the further accretion of karma by abandoning action, and secondly by penance (tapas) based on austerity, the already accumulated karma can be wiped out.
The doctrine certainly does not lie in the province of science,

since we cannot falsify it. Observe, however, that the Popper's theory is used to decide whether a theory is scientific or not. It does not in any way confirm or deny the assertion which pertains to non-science.

In Chapter 5 it was mentioned that in a wider sense any systematic study can be called science. Suppose you study many religions and call it the 'science of religions'. You might think that Popper's criterion is not applicable to this science. But this is only an illusion. Suppose you assert that Hindus believe in rebirth. Your assertion is falsifiable; we can go through the religious texts and find out whether Hindus do believe in rebirth or not. What we cannot falsify is the actual belief in rebirth, which is of no relevance in deciding whether the 'science of religion' is really a science. Of course if the method of your study has internal inconsistencies, so that your claim cannot be falsified, it will cease to be a scientific statement.

I.3. *X* claims that he is an incarnation (*avatāra*) of Viṣṇu. He claims that he can visit other worlds and often describes the events which take place in these worlds. His claim is not falsifiable and has no place in the province of science. However, there is no need for us to deny that he is an avatāra. Note that any such denial by sceptics is itself not falsifiable and hence does not belong to the domain of science. The only value of our opinion about *X*'s status is no more than our faith.

15.2 Mantra Śāstra

It was mentioned earlier that a śāstra in the widest sense means a body of knowledge. However, those who use the word mantra śāstra do not just mean by it the study of mantras and ritual. The word conveys a meaning similar to that implied in the physical and chemical sciences or in engineering. Mantra śāstra is a science which can be used to acquire siddhis or extraordinary and supernatural powers. We may say that mantra śāstra uses ritual and mantras as forces to bring about the desired effects.

Despite the widespread belief in mantra śāstra, there does not seem to exist a traditional treatise on mantra śāstra nor was it studied as a separate discipline like, say, gāyana śāstra or musicology. This has to do with the origin of the Vedas and tantra.

According to the Tantra śāstra text the four Vedas emanated from the four mouths of Śiva and from the fifth mouth emerged tantra (āgama). There is thus a school which believes that the Vedas and tantras were created simultaneously and śāstras were developed subsequently by various ṛṣis. The Atharva Veda is full of charms, magical formulas and exorcistic chants. The use of the Atharva Veda was entrusted to a special ritualist whose job it was protect the priests reciting other Vedas and the yajamāna and his wife. Since the Atharva Veda was considered as the ultimate authority, it is believed, there was no need for a separate mantra śāstra text. This also explains why mantra śāstra was not taught as a separate subject.

According to the *Gopatha Brāhmaṇa* the Atharva has five subordinate Vedas (upavedas) which were created when Brahma was looking in different directions. Snake-veda (sarpaveda), ghost-veda (*piśācaveda*), history-veda (*itihāsveda*), *āgama* (tantra) and Purāṇa (urdhvāmānya).

The *Gopatha Brāhmaṇa* describes the application of the Atharva ritual in five kinds of sūktas which include hundreds of topics from different areas. A brief summary will give you an idea of the scope of the use of ritual.

Kauśikasūtra—weaponry, counterattack, cure of many physical and mental diseases, exorcism; rituals relating to agriculture and navigation, expiation of sin, growth of hair.

Nakṣatrakalpa—'protection rituals', weaponry including missiles, fulfilment of wishes, seismology.

Vaitāna saṅkalpa—Several well-known yajñas like Vājapeya, Agnicayana, Aśvamedha, Rājasūya etc., some of which have been mentioned earlier.

Āṅgirasakalpa—Several mantras for specific gods and goddesses, Ganeśa, Lakṣmi etc.

Śāntikalpa—Śanti means peace and a 'sānti ritual' is performed to avoid the wrath of gods and planets.

According to mantra śāstra the rituals are effective only when performed in the prescribed manner. The right mantras have to be selected to suit the performer's constitution and they have to be subjected to certain saṃskāras as mentioned earlier.

Besides the Atharva, hundreds of tantra texts and other commentaries are used as the sources of mantra śāstra.

In this context it is necessary to mention 'astraṣ' which are weapons or missiles 'driven' by mantras, sometimes mantras themselves might constitute astras. Astras differ from the conventional weapons called 'śastra' in that the latter use physical energy. The mace, sword, bow and arrow are examples of śāstra. Astras are not only used as missiles but also as anti-missile weapons. A typical battle scene between two armies led by *A* and *B* might progress as follows :

A launches a fire-missile (*agni-astra*) which makes the fire rage on the enemy side. *B* retaliates with the rain-missile (*parjanya astra*) which causes rainfall and the fire is extinguished. *A* then launches a wind missile (*vāyu-astra*) which makes a terrible wind blow over the enemy camp. *B* may send a counter astra which stops the wind from blowing.

You will observe that some of the mantra śāstra claims are testable while some are not. For example, we can test if the agni-astra really works or not, provided of course, the putative mantras and rituals are made available to us. However, some claims are not scientific. For example, the claim that a certain ritual can drive away the ghosts from your 'haunted' house is not scientific since it cannot be falsified.

If for convenience we include yoga in rituals and mantras in mantra śāstra, we may say that those who believe in mantra śāstra believe that its application can bring about one or more of the following changes:

1. Psychophysiological changes
2. Transcendental changes.
3. Miracles.

Psychophysiological changes—These include a sense of well being, peace of mind, indescribable ecstacy, sometimes described as heavenly bliss in the state of samādhi, and cure of various psychological and physical ailments.

Some of these claims have been substantiated. Prayer, confession, hypnosis, suggestion and psychotherapy are known to lead to a sense of well-being especially among those who have faith in such methods. But what about the cure of diseases?

Most physicians now regard the body and the mind as inseparable and that the biochemistry of our body is dependent on our awareness. Biofeedback and meditation experiments have proved that even the so-called involuntary functions such as heartbeat, breathing, bloodpressure, digestion and even hormone regulation can be controlled consciously.

A study by Dr. Bal K Anand of All India Institute of Medical Sciences, New Delhi is interesting. About 400 yogis were tested under controlled conditions. The results were not as spectacular as the believers in yoga would expect, but a few yogis did demonstrate extraordinary abilities such as slowing down metabolism, reducing the heartbeat, materializing perspiration on the face without working a muscle etc.[2] Some medical practitioners like Deepak Chopra make far-reaching conclusions : intelligence is not confined to the brain, but pervades the whole body. They argue that RNA takes bits of information from DNA and carries this intelligence to different molecules.

Researchers conducted by David Spiegal seem to confirm that patients suffering from cancer benefit from psychotherapy. Other researchers have found similar results in patients suffering from other ailments like, arthritis, asthma, pain etc.[3] It is reasonable, therefore, to assume that mantra śāstra should bestow similar benefits especially when the patient has faith in the therapeutic system. It may even be surmised that if rituals are performed for the benefit of the patient who does not directly participate in the ritual activity, some relief may be expected if she has faith in mantra śastra and is aware that the rituals are being performed to improve her health.

Transcendental effects—These include liberation from the cycle of birth and death, a place in heaven, prosperity in the next life, meeting gods, conversation with ghosts etc. This category can be dismissed as belonging to the province of non-science since such claims cannot be falsified. This is the area where belief, not science, prevails.

Miracles—Miracles are acts or events which exceed the known powers of nature, and are usually attributed to supernatural powers or siddhis. The Atharva Veda, tantra, yoga and other texts describe hundreds of miracles which can be performed through rituals and siddhis. They include levitation, walking on water, entering someone else's body, materializing or de-materializing substances, the art of vanishing, the art of being at different places at the same time, killing a person thousands of miles away, metamorphosing someone into a parrot; the list is endless and includes all those phenomena called psi or paranormal.

Miracles are particularly interesting because they can be scientifically tested. However, the trouble with miracles is that most of them seem to have taken place in the past and thus cannot be commented upon. For example, those who believe in mantra śāstra can contend that the Vedic ṛṣis performed many feats but the science was subsequently lost. Miracles are mentioned in many religious scriptures, but religions sometimes have an ambivalent attitude towards them. Among Christians the Protestants hold that miracles ended with the death of the apostles. The Roman Catholicism, on the other hand, refutes this contention and even today requires evidence of the miraculous powers by a person considered for canonization as saint. Miracles seem to be declining in the West since the 18th century. But in India, even in the 20th century there were yogis, babas (holy fathers) and godmen who claimed to possess supernatural powers. Many of them had millions of followers from all over the world. Since supernatural powers can be tested, we shall briefly consider a few cases and try to determine whether their feats have been scientifically verified.

15.3 Supernatural Powers

Paramahansa Yogananada (1893-1952) was a renowned yogī who specialized in Kriyā Yoga (Chapter 3). He had innumerable followers in India and America. His autobiography was first published in the US and has been immensely popular. He established spiritual centers in India and the US. The headquarters of his self-realization Fellowship are located atop Mt. Washington, Los Angleles, California.

Yogananda describes a number of miracles performed by other yogis. Among them was his guru Sri Yukteshwar who is reported to have performed a number of feats. (1) He cured a veterinary surgeon suffering from diabetes which was considered a hopeless case by doctors. (2) He happened to be in Calcutta and Serampore (two different places) at the same time (3) When he was dying, Yogananda, who was then America, heard his voice asking his disciple to return to India (4) On a festive day a religious procession had to be taken out. The day was extremely hot and the students had to go barefooted. The guru assured Yogananda that the Lord would provide an umbrella of clouds. As soon as the procession started, there were dark clouds in the sky followed by a light shower bringing down the temperature. (5) In his book (Chapter 43) Yogananda describes the resurrection of his guru. The guru appeared before him in his hotel room in Bombay and imparted to him the knowledge of the astral world and after-life.

Yogananda also mentions Babaji, a yogi who had been living for several centuries. He is believed to have given yoga initiation to the monist Śaṅkara (788-820CE) and saint Kabir (15th century) Babaji also resurrected a devotee in the 19th century and met Yogananda when the latter was about to leave for America.

Yoganada himself was believed to have supernatural powers. After his death his body was kept in a mortuary at Los Angeles. The mortuary Director Harry T. Towe is reported to have observed in a notarized letter "The absence of any visual signs of decay in the dead body of Paramahansa Yogananda offers the most extraordinary case in our experience... No physical disintegration was visible in his body even twenty days after his death..."[4]

Yoganandas's autobiography is being used in 100 universities and colleges for courses in comparative religion, psychology, literature, philosophy, sociology and biology.

Sri Sathya Sai Baba – Among the miracle men of the twentieth century, Sathya Sai Baba (1926-) is without doubt the most renowned. He has millions of devotees all over the world. They include scientists, judges, businessmen and politicians.

Sathyanarayana was born in a small hamlet called Puttaparthi. It is reported that at the time of his birth at midnight the tambura (a stringed instrument) in the house automatically started twanging and the maddala (a percussion instrument) began to beat rhythmically, "as if an expert Hand was handling it."[5]

In his childhood he became quite famous for his 'celestial plays' (*līlās*). He used to materialize sweets and peppermints from empty bags and distribute them among children. Once a teacher punished him for not taking down the notes in class. The boy was made to stand on bench. At the end of the period, it was found that the teacher did not vacate the chair. When his colleague who was to take the next class entered and asked him what the matter was, he did stand up, but up went the chair along with him – the chair had stuck to him.

Sathyanarayana soon declared that he was Sai Baba – a saint of the 19th century who lived in Shirdi in the State of Maharashtra and performed many miracles. The boy asked the people to worship him.

He was subsequently treated as the incarnation of Sai Baba of Shirdi.

Sri Sathya Sai Baba is believed to have enabled many people to see visions. Once he took a person to a river and asked to watch the reflection. The person first saw Baba, then only a halo followed by a sequence of nine incarnations (*avatāras*) of Viṣṇu. He also saw the tenth avatara which Hindus believe would appear in the future as Kalkī on the horseback. When the man saw Kalkī mounted on a horse, the rider had the form of Baba.

Once Baba was on the sea shore with his devotees. Suddenly, he walked straight into the sea disappearing behind the waves. The dazed devotees saw a vision of the Lord on the serpent Śeṣa reclining on the waves. Since this is the normal posture of Viṣṇu described in Purāṇas, the anecdote implies that Baba is Viṣṇu's avatāra.

While Baba materialized a number of things by a wave of the hand, which he gifted to his devotees, *vibhūti* or 'sacred ash' was his favourite. The devotees used the vibhūti given by him as a specific against illness. Hundred of devotees have reported that vibhūti exuded from Baba's photographs which they kept in their homes.

On one occasion, he is reported to have converted water into petrol to be used for the stranded car in which he was traveling. On another occasion he metamorphosed water into diesel which was used for running a dynamo. Baba often 'left' his body to see his devotees, miles away, who were about to die.

Although Baba does not seem to perform miracles regularly any more, his popularity has not waned. He has become a living legend and hundreds of thousands of devotees from all over the world visit Puttaparthi every year where his headquarters are located.

Uri Geller—A twentieth century miracle man from Israel, Geller was believed to have performed such feats as bending nails and keys, entering flying saucers and teleporting thousands of miles in a matter of seconds. However, Geller's fame seems to have ended after the publication of James Randi's book, *The Magic of Uri Geller* in which Randi questioned his supernatural powers.

The credibility of such claims can be ascertained only when these feats are performed under controlled conditions. Unfortunately, most yogis and paranormals are reluctant to subject themselves to scientific scrutiny.

In this context we must mention Dr. Abraham Kavoor (1898-1978), an India - born rationalist, atheist and a naturalized citizen of Sri Lanka. He was also the President of Ceylon Rationalist Association. He waged a sustained war against superstition and exposed many charlatans claiming supernatural powers. He offered an award of 1,00,000 Sri Lankan rupees to anyone who would demonstrate any of the 23 miracles listed by him. This open challenge was published all over the world for nearly 15 years. "I have not lost a single cent" he says, "Instead I have gained a few thousand rupees, the forfeited earnest money deposits of contestants who failed to turn up in the end."[6] One of the conditions laid down by Kavoor was that the miracles must be demonstrated in fraud-proof conditions. One of the paranormals who accepted his challenge but backed out later was Kjell Eide, a Swedish miracle man. Kavoor also challenged Uri Geller offering him $16,000, but the latter did not accept the challenge.

Sathya Sai Baba has never responded to Kovoor's challenges. His devotees contend that Bhagawan (God) need not condescend to subject himself to such tests.

Scientific research in parapsychology commenced more than a century ago. The first society of Psychical Research was established in London in 1882. Psi phenomena acquired respectability in early 20th century when Dr. J. B. Rhine and his colleagues conducted research at Duke University, North Carolina under the renowned psychologist William McDougall on ESP (extra-sensory perception) and PK (psychokinesis) at the university, and Rhine became its Director. Rhine's publications earned him many supporters, many of them noted scientists like S. G. Soal, N. V. Peal and B. Wiesner. However, subsequent researchers in parapsychology conducted by Christopher Scott, Dennis Hyde and E. Roux have failed to confirm the validity of paranormal phenomena as claimed by Rhine and his associates. Scientists do agree that research in parapsychology belongs to the domain of science (recall Popper's test) but assert that the claims have been falsified.

From the above discussion it may be inferred that supernatural powers have not been conclusively demonstrated under controlled conditions. However, a grey area must be mentioned. While it can be asserted that miracles cannot be repeated – for this is what laboratory experiments intend to show – can we assert that miracles never took place or that they do not take place once in a while? The question is difficult to answer for the simple reason that all inductive judgements as explained in Chapter 4 are probabilistic.

Suppose you believe in deism, the doctrine that God set the universe in motion, but does not interfere in its working. Then miracles cannot happen if we add a premise that the universal laws do not change. But if you are a theist and believe that God can intervene in the working of the universe if he feels necessary, miracles can take place occasionally which will not be reflected in inductive methods. The ambiguity is further compounded by the fact that neither deism nor theism lies in the domain of science.

Leaving aside the last problem, we may conclude that the experiments to prove miracles or supernatural powers have either failed or those who claim to possess such putative powers have not been subjected to scientific investigation. This reflects the status of supernatural powers vis-a-vis science.

15.4 Pseudoscience

Psendoscience is a pretended or spurious science. My belief that God can send rain if I sincerely pray to him is not pseudo-science, it is superstition. But if I contend that my incantations create vibrations which have the effect of rearranging the molecules to produce rain, I am making a pseudo-scientific statement.

Pseudo-science has usually three sources, fraud, scientization and spurious interpretation.

Fraud—A person who claims that he can manufacture a cheap fuel from plants, which can be used as a substitute for petrol, is practicing fraud if he knows that such a thing is not possible. Usually his goal is to earn money rather than fame. Though he may be able to dupe a few gullible investors, he is bound to be exposed sooner or later. Since frauds pertain to the province of penal law, we need not discuss them further.

Scientization—Those who believe in the power of mantras sometimes claim that every mantra gives rise to vibrations similar to electromagnetic waves. It is well known that the electromagnetic waves can be used in several ways. They help us in transmitting messages and pictures to distant places, they help us to use remote control and manipulate missiles, planes and satellites. Through artificial satellites we can take pictures of different heavenly bodies. In other words these waves do for us everything that falls under ESP and PK, and in the future, they may be able to do many feats we are not able think of today.

The vibrations emanating from mantras uttered, muttered or said in silence create similar waves, which can do the same tasks that the electromagnetic waves do. They might act in a slightly different manner. For example a guided missile sent to destroy the enemy aircraft has a physical form. The mantric waves on the other hand re-assemble the molecules and atoms in such a way that they can create enough heat or śakti at the exact time and the right place, which will burn the aircraft.

Scientization is a device to make superstitions more respectable. If it is used in theories that relate to rebirth or ghosts, we may simply ignore them since they lie outside the ambit of science. When scientization is used to explain supernatural powers, their validity can be tested, But in view of what has been said about miracles earlier, scientization has no value if such powers cannot be demonstrated under laboratory conditions.

Interpretation—It was mentioned in Chapter 6 that hermeneutics and interpretative techniques can prove almost anything. Scientific progress has created a dilemma for us. While we have been conditioned to revere our scriptures, our rational faculty accepts scientific theories. However, since scriptural pronouncements are often inconsistent with scientific results, the only way in which we can reconcile our double allegiance is through re-interpretation of scriptures so that they appear to conceal profound scientific theories behind their exterior. This is how some biblical passages have been interpreted.

One of the most interesting books which use interpretative techniques to prove that the Vedas conceal modern scientific theories is Dhananjay Deshpande's work, *The Vedic Science* ('Vedanteel Vidnyan'). According to the author the Nāsadīya Sūkta which we mentioned in Chapter 6 embodies the big bang theory. The description of Uṣas (Dawn) relates to the period between the big bang and the formation of the sun. Maruts (wind gods) mentioned in the Rig Veda hide such secrets as the corona, solar wind and flares. The yajñas are not mere sacrificial fires, they were scientific laboratories where advanced research was conducted. The Vedic scientists knew the structure of many atoms such as oxygen, sodium, carbon, lithium and were familiar with the concept of atomic numbers. They also knew the three isotopes of hydrogen (hydrogen, deutorium, tritium). They had also discovered antimatter and black holes. The Vedic scientists also appeared to know the distinction between what we call Euclidian geometry and Riemannian geometry, and possibly were familiar with the Einstein's general theory of relativity especially the fact that the space-time is not flat, but curved due to the distribution of mass and energy.

The author's interpretations are based on a 1-1 correspondence between what the Vedas say and what they actually mean. I shall briefly discuss the knowledge of magnetism which the Vedas are believed to impart. The theory has a patent flaw. The interpretation is based on maṇḍala 1, sūkta 164 of the Rig Veda. The relevant data on which the interpretation is based is (in brief) as follows :

1. ...... His cows produce milk in their mouths and drink their own milk with their legs. (R. V 1-164-7)
2. Mother earth offers her body to father God (RV 1-164-8)
3. Mother Universe is linked to the South and she is pregnant (RV 1-164-9)
4. With one leg she holds the Nature below, and with her other leg she supports the heavens above. (RV 1-164-17)
5. The seas emanate from her: All directions live because of her. The universe is sustained by her ever-flowing milk (RV 1-164-42) [7]

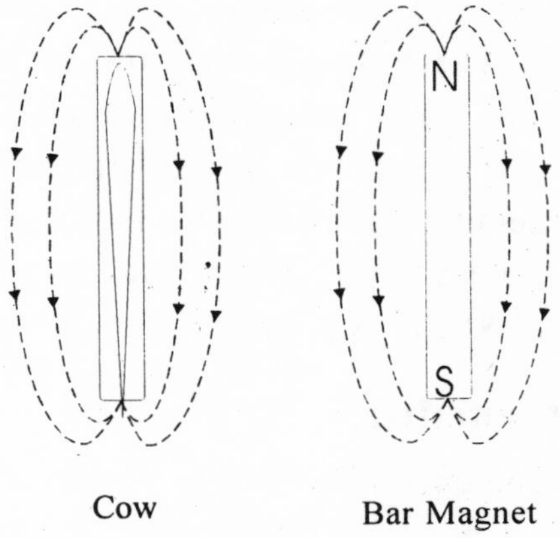

Fig. 15.1 Magnetism in the Vedas

Interpretation—The cow symbolizes a bar magnet. Her mouth in the north represents Father, her legs in the south, Mother. Father (heaven) and Mother (earth) make love to each other and the earth becomes pregnant. The cow's mouth (Father) is the source of semen (milk) which flows from North to South (earth). The direction is significant; it shows that Mother accepts Father's seed. This is in exact correspondence with the south pole "accepting" magnetic lines from the north pole. The interpretation appears a bit confusing in the beginning, but its analysis leads to three sets or classes whose elements have a 1-1 correspondence as follows:

Analogy

Class I	*Class II*	*Class III*
1) Cow Mouth, the source of milk	heaven (Father) and earth (Mother) Father, the source of semen	bar magnet north pole, the source of magnetic energy
2) Legs	Mother	south pole
3) Milk	semen	magnetic lines or energy
4) Flow of milk from mouth to legs	flow of semen from Father to Mother	flow of magnetic energy from the north pole to the south pole.

There are many discrepancies in his theory but the most important inconsistency is pointed below :[8]

The serious flaw lies in the analogy between the "Mother 'accepting' the semen from Father" and "the south pole receiving magnetic energy from the north pole". The author is under the misconception that the north pole of a magnet 'generates' energy which is 'attracted' by the south pole. In fact, the direction of the magnetic lines is purely conventional; it is the direction in which a hypothetical isolated north pole would travel. The north pole was treated as positive by physicist Willian Gilbert in 1600 CE as a matter of convenience.

15.5 Vedic Mathematics

The discussion on ancient Indian Science will remain incomplete if we do not mention a most intriguing work *Vedic Mathematics* by Jagadguru Swāmī Śrī Bhāratī Kṛṣna a Tīrthaji Mahārāja (1884-1960) who held the title of Śaṅkarācārya of Govardhana Maṭha, Puri.

Apart from being the head of the monastery the Swami was a brilliant scholar in mathematics, Sanskrit, philosophy and religion. He passed his matriculation examination with first rank, won the highest place in the B.A. examination and obtained the M.A. degree from the American College of Sciences, Rochester New York, receiving highest honors in all subjects including mathematics.

According to the author the book is based on "sixteen simple mathematical formulas from the Vedas". The book lists 16 sūtras and 13 sub-sūtras (corollaries) which are used in solving a number of problems.

For example, the first sūtra is "*Ekādhi kena Pūrveṇa*" which means "By one more than the previous one". Unlike the mathematical formulas we learn, the sūtra is not intelligible, it has to be interpreted in the proper context. However, the interpretation does not appear far-fetched when explained in mathematical language. It can be used consistently to convert vulgar fractions into their decimal forms by a method which is much quicker than the conventional procedure. However, only the fractions of the type 1/19, 1/29 ... in which the unit's digit in the denominator is nine can be used.

The second sūtra 'nikhilam' and the third 'ūrdhva-tiryagbhyām' are used for multiplication and division. The same sūtra can sometimes be used for more operations than one.

The author furnishes a number of 'short-cuts' based on the sūtras which can be used in solving problems in different areas of mathematics: algebra (factorization, quadratic and cubic equations, partial fractions), geometry (Pythagoras' theorem, Apollonius' theorem, analytical conics), calculus (differentiation and integration) and arithmetic (squareroots and cuberoots). Interestingly it provides no less than five proofs of the Pythegoras' theorem.

Some of the features of Vedic Mathematics may be mentioned.

1. There is no systematic development of the subject, the knowledge is contained in sūtras which can handle only specific topics and types.
2. The same sūtra can be used for more operations than one.
3. Some methods are definitely much shorter than the ones used in conventional mathematics.

4. The sūtras are not transparent, but need to be explained.

The book appears to be a collection of a number of 'short-cuts' in mathematics rather than a systematic and progressive development of any branch of mathematics. Nevertheless it does constitute science.

However, the main question which is relevant for our purpose is, on what grounds it should be called "Vedic" mathematics. Was it really contained in the Vedas?

The author uses the word Vedas in a broad sense which include 'Sthāpatya Veda' ("engineering, architecture and all branches of mathematics"). According to him the sūtras used in his book are contained in the appendix (*pariśiṣṭa*) to the Atharva Veda. But Manjula Trivedi, his disciple, agrees in the note included in the book that these sūtras are not found in the present recension of the Atharva Veda. According to her the swami reconstructed the formulas on the basis of "intuitive revelation from the material scattered here and there in the Atharva Veda". She also mentions that the swami used to say that the formulas were reconstructed from the Atharva Veda after "assiduous research and 'tapas' for about eight years in the forests surrounding Sringeri".

There does not seem to be any collateral evidence to show that the Vedic society knew anything about algebra, geometry calculus and such advanced topics mentioned in *Vedic Mathematics*. The Vedic origin of these sutras appears apocryphal.

The sūtra mathematics, however, seems to be the product of unusual mathematical ability and extraordinary intuition. It may be conjectured that the swami himself was the author of the sūtras. However, it looks strange that he should disown the authorship of such a valuable contribution. But religious faith coupled with humility can have strange consequences. It is not difficult to believe that the swami persuaded himself into believing that he was merely reconstructing the sūtras from the material contained in the Atharva Veda. One finds a parallel in the Indian mathematical genius Srinivas Ramanujan (1887-1920) who often claimed that goddess of Namakkal appeared in his dreams and provided him mathematical formulas which he subsequently wrote down and verified after he woke up in the morning.

15.6 Siddhis and Science

In Chapter 3 we mentioned several siddhis which, according to Patañjali's Yoga Sūtra, can be acquired by a yogī. In view of what has been discussed in this chapter, the status of these siddhis may be briefly stated.

Siddhis	*Status*
1. Knowledge of earlier births.	Not falsifiable, hence non-science
2. Knowledge of other people's transactions	Falsifiable
3. Ability to make oneself invisible	Falsifiable
4. Clairvoyance	Falsifiable
5. Knowledge of the universe	Not falsifiable, hence non-science. The 'knowledge of the universe' is broad enough to connote transcendental knowledge.
6. Ability to enter someone else's body	Not falsifiable, hence non-science
7. Ability to walk on the water or bog	Falsifiable
8. Ability to fly	Falsifiable

Siddhis 2, 3, 4, 7, 8 pertain to the domain of science, but have not been demonstrated by anyone under controlled conditions.

16

THE SCIENCE OF RITUAL

16.1 Indian Science of Ritual

We are now ready to examine whether there can be a science of ritual. This should be done in the light of the earlier finding that the semantic approach sometimes leads to ambiguities (Introduction, Chapter 14.). The structural approach, on the other hand, leads to many uniform patterns shared by different religious rituals (Chapter 11.).

In *Ritual and Mantras* Staal shows that there existed in ancient India a science of ritual embodied in the Śrauta Sūtras. He shows that there is considerable resemblance between Indian linguistics and śrauta rituals. Both these sciences use the medium of sūtras. A sūtra means a 'thread' or a 'string' but connotes a terse aphorism.

Linguistics and Śrauta Sūtras have similar abstract concepts such a rules, metarules (paribhāṣā) and ordered sequences. The Śrauta rituals display a hierarchical structure, a fact that was recognized by Indian ritualists and later acknowledged by Western scholars, like Willam Caland. For example Agnicayana which was mentioned in Chapter 11 is a complex ritual comprised of a hierarchy in which Darśapūrṇamāsa (Full and New moon Ceremonies) is the simplest ritual followed by Paśubandha, Agniṣṭoma and Agnicayana, the last ceremony being the most elaborate. These structures can be explained with the help of rules similar to phase-structure rules, transformation rules and self-embedding rules.[1]

In order to show that Śrauta Sūtras constitute science Staal assumes that any science has the features similar to those we mentioned in Chapter 5. However, he does not include 'generalization' as one of the features. This approach makes ritual science narrow and closely linked with linguistics. It does not enable us to generalize the concept of ritual science and link it up with rituals in general and animal rituals mentioned in Chapter 8. While it underscores certain processes common to natural language and śrauta rituals, it cannot explain the fact that structurally language (except verse) and rituals are poles apart. As explained earlier (Chapter 13) we do not normally use iterations, refrains, chorus, relays or palindromes, when we communicate with others. In fact we shall show that the sūtra style is calculated to hide refrains and iterations

To understand the sūtra technique consider *A*'s weekly schedule of meals detailed in Table 16.1

	Breakfast* *7 A.M.	***Lunch* *12 Noon***	***Dinner* *8 P.M.***
Sunday	pizza	rice, curry, fruit (mango if available)	milk, fruit
Monday	bread, fruit	rice, curry, fruit (mango if available)	milk, fruit
Tuesday	bread, fruit	rice, curry, fruit (mango if available)	-
Wednesday	fruit	rice, curry, fruit (mango if available)	milk, fruit
Thursday	bread, fruit	rice, curry, fruit (mango if available)	milk, fruit
Friday	bread, fruit	rice, curry, fruit (mango if available)	kabab, icecream, coffee
Saturday	bread, fruit	eggs, icecream, coffee	milk, fruit

Table 16.1 A's Weekly Schedule of Meals

If this schedule is translated into the sūtra form, it would appear as:

1. *A*'s meals – breakfast 7 A.M., lunch 12 noon, dinner 8 P.M.
2. Breakfast – bread, fruit; lunch-rice, curry, fruit; dinner - milk, fruit, unless otherwise stated.
3. Saturday lunch- eggs, icecream, coffee, Friday dinner- kabab, icecream, coffee.
4. Breakfast – Sunday only pizza; Wednesday, no bread.
5. Lunch – mango is the preferred fruit.
6. No dinner on Tuesday.

The sūtra style is not uncommon in modern times. Similar constructions are found in legal enactments. The students of law often encounter such expressions as "provided that", "unless otherwise stipulated", "notwithstanding anything contained in section ...", "subject to section...", etc. These phrases provide exceptions, provisos and deviations from the general rule. They bring about economy in the same way as sūtras do.

To see how the sūtra is economical let us write Table 16.1 in the form of a sequence

P/RCF/MF//BF/RCF/MF//BF/RCF/-
//F/RCF/MF//BF/RCF/MF//BF/RCF/KICo//BF/EICo/MF//

where P= pizza, R= rice, F= fruit etc,

The structure is full of refrains : R, C, F, M, B, I, Co. There are also composite refrains such as RCF, MF etc.

The ritual sūtras effect economy, but at the same time they conceal structural patterns.

We shall now briefly discuss sandhi and transformation in grammar (not to be confused with the geometrical transformations mentioned in Chapter 7) and show that they have parallels in rituals in general.

Sandhi. In Sanskrit when two words combine, the morphemes entering into the resultant word undergo phonetic changes depending upon the presence of other morphemes. Consider the following examples.

1. Jagat + nātha –Jagannātha (Lord of the world)
2. Nara + īśa- Nareśa (Lord of the world)
3. Kamala + īśa – Kamaleśa (Lord of the world)
4. Nara + Indra – Narendra (Best of men)
5. Rājā + Indra – Rājendra (King of Kings)

This process is called 'sandhi'. The sandhi of the type 2 through 5 may be written as

a or ā + i or ī → e i.e. a or ā → e when i or ī follows

This is a context - restrictive rule.

Some of these rules may be amenable to generalization.

For example the rules

u → va when 'a' follows

i → yu when 'u' follows

can be generalized as

Vowel → corresponding semi vowel when a different vowel follows.

However, similar context-dependent changes are also found in almost all rituals. Consider the following examples

I.1. Suppose a foreign dignitary, when he visits your country, is given a 19, gun salute. This is modified into a 21-gun variety when the dignitary happens to be the Head of the State.

I.2. In your daily routine you have a modest 3 course dinner without dessert. However when your mother-in-law is invited, the dinner becomes a major 5-course event followed by dessert and coffee.

We have already mentioned that embedding is present in almost every long ritual.

Transformation—This was mentioned in Chapter 10. In fact, this mechanism is present in almost every activity that can be called a ritual. Consider the following figure which shows the activities of a bank cashier.

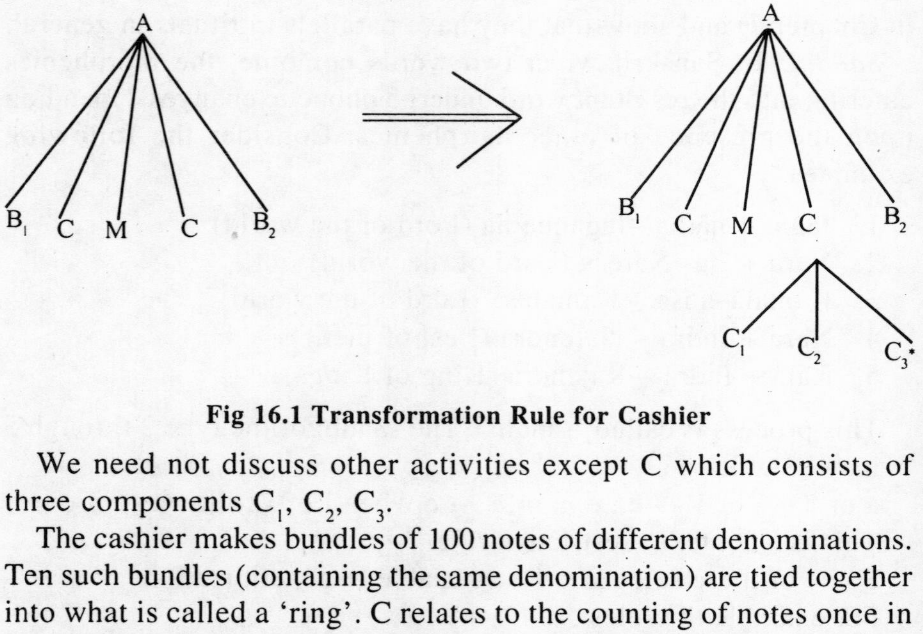

Fig 16.1 Transformation Rule for Cashier

We need not discuss other activities except C which consists of three components C_1, C_2, C_3.

The cashier makes bundles of 100 notes of different denominations. Ten such bundles (containing the same denomination) are tied together into what is called a 'ring'. C relates to the counting of notes once in the morning before the start of business and once after the business is closed. Its components are as follows :

C_1 – count the rings (each denomination)
C_2 – count the bundles in each ring
C_3 – count the notes from one or two bundles selected at random.

Once in a month the cashier changes his procedure which makes counting elaborate. The first C is unchanged. In the second C there are no changes as far as C_1 and C_2 are concerned. However, C_3 changes to C_3*

C_3* - Count the notes from each bundle. The figure depicts the transformation rule for the cashier.

In fact, context – restrictive rules, embedding and transformation rules seem to be inseparable from all human activities. They represent the modifications of our behaviour in response to new situations. They may have a profound significance in linguistics, but as criteria for rituals their importance seems to be limited. Pre-planned behaviour is often modified even when the activity is not categorized as ritual. When such modifications are stylized they may be said to introduce a second (lower) order ritualization of which transformation rules and context-restrictive rules are examples.

It is the absence of the GRS in language- especially iteration, refrain and pattern completion which makes it distinct from rituals. However a few characteristics like recursion and self-embedding which are the potential "creators of infinity" seem to be shared by language with śrauta as well as compulsive rituals.

16.2 The General Theory of Rituals

As mentioned earlier our hypothesis will not be confined to śrauta / Vedic rituals, but will cover a wider field. In earlier chapters we considered mantras and rituals from Vedic, Puranic and tantric sources all of which are used in the present day religious ceremonies. The fact that religious rituals have features common with the rituals in general and that animals too perform rituals should make us wonder whether ritual science can be so narrow as to be applicable to say, only Vedic rituals. We also recall what we said in Chapter 14, that any theory which purports to explain the science of ritual must take into account six other findings : similarities between Vedic, Purāṇic and tantric rituals, similarities between religious rituals and rituals in general including music, dance etc., compulsive rituals, animal rituals and the absence of meaning in some mantras.

To begin with we can suggest a hypothesis relating to religious rituals. We assert that they display some or all of the ten structural patterns (GRS) mentioned in chapter 8. We have to show that the hypothesis meets the criteria mentioned in chapter 5 viz. empirical adequacy, abstraction, consistency, provisional status and generalization.

1. *Empirical Adequacy* – In Chapter 11 and 12 we found that the religious rituals displayed GRS in various degrees. While iteration and refrain are universal, palindrome, embedding and pattern completion appear in longer ceremonies. The remaining structures appear in frequency depending upon the type of ritual. Some of these patterns also have spatial correlates such as the mirror and rotational symmetry found in the yantras used in tantric rituals.

   It must be borne in mind that ritual science is one of the human sciences and our hypothesis cannot be more precise such as is found in exact sciences.

   We were also able to discover that worship rituals or ceremonies are homoeomorphic or structurally similar. This enables us to make the second hypothesis which is not general but is applicable to worship ceremonies viz such a ceremony or the puja has the form

   P = AWBCDXFGHI.........................(1)

   where the different letters have the meaning as mentioned in Chapter 12. We discussed at length the predictability of the formula and the fact that it is used to design new worship rituals. The most important reason for predictability and 'designability' of the worship ceremony is not only the preponderance of ritual constants like **A** (First Quintet), **B** (Middle Septet) etc. which are manifest in the above formula, but also inessential constants like **J** (Minor Pūjās), **L** (Sarasvatī Pūjā) etc. which are embedded in other ritual components and hence do not appear explicitly in the formula.

   As mentioned in Chapter 12, there are a few ritual constants even in the rites of passage. It may be possible to devise a general formula for these ceremonies despite their apparent dissimilarities. But this is only a conjecture.

2. *Abstraction* – The degree of abstraction varies from one science to another. In mathematics and physics it is the highest, and as explained earlier the abstractions such as points and photons may have a dubious existential status. But abstractions afford a powerful tool in establishing new theories and integrating them

at different levels. Abstraction in descriptive sciences such as chemistry and geology is not manifest, but it does exist in the form of classification. In zoology, for example, species, genus etc are abstractions in some sense. Formula 1 for worship ceremony has symbols which are to some degree abstractions. The method which identifies ritual constants is also a process of abstraction which enables us to represent different ceremonies in a compact way.

Ritual instinct is also an abstraction which will help us to integrate religious rituals, social rituals, compulsive rituals and animal rituals.

3 *Consistency* – Since ritual rules are descriptive of what people actually do, procedural inconsistency is a rarity. Of course, there may be more manuals than one which are referred to by practitioners. In such cases we can always speak of different schools. Though these schools may clash with one another, each of them is usually internally consistent.

It might be thought that 'or' sometimes leads to inconsistency. For example in

1. Recite mantra X or mantra Y
2. Recite mantra X 100 times or more.

Here 'or' merely offers options and does not lead to ambiguities. There are also no inconsistencies involved in the hypothesis related to ten structural patterns or the worship formula.

The former might have an element of vagueness but we have already made it clear that in human sciences like ritual, we cannot expect an exact formula such as is found in, say, physics.

4. *Provisional Nature* – Any scientific theory is provisional and needs to be revised in the light of new evidence. Fortunately ritual science is better placed than natural science in this respect. In our general hypothesis the two characteristics, iteration and refrain appear to be universal. If we encounter any peculiar features such as are found by Staal in śrauta rituals, they only characterize a particular type of rituals without nullifying our hypothesis relating to ten ritual patterns. Of course at a later date if someone discovers that all these 10 patterns can be

described with the help of fewer parameters, our hypothesis can be revised accordingly.

There is another reason why rituals science needs revision. Rituals not only change from one place to another, they also tend to change over time. Revision of manuals is all that is necessary. Unlike in physics where our theories are tailored to reflect natural law, in ritual science theories merely reflect what people do. Newer formulas to replace (1) may have to be derived, but the basic hypothesis based on GRS will not require revision.

5 *Generalization* – The doctrine of stratification of a scientific system implies a gradual shift from special laws to general laws. The most general law involves the minimum number of characteristics which are common to all subordinate laws. In Chapter 8 we studied social rituals or rituals in general having ten structural patterns. We have also found iteration and refrain are common to all of them. There is a hierarchy of rituals shown by the Venn diagram (Chapter 14) in which the outermost circle shows the rituals in general. Religious rituals appear as its subclass and Vedic rituals are a subclass of religious rituals.

Thus, our first generalization is from the religious rituals to the rituals in general which will also include verse, music, dance, gymnastics etc. Animal rituals afford further generalization. While we know that animals perform rituals, their structural analysis is yet to be studied in detail. Yet, iteration and refrain are pronounced while palindrome, chorus and cycle too appear to be present. This data is sufficient for us to elevate the ritual science to a higher level. In the Venn diagram shown in Chapter 14, animal rituals form a superclass of human rituals and are shown by an outer circle. (Figure 14.1) The word animal of course, connotes human beings in this case.

Two structures, iteration and refrain are certainly present in all rituals and can be treated as the essential patterns in ritual science. For want of a better term we can call this essential core of call rituals 'rhythm'.

Table 16.2 shows various features of religious ritual, verse, music, dance, and compulsive rituals, which are compared with language. The features include 10 GRS and meaning. We have added dance tentatively though we did not analyse its structure. But any one who is familiar with dance, Indian or Western, classical, folk or social (ballroom) should have no doubt that it has the features mentioned in the table. Gymnastics is another activity which would show patterns similar to those of dance.

Features	*Language*	*Verse*	*Music*	*Dance*	*Religious Rituals*	*Compulsive Rituals*
Iteration	No	Yes	Yes	Yes	Yes	Yes
Refrain	No	Yes	Yes	Yes	Yes	Yes
Palindrome	No	Some-times	Some-times	Yes	Yes	Yes
Embedding/ Self embedding	Yes	Yes	Yes	Yes	Yes	Yes
Multiplets	Rare	Rare	Yes	Yes	Yes	Yes
Relay	No	Some-times	Yes	Yes	Yes	-
Cycle	No	Rare	Yes	Yes	Sometimes	Yes
Overlapping	No	-	Yes	Yes	Sometimes	Yes
Pattern completion	No	No	Yes	Yes	Yes	Yes
Chorus	No	Yes	Yes	Yes	Yes	-
Meaning	Yes	Yes	No	Sometimes	Sometimes	-

Table 16.2 Features of Language and Rituals

The first thing that strikes us is that language is the *odd man out* - it does not even possess the essential ingredients of ritual in general - iteration and refrain. This is despite the fact that it has certain processes common with śrauta rituals and even rituals in general as mentioned earlier in this chapter.

All other heads; verse, music, dance, mantras and religions rituals and compulsive rituals deserve to be called structured subclasses of rituals in general. A few more observations can be made. Music and dance are the closest relatives of religions rituals. But music and dance are closer to each other than they are to religions ritual. Verse appears to be at some distance from other rituals.

Conceptually therefore it is possible to conceive rhythm represented by iteration and refrain as the essential characteristics which bind verse, music, gymnastics and other rituals together. This is a generalization similar to that found in physics in which the gravitational law encompasses Kepler's law and the laws relating to falling bodies.

Animal rituals and compulsive rituals can be accommodated in our model admirably if we posit the existence of ritual instinct which manifests as rhythmic and ritual activities. In view of what we have said about animal rituals, compulsive rituals and instinct in Chapter 8 and 14, the hypothesis regarding ritual instinct appears well-justified.

Ritual instinct enables us to effect further integration and generalization through abstraction. The number of parameters involved in the general theory of rituals is reduced to just one. Ritual instinct plays the same role of abstraction as the gravitational force plays in physics. Moreover, it also permits us to treat some rituals such as śrauta and compulsive rituals as pure structures vindicating Staal's observations that rituals are without any meaning or goal.

The task of expressing ritual instinct in biological terms must be left to biologists and geneticists. Since an instinct is belived to be genetically determined, genetic research may be able to help us in this task. It must, however, be emphasized that the validity of the science of ritual does not depend on the 'genetic localization' of ritual instinct. The instinct can still be treated as an abstraction similar to points and photons, which serves the purpose of unifying different classes of rituals.

NOTES

(Authors cited below are listed in the Bibliography)

Introduction

1. Śaṅkarācārya (108) (1996), p.35
2. Staal, Preface, p.XIII

Chapter 1 Vedic and Ancient India.

1. Basham, p.235
2. Dowson, p.310
3. According to Basham, p.239, 'brahman' implies "a sort of supernatural electricity known to students of primitive religion as *mana*"
4. Basham, p.143. Some authors like Bose and Dowson do not mention the fifth class, and most Hindus perceive the 'untouchables' as belonging to the śudra class.
5. Basham, p.149
6. Many scholars are reluctant to use 'salvation' as equivalent to liberation. The former implies deliverance from sin or evil, while the latter connotes seeing the Ultimate Reality, freedom from the cycle of birth and death, etc.

Chapter 2 Rituals and Mantras

1. Staal, p.67
2. Frazer, Chapter LXIII, LXIV
3. Tigunait (1983), p.187
4. Ibid., p.193.
5. Four mahāvākyas relating to the concept of Brahman were mentioned in Chapter 1.
6. Quoted in Śaṅkarācārya (108) (1996), p.55
7. There are many other interpretations of AUM. For example A – U – M stand for absence of desire, fear and anger. The whole word symbolizes a perfect man. See, for example, Iyangar, p.50

8. Quoted in Bahsam, p.141
9. Quoted in Bapat, *Gorakshanatha Yoga,* p.230

Chapter 3 Tantra and Yoga

1. A map of the existing tantra shrines will be found in Tigunait (1999), p.31
2. See, for example, Tigunait (1999), p.71. For nyāsa see Desai (2002), pp.29-30
3. A fuller discussion on the kaula school will be found in Tigunait (1999), pp.106-114
4. Woodroffe, p.1

Chapter 4 Knowledge

1. See, for example, Russel's *The Principles of Mathematics*.
2. Strictly speaking "x is a cat", "x is a mammal", etc. are called 'propositional functions'. However, these technicalities may be ignored. Syllogism in its general form appears as in (1).
3. Rand (1990), Chapter 3 discusses this aspect in depth.
4. A more detailed discussion on this topic will be found in Staal, Chapter 27.
5. Russel discusses these postulates in detail in *Human Knowledge*, Chapter IX
6. Capra (1993), p.154
7. See, for example, Penrose, p.251

Chapter 5 Science

1. Einstein (1979), p.293 in his paper "Physics and Reality."
2. Hawking, p.9
3. See for example, Stonier and Hague, p.468
4. See Chakravarti, p.153
5. Einstein (1979), p.227 from his speech "Principles of Research."
6. Hocket, p.260

Chapter 6 Meaning and Interpretation

1. The phrase *the meaning of 'meaning'* is believed to be due to philosopher Ludwig Wittgenstein.
2. Freud, p.174
3. Russel, *An Enquiry into Meaning and Truth,* p.12

4. Schlick in "Meaning and Verification" reproduced in Peterfreund (1967), pp.255-288
5. Russel, *Human Knowledge,* p.164
6,7. James in "Pragmatism" reproduced in Peterfreund (1967), p.141
8. Staal, p.31
9. Webster, p.264
10. Ibid., p.265
11. O'Flaherty, pp.25-26. Authors referred to here are mentioned in the Bibliography.
12. Quoted in Staal, p.417

Chapter 7 Structure

1. Capra (1993), discusses symmetry found in elementary particles in Chapter 7

Chapter 8 Rituals in General

1. Frazer, p.19
2. Berne, pp.17-18
3. Morris (1984), pp.113-114
4. Ibid., p.126
5. Schwartz, p.52. The neo-striatum and globus pallidus form the striatum. The striatum is part of the basal ganglia or the extrapyramidal motor system, responsible for stereotyped patterns of movement. See also Longstaff, p.86, 257 and Amen, Chapters 5 and 9

Chapter 9 Language

1. Julie Cohen, "When Animals Talk" in the *The Sunday Times Magazine*, reproduced in *The Readers' Digest*, Dec. 2001
2. The scanning rules are, however, more complicated, but need not be considered for our analysis.

Chapter 10 Music

1. Gajendragadkar (2000), p.10
2. Staal, pp.169-170
3. Ibid., p.168
4. Ibid., pp.171-172
5. Ibid., p.174

6. Ibid., p.172
7. Gajendragadkar (1992), Ex.2, p.211
8. Ibid., Ex.5, p.233
9. Ibid., Ex. 7, p.211

Chapter 11 The Structure of Religious Ritual

1. A brief description of Agnicayana will be found in Staal, Chapter 8. Its structural aspects are discussed in Chapters 9 through 12.
2. Ibid., p.86
3. Ibid., Chapter 12
4. Desai, p.30. The Gāyatrī mantras associated with other gods and saints appear to be expressible by a formula :
   Om X vidmahe / Y dhīmahi / Tannaḥ Z
   where X, Y, Z are names / epithets of the gods or saints. For example, in case of the 20th Century saint Sai Baba, X = Srīsāinātha Y = Srīkṛṣṇarupaya (compared with Kṛṣṇa), and Z = Sai.

Chapter 12 Major Religious Rituals

1. Also called Upāṅga-devatā-sthāpanam Pūjanam. See Umeshanand (2000), p.32

Chapter 13 Mantras and Language

1. Staal, p.281. More structures will be found in Staal, Chapter 23.
2. Ibid., Chapter 17. Stobhas are meaningless syllables from the Sama Veda. Staal devotes an entire Chapter (19) to their syntax.
3. C. Hooykaas (1973), *Balinese Buddha Brahmins*, quoted in Staal, p.261
4. Staal, p.266
5. A Venn diagram shows a group of circles representing logical sets or classes and their relationship (language, rituals etc. in the present case.) named after John Venn, English logician (1834-1923). The selection of circles is a matter of convenience which leads to many problems. For example, the subsets 'meaningful and meaningless mantras' are not circular.

Chapter 14 The Interpretation of Rituals

1. Staal, p.117
2. Ibid., p.122
3. Ibid., p.123
4. Ibid., p.131
5. Ibid., Chapter 18
6. Ibid., p.40
7. See Guilford, p.70
8. Eyesenck, p.155
9. Guilford, pp.104-114
10. Morris (1984), Chapter 3
11. Schwartz, p.52

Chapter 15 Science, Non-science and Pseudo-science

1. Kavoor, p.85
2. Eyesenck, p.332
3. Chopra (1993), p.28
4. Quoted in the note "A Yogi in Life and Death" in Paramahansa (1975)
5. Kasturi, p.7
6. In the opening note in Kavoor.
7. Deshpande's own translation in Marathi is used in the data for convenience.
8. It is not clear whether Deshpande is referring to geomagnetism. Since he shows the magnetic north pole at the geographical north, one hopes he is not thinking of the earth's magnetism.

Chapter 16 The Science of Ritual

1. For details of the s̄rauta structure and its comparison with linguistic syntax see Staal Chapters 11-12. In Chapter 26, he builds the science of ritual drawing heavily from ancient Indian sources. The analysis of *Āpastamba Śrauta Sūtra* in this Chapter is particularly illuminating.

BIBLIOGRAPHY

Abraham, Francis, John Henry Morgan (1985). *Sociological Thought From Compte to Sorokin.* Macmillan, Delhi.

Abraham, M.H. (1993). *A Glossary of Literary Terms.* Prism Books, Bangalore.

Acharya, S.S. (2001). *Rig Veda Vol. I – IV.* Sanskriti Sansthan, Bareli.

(1998). *Sāma Veda.* Sanskriti Sansthan, Bareli.

(2001). *Yajur Veda.* Sanskriti Sansthan, Bareli.

(1998). *Atharva Veda Vol. I – II.* Sanskriti Sansthan, Bareli.

Amen, Daniel G. (1998). *Change Your Brain, Change Your Life.* Times Books, N.Y.

Basham, A.L. (2001). *The Wonder That Was India.* Rupa & Co., New Delhi.

Bapat, K.M. (-). *Gorakshanath Yoga.* Raghuvanshi Prakashan, Pune.

Bapat, K.M (1996). *Svayampurohita.* Raghuvanshi Prakashan, Pune.

Berne, Eric (1968). *Games People Play.* Penguin, Middlesex.

Bose, A.C. (1970). *The Call of The Vedas.* Bharatiya Vidya Bhavan, Mumbai.

Capra, Fritjof (1983). *The Turning Point.* Flamingo, London.

(1993). *The Tao of Physics.* Flamingo, London.

Chakravarti, Mohan (2000). *Indrajal.* Kshirasagar and Co., Pune.

Chidbhavananda, Swami (1965). *The Bhagvad Gita.* Sri Ramakrishna Tapovanan, Tirupparaitturai.

Chopra, Deepak (1993). *Ageless Body, Timeless Mind.* Harmony Books, N.Y.

(1990). *Quautum Healing.* Bantam Books. N.Y.

Desai, C.G. (2002). *Gayatri Mantra Sadhana.* Manorama Prakashan, Mumbai.

Deshpande, Dhanajay (2001). *Vedanteel Vidnyan.* Popular Prakashan, Mumbai.

Dondo, Mathurin (1967). *Modern French Course.* Oxford University Press, Calcutta, (London).

Durant, Will (1953). *The Story of Philosophy.* Pocket Books, New York.

Einstein, Albert (1979). *Ideas and Opinions.* Rupa & Co., Calcutta.

Frazer, James (1993). *The Golden Bough.* Wordsworth Editions, Hertgordshire.

Freud, Sigmund (1960). *A General Introduction to Psycho-analysis* . Washington Square N.Y.

Gajendragadkar, Arvind (1992). *Vadyavadanache Sampurna Guide*, Unmesh Prakashan, Pune.

(1991). *Sangeetashastrache Guide.* Devadatta Prakashan, Pune.

Guilford, J.P. (1964). *General Psychology.* Affiliated East-West, New Delhi (Van Nostrand)

Hawking, Stepen W. (1989). *A Brief History of Time.* Bantam, N.Y.

Headington, Christopher (1983). *Illustrated Dictionary Of Musical Terms.* Hamlyn Paperbacks, Middlesex, England.

Hocket, Charles F. (1970). *A Course in Modern Linguistics.* Macmillan, N.Y.

Iyengar, B.K.S. (1992). *Light on Yoga.* Harper Collins, New Delhi.

Jeans, James (1960). *An Introduction to The Kinetic Theory of Gases.* Cambridge University Press, Cambridge.

Kasturi, N. (1962). *Sathyam – Sivam –Sudaram.* Sanathana Sarathi, Mangalore.

Kavoor, Abraham T. (1990). *Gods, Demons And Spirits.* Jaico, Bombay.

Longstaff, A. (2002). *Neuroscience.* Viva Books, New Delhi.

Morris, Desmond (1984). *The Naked Ape.* Laurel, N.Y.

(1994). *The Human Zoo.* Vintage, London.

Narayan, Shanti (1961). *A Text Book of Modern Abstract Algebra.* S.Chand & Co., New Delhi.

O' Flaherty, Wendy Doniger (2000). *The Rig Veda.* Penguin, New Delhi.

Page, Leigh, Norman Isley Adams. (1955). *Principles of Electricity.* S.Chand and Co., Delhi.

Paramahansa, Yogananda. (1975). *Autobiography of a Yogi.* Jaico Publishing House, Mumbai.

Penrose, Roger (1991). *The Emperor's New Mind.*Penguin, N. Y.

Peterfreund, Sheldon P., Theodre C. Denise (1968). *Contemporary Philosophy and Its Origins.*East-West, New Delhi.

Phadake, V.K. (1993). *Devapuja Kashi Karavi.* Anjali Publishing House, Pune .

Rand, Ayan (1984). *Philosophy. Who Needs It.* Signet (Penguin), N.Y.

(1990). *Introduction to Objective Epistemology.* Meridian (Penguin), N.Y.

Russel, Bertrand (1992). *Human Knowledge.* Routledge, London.

(1982). *The Principles of Mathematics* . Routledge, London.

(1995). *An Inquiry into Meaning and Truth.* Routledge, London, (N.Y.)

(1993). *Introduction to Mathematical Philosophy.* Routledge, London.

(1994). *Mysticism and Logic.* Routledge, London.

(1995). *The Analysis of Mind.* Routledge, London.

(1993). *Our Knowledge of the External World.* Routledge, London.

(1994). *Philosophical Essays.* Routledge, London.

(1999). *History of Western Philosophy.* Routledge, N.Y.

Saha, M.N., B.N. Srivastava (1958). *A Treatise on Heat.* The Indian Press, Allahabad.

Salman, Wesley C. (1963). *Logic.* Prentice Hall, N.J.

Śaṅkarācārya (1978). *Ātmabodha.* Sri Ramakrisna Math, Madras.

Śaṅkarācārya, Bhāratī Kṛṣṇa Tīrthajī Mahārāja (1992). *Vedic Mathematics.* Motilal Banarasidass, Delhi.

Śaṅkarācārya (108), Śrīyogeśvarānandatīrtha (1996). *Mantraśāstra.* Keshav Bhikaji Dhavale, Mumbai.

Sasine, Jayvijay (1999). *Kundalinichya Shodhat.* Vedanta Publishers, Mumbai.

Schwartz, Jeffrey M. (1996). *Brain Lock.* Harper Collins, N.Y.

Simmons, G.F. (1963). *Introduction to Topology and Modern Analysis.* Mc Graw Hill N. Y. (Kogakusha Tokyo).

Staal, Frits (1996). *Ritual and Mantras: Rules Without Meaning.* Motilal Banarasidass, Delhi.

Stern, Paul J. (1966). *The Abnormal Person and His World.* Affiliated East-West, New Delhi.

Svanandasarasvati (-). *Patañjala Yogavidyā.* Raghuvanshi Prakashan, Pune.

Swami Ashokananda (1995). *Avadhūta Gītā of Dattatreya.* Sri Ramakrishna Math, Madras.

Thirketlle, G.L. (1968). *Advanced Economics.* Macdonald & Evans, London.

Tigunait, Pandit Rajmani (1983). *Seven Systems of Indian Philosophy.* The Himalayan International Institute of Yoga science and philosophy of the U.S.A., Honesdale.

(1996). *The power of Mantra & The Mystery of Initiation.* The Himalayan International Institute of Yoga science and philosophy of the U.S.A., Honesdale.

(1999). *Tantra Unveiled.* The Himalayan International Institute of Yoga science and philosophy of the U.S.A., Honesdale.

(1997). *From Death to Birth.* The Himalayan International Institute of Yoga science and philosophy of the U.S.A., Honesdale.

Unmeshanand (1997). *Shastra Ase Sangate Part I.* Vedwani Prakashan, Kolhapur.

(1999). *Shastra Ase Sangate Part II.* Vedwani Prakashan, Kolhapur.

(1997). *Tumche Pourohitya Tumhich Kara, Part I.* Vedwani Prakashan, Kolhapur.

(2000). *Tumche Pourohitya Tumhich Kara, Part II.* Vedwani Prakashan, Kolhapur.

Webster, Rechard (1995). *Why Freud Was Wrong.* Basic Books, New York.

INDEX

R

S